INTERNATIONAL TRADE

Existing Problems and Prospective Solutions

Edited by Khosrow Fatemi

Taylor & Francis

New York • Bristol, PA • Washington D.C. • London

USA	Publishing Office:	Taylor & Francis New York, Inc.
		79 Madison Ave., New York, NY 10016-7892
	Sales Office:	Taylor & Francis Inc.
		1900 Frost Road, Bristol, PA 19007
UK		Taylor & Francis Ltd.
		4 John St., London WC1N 2ET

International Trade: Existing Problems and Prospective Solutions

First published 1989
Printed in the United States of America

Library of Congress Cataloging in Publication Data

International trade : existing problems and prospective solutions / edited by Khosrow Fatemi.
    p. cm.
  Includes bibliographical references.
  ISBN 0-8448-1626-4.—ISBN 0-8448-1627-2 (soft)
  1. International trade. 2. Developing countries—Commerce.
I. Fatemi, Khosrow.
HF 1379.I583   1989
382—dc20

89-20173
CIP

To Sandra Richard,
my distinguished colleague
and dear friend.

Contents

Part Three. Special Issues

Preface

The main purpose of this book is to discuss some of the major theoretical as well as practical problems of international trade and to propose some solutions.

Following an introduction, the book is divided into three parts and eleven chapters. Part One consists of four chapters, two on the environment of international trade and two on the operations of multinational corporations. In Chapter 2, Jack N. Behrman discusses the growing importance of the world economy—in contrast to individual national economies—as an element of the environment of international trade. In Chapter 3, H. Peter Gray makes a similar observation, pointing out that as we enter the last decade of the twentieth century, national economies and financial markets have become closely integrated to a point that the global macro economy and macroeconomic interdependence must now be treated as independent actors and separate from national economies.

In Chapter 4, Franklin R. Root discusses the environmental risks that multinational companies face, and in Chapter 5, John H. Dunning provides a detailed analysis of the theory of international production, including an exhaustive survey of literature.

Part Two has four chapters devoted to the role and impact of the developing countries on international trade and the global efforts aimed at facilitating the expansion of LDC's trade. In Chapter 6, Craig MacPhee evaluates the benefits for the developing countries of the last (Tokyo) round of MTNs, and in Chapter 7, K. A. Koekkoek provides an analysis of some important aspects of the next (Uruguay) round of trade negotiations.

In Chapter 8, Khosrow Fatemi measures the significance of the LDC debt and specifically discusses the debt-equity swap as one of the more promising approaches to solving the global debt crisis. In Chapter 9, James Lutz analyses the significance of the Newly Industrialized Countries (NICs) in the global economy.

Part Three of this book consists of three chapters each dealing with one of the important issues facing international trade. In Chapter 10, Bernard Sarachek discusses what could potentially be one of the most significant international economic events of the last quarter of the twentieth-century—a single European market. In Chapter 11, Darwin Wassink and Robert J. Carbaugh analyze the welfare effects of international joint ventures in the world automobile industry, with specific emphasis on competing U.S. and foreign firms operating in the American auto industry. In Chapter 12, Catherine Mann provides an estimation of the effect of foreign competition in prices and market share on employment in selected import-sensitive industries in the United States.

Acknowledgments

I would like to express my appreciation to all the authors for their contributions to this volume. Their support of this project and their willingness to write new pieces or update earlier writing were far beyond my expectations.

My thanks are also due to Ralph Salmi, International Studies editor at Taylor and Francis New York. His support was instrumental in making this book a reality. My thanks are also due to my secretary, Bertha Cabrera, and my graduate assistant, Michelle Walter.

Finally, a very special note of appreciation to my wife, Marcella, for her unwavering encouragement and support.

Needless to say, none of the above bears any responsibility for the contents of this book. That rests with the editor and the individual contributors of each chapter.

Chapter 1

INTRODUCTION

Khosrow Fatemi

The growing importance of international trade has been one of the major features of the last two decades of the twentieth century. However measured and whatever the cause, the significance of international trade in global economics—and, therefore, international politics—has increased dramatically over the past twenty years.[1] This growth has created new opportunities—and problems—for the policymaker and the practitioner, as well as the scholar of the field. Several nations, most notably the newly industrialized countries and a small number of others, as well as hundreds of multinational companies around the world have been able to improve their economic status dramatically by seizing this opportunity. The Republic of Korea, for example, registered annual increases of 27.1% and 14.7% in its GNP during the 1970s and 1980s, respectively. Comparative figures for Japan, the fastest growing industrial country during the period, were 15.2% and 5.3%.[2] Many other countries in this trade-oriented category registered similar, albeit smaller increases. In contrast, those countries that were unable, or in some cases unwilling, to capitalize on the opportunities that the rapid expansion of global trade provided them, have seen their economies stagnate, their currencies depreciate substantially, and their foreign reserves depleted. In short, their economies are in shambles. Mexico, Brazil, and other debt or nations fall into this category, as do many other less-developed countries (LDCs) without a serious debt problem. (What is postulated here is not that international trade created the debt problem; rather, that the failure of many debtor nations to use international trade to generate economic growth has accentuated this problem and has placed them in a quagmire.)

One of the most distressing and persistent problems associated with international trade during the last two decades has been the inability of the deficit countries to balance their foreign trade and the unwillingness of the surplus countries to help in this effort. In general, global trade is a zero sum game—that is, total trade for the world is always

---

[1]Between 1973 and 1988, total exports for all countries of the world increased from $520 billion to over $2.5 trillion for a cumulative increase of 400%. Source: *Direction of Trade Statistics* (various annual and monthly issues).

[2]Source: *International Financial Statistics* (various issues), lines 99.a and 99.ac.

in balance—and any one country's surplus must be matched through an *equal* deficit by other countries.[3] However, the overall economic impact of a persistent deficit in one country far exceeds the "benefits" of an equal surplus by another country. The reason is that whereas the successful exporting countries may be able to use their accumulated surpluses to their advantage and benefit to some extent, the deficit countries are hampered by their inability to eliminate this problem to a much greater extent.

After many years of deficit, different countries have reacted—and are reacting—to their trade imbalance. The abundance of protectionist cries notwithstanding, in the industrialized countries, the reaction has so far been moderate and generally limited to allowing—often forcing—their currencies to depreciate. The problem is that for some, most notably the United States, depreciation of their currency has not been sufficient, or sufficiently large, to alleviate the problem. For example, during the 1980s the parity of the American dollar underwent two distinct phases. First, between the first quarter of 1983 and the first quarter of 1985 the American currency appreciated between 10–45% against different currencies (see Table 1.1). During the second period, from the first quarter of 1985 to the fourth quarter of 1987, the dollar fell by 28–49%. These fluctuations, however, had little impact on the U.S. trade balance.[4] The American trade deficit increased from $69.4 billion in 1983 to $148.6 in 1985 and $173.6 billion in 1987, and showed very little causal relationship with the fluctuations of the dollar. Ironically, despite this very large deficit, the American economy functioned fairly well during this period. In contrast, Japan, the leading industrialized surplus country, accumulated $346 billion in trade surplus in the 1980–1988 period. And again, the fluctuations of the Japanese currency seem to have had little to do with Japan's accumulation of surplus, which has been steadily increasing regardless of the fate of the yen.

Among the developing countries, the impact of the trade imbalance has been more pronounced and, for the deficit countries among them, more devastating. During the 1970s and 1980s Mexico and Brazil each accumulated over $100 billion in foreign debt. For either country, the foreign debt exceeds its annual GNP and is several times its foreign exchange earnings per year. When measured as a percentage of GNP or foreign exchange earnings, several other countries are in a similar situation, even though their total debt may be significantly smaller.

In many countries the impact of a trade imbalance has been to aggravate the country's debt problem. These two problems—as well as some of the solutions used to alleviate them, such as crippling import controls—have severely suffocated economic growth in these countries. It would be an oversimplification to attribute the problems of the debtor nations, or the developing countries in general, solely or completely to their foreign trade picture. Nevertheless, it is a certainty that the trade deficit is the major cause of

---

[3]Actually, total global exports and imports differ, slightly because of such factors as statistical discrepancy, underreporting or overreporting of trade by different countries and companies, and how different countries treat freight and insurance. This difference is, however, marginal and does not alter the premise of this section.

[4]For a analysis of this point, see Khosrow Fatemi, "U.S. Trade Imbalance and the Dollar: Is There a Correlation?" *International Journal of Finance*, May 1989.

Table 1.1

Dollar Fluctuation against Major Currencies (1983–1987)

Currency	First Quarter 1983	First Quarter 1985	Fourth Quarter 1987
A: Absolute Values[1]			
SDR	0.916	1.034	0.745
British pound	0.653	0.897	0.570
French franc	6.887	9.960	5.755
German mark	2.408	3.256	1.706
Japanese yen	235.7	259.7	135.8
Swiss franc	2.015	2.756	1.403
B: Percentage change from preceding period			
SDR		+12	−28
British pound		+37	−36
French franc		+45	−42
German mark		+35	−47
Japanese yen		+10	−47
Swiss franc		+37	−49

[1]Number of each currency per dollar during each quarter (period average).
Source: *International Financial Statistics*, various monthly issues.

the economic problems of many of these countries, and the prospects for finding short-term solutions for either problem are not very good.

RAW MATERIAL PRICES

After a decade of turbulence in the 1970s, commodity prices remained relatively stable during the 1980s. This has helped the economies of exporters of manufactured goods but has negatively impacted those countries dependent on raw material exports. This is true even for oil-exporting countries, which not long ago seemed to be the only bright spot among the LDCs. It is very important to note that the calm of recent years has been misleading and may, in fact, have resulted in a dangerous complacency. For the underlying problem of imbalance has not been resolved, and in part because of this failure, the global trading system is extremely fragile. This fragility was best substantiated in 1989 by the sharp increase in oil prices following the Valdez oil spill.[5] The 19.4% increase in retail gasoline prices may have been used and exacerbated by the greed of the oil companies and distributors, but it was the market's high propensity to panic that allowed them to increase their prices by as much as they did. In a more

---

[5]In April 1989 an oil tanker hit a reef in Valdez, Alaska, and spilled several million gallons of oil into the water. As a result there was a temporary suspension of oil shipments from Alaska for a few days. Almost immediately, distributors on the U.S. West Coast increased their prices, and shortly thereafter prices started to climb throughout the country, even though eastern and southern states have no appreciable imports from Alaska. In the six weeks that followed the Valdez accident, the average price of gasoline in the United States increased from $1.08 per gallon to $1.29, for an increase of 19.4%.

stable market, the increase in oil prices would have been more proportional to the problem.

PROTECTIONISM AND REGIONAL INTEGRATION

One of the many reactions shown to the trade problem has been a gradual move toward protectionism, most seriously manifested in the form of regional integration. The most important regional integration is, of course, the creation of a "single market" in Europe by 1992. The Commission of European Communities estimates that the cost of market fragmentation among the twelve members—and therefore the potential benefit of the Single European Act—is about ECU 200 billion, or approximately $250 billion (CEC, 1988, p. xviii). This reduction in cost is being accomplished by the removal of "[1] physical barriers—like intra-EC border stoppages, customs controls and associated paperwork; [2] technical barriers—for example, meeting divergent national product standards, technical regulations and conflicting business laws; and entering nationally protected public procurement markets; and [3] fiscal barriers—especially differing rates of VAT and excise duties" (CEC, 1988, p. 4). Unquestionably, the above steps will streamline intra-European trade and will result in a substantial benefit for all the parties to this agreement. Part of this benefit will be in the form of increased efficiency through the reduction of bureaucratic hurdles and the elimination of waste. This benefit, however, will be provided exclusively to the member states and will place nonmembers at a distinct competitive disadvantage.

Europe-1992 is the largest regional integration, but not the only one. On January 1, 1989 the Canada-U.S. Free Trade Agreement went into effect. The most important feature of this agreement is the provision that will eliminate all tariffs between the two countries in ten years. Additionally, under other provisions of the pact, import quotas and export controls are prohibited and many other nontariff barriers are removed or liberalized. Finally, the pact requires the two governments to liberalize the laws governing trade in services and direct investment flows (Fatemi, 1989; Morici, 1989). As in the case of Europe, this agreement will provide the exporters from member countries a competitive advantage over competing firms from other nations. Similar attempts are being made—so far less successfully—to create integrative alliances elsewhere. For example, the Far Eastern countries are becoming much more regionally oriented and dependent on trade with Japan than ever before.[6]

All integration attempts are genuine efforts at reducing trade barriers, and as such should be applauded. However, they are all "discriminatory" in that by giving preferential treatment to some countries—members of the union—they are creating trade barriers for others. One of the advantages of the Canada-U.S. Free Trade Agreement, for example, is that it gives business enterprises in the two countries unlimited access to the markets and resources of the two countries. This also means that a competing firm from, say Sweden, will now find itself at a distinct competitive disadvantage. Until

---

[6]See, e.g., *Fortune*, May 22, 1989, pp. 48–56.

the Free Trade Agreement between the United States and Canada went into effect, the Swedish and American household furniture imported into Canada were both subject to a 14.3% tariff. By the time the agreement is fully operational, Swedish manufacturers of household furniture will be subject to a 14.3% tariff, contrasted with duty-free imports from the United States. Needless to say, it will become increasingly difficult for the firms from nonmember countries to be price-competitive with producers from member countries.

References

Commission of European Communities, 1988. *The European Challenge, 1922: The Benefits of a Single Market (The Cecchini* Report). London: Wildwood House.

Fatemi, Khosrow. 1989. The Canada-U.S. Free Trade Agreement and Its Implications on U.S. Business. Paper presented at the Conference on the Free Trade Agreement and its Implications on the Business Community and the Accounting Profession, Montreal, April 30.

Morici, Peter. 1989. Canada-U.S. Free Trade Agreement. *International Trade Journal,* 111 (4), Summer, 347–373.

Part One

The Environment of International Trade and the Multinational Companies

The first two chapters of Part One analyze the impact of the global economy, and each proposes a new framework of analysis for the study of the new role of the international economy. In Chapter 2, Jack Behrman provides a systemic approach to the international economy by examining the economic implications of some highly significant events that have occurred in international economic relations in recent years and have resulted in a continuous restructuring of the world economy. Behrman maintains that this restructuring has manifested itself in the form of the de-linkings of several former causal relationships. As a result of this restructuring, the world economy has become more integrated and more important than any single country, and consequently a dominant force in international economic affairs. Behrman further argues that this trend will continue and the world economy will become even more integrated, almost inexorably, and national economies must adjust to it. He further maintains that the significance of these changes has not yet been sufficiently recognized, either in the theories of international trade and investment or the policies of national governments. To alleviate this problem and enhance the recognition of the restructuring of the global economy, Behrman proposes a new "ordering principle" for the governments of major industrial countries, especially that of the United States, to follow. He further recommends that his proposed policy of "structured investment with free trade" be implemented on a regional or bilateral basis.

In Chapter 3, H. Peter Gray uses the premise of greater global economic integration and provides a different perspective of its causes and effects. He argues that as we enter the last decade of the twentieth century, national economies and financial markets have become so closely integrated that some concept of a global macro-economy—separate from national economies—and of macroeconomic interdependence is now necessary. To accomplish this objective, that is, to create a basis analytical framework for the study of macroeconomic interdependence in the modern world, Gray develops an analytical model. In particular, his framework, which draws heavily on a flow-of-funds analysis of international payments, examines the international transmission of aggregate demand through the phenomenon of economic "locomotion." It also assesses the implications of the international balance sheet position for economic locomotion and addresses the issue of the effects of the huge international debtor position of the United States on its ability—and other nations' willingness—to play the locomotive.

In Chapter 4, Franklin R. Root provides an analysis of one specific aspect of the international economy, that is, the environmental risk as faced by multinational corporations. He divides the environmental factors into "transactional," over which MNCs have direct influence, and "contextual," in which the MNCs operate and over which they have no control. He defines each element and provides a listing of the actors in each category that influence the operations of multinational corporations. Moreover, Root examines the responses that MNCs make to environmental risk, and continues by schematically applying his model to the study of country risk and proposing a country-risk management model for MNCs to follow. He concludes that to maintain viability in most countries, MNCs must be viewed as indispensable and as making a net positive social contribution beyond the capability of local firms. He then makes several specific proposals for MNCs to achieve this objective.

In Chapter 5, John H. Dunning provides an in-depth analysis of the theory of international production. He starts with an exhaustive survey of literature and traces the evolution of this theory during the last three decades. He points out that what distinguishes the theory of international production from new classical models of trade is that the latter are concerned only with the *location* of foreign production, whereas the theory of international production takes into account the location as well as the *ownership* and *organization* of these activities. Dunning's pioneering work in the development of the theory of international production draws upon, and integrates, two strands of economic theory: (1) the theory of international resource allocation based on the spatial distribution of factor endowments, which chiefly addresses itself to the location of production; and (2) the theory of economic organization, which is essentially concerned with the ownership of that production and the ways in which the transactions relating to that production are organized.

Following his analysis of the theory of international production, Dunning concludes by identifying some new challenges that lie ahead for any further intellectual development of this theory. Specifically, he raises the question of how to incorporate into the framework of analysis some recent changes in the cross-border relationships involving multinational companies.

Chapter 2

RESTRUCTURING AND REORDERING THE WORLD ECONOMY*

Jack N. Behrman

INTRODUCTION

During the past few decade three highly significant events have occurred in international economic relations: the world economy has been restructured, becoming more important than any single country and therefore dominant in economic affairs; the rules for ordering policy decisions have atrophied with the demise of the Bretton Woods Agreements; and the last two major closed economies (the Soviet Union and China) have decided to adopt more open strategies. These three events signal further radical changes in international economic relations, requiring a reordering of rules and institutions and a restructuring of patterns of trade and investment.

Peter Drucker (1986) has already noted the de-linking of several former causal relationships: resources from industrial advance, domestic employment from technological advance, and financial movements from trade. Other de-linkings have occurred in the past thirty to forty years, including the severance of colonial relationships, the partial withdrawal of two major economies from the international economy, the withdrawal of others into highly protected development patterns, which include constraints on foreign direct investment, and attempts to de-link national monetary and fiscal policies from those of other countries through the adoption of fluctuating exchange rates.

Each of these events, coming over the period since World War II, has led to significant changes in the world economy. The significance of these changes has not yet been sufficiently recognized, either in the theories of international trade and investment or the policies of national governments. But transnationals are progmatically adjusting and increasing cross-national ties. The fundamental signal is that the world economy will continue to become more integrated, almost inexorably, and national economies must adjust to it. Contrarily, national policies are still being formulated as though they can alter the nature of the world economy and thereby their own costs and benefits.

---

*Reprinted from *The International Trade Journal,* Vol. III, no. 1, fall 1988.

RESTRUCTURING

The de-linking of resources from industrial development is signaled by the substitution of low-cost, readily available materials for use in manufacturing compared to the heavier and more costly minerals and metals. While the developing countries were a source of natural resources, they were drawn into industrial advance partly by the growth in the advanced countries; though there was considerable debate as to whether the income resulting was equitable to the developing countries, they were at least benefited by industrial advance elsewhere. Without this stimulus they must look to their development though modernizing agriculture and industry, copying the advanced countries.

The de-linking of employment from technological advance signals that the mere acquisition of higher technologies on the part of any country—developing or advanced—does not necessarily help resolve significant problems of unemployment. Technological advance does not directly provide new employment for large numbers of peoples, though it does upgrade the levels and skills of employment. Still, the higher tech industries are needed as an engine of industrial development within each country, and this spreading will accelerate the increasing similarity of national economies. But, increasingly, employment will be stimulated by domestic growth in services and basic infrastructure rather than by high-tech industry.

The de-linking of financial movements from trade has had several important effects: one is the tying of financial markets around the world more tightly together and generating similarity (though not cooperation) in operations and objectives in national financial institutions. The ready flow of funds has also tied national monetary and fiscal policies together in ways not anticipated by governments. Financial movements that were previously seen as following the imbalances of trade are now themselves generating these imbalances through shifts in demand and prices. Thus financial movements are becoming more active than passive in the balance of payments.

The de-linking of colonies from the mother countries has generated a host of new nations that have strong desires for independence, reflected in a move toward protection and import substitution but also in political divorce from the more advanced countries and in the formation of a bloc of countries having somewhat similar interests in re-balancing economic wealth and political power. Thus they will exercise their diplomatic strength to maintain and support their interests against the former mother countries. This separation has not been complete; a number of the African countries have remained tied, at least economically, to the former mother countries and have obtained special privileges from the European Community. With the number of nation states reaching 170 and some 140 represented in the United Nations, the number and composition of governments that would demand a voice in any new ordering of the world economy are substantially greater than before, complicating the process of formulating new rules; any worldwide negotiation is probably fruitless save as an educational exercise.

A number of countries were more or less closed economically during several decades in the post-World War II period. Many sought to de-link themselves even from the world economy so as not to be influenced in their development or modernization by ties to the advanced countries. This was seen in the policy of import substitution with reference to trade and in a number of regulations on the inflow of technology and foreign direct investment. Advice was taken by many of them to substitute debt for equity investment to support the development process and as a means of reducing dependence on the advanced countries. The two major prescriptions of import substitution and debt financing have backfired on virtually every country. The more successful countries (notably the "Four Tigers" of Southeast Asia) followed more open and export-led development with attention to the creation of appropriate infrastructure and agricultural bases.

The two major countries that were most closed but unburdened by external debt were the USSR and China, yet both have in the past decade determined that openness is a better policy, resulting from their inability to maintain sufficient economic growth and the evident stimulus of the world economy to national growth. Each has recognized that to achieve levels of efficiency and standards of living similar to those in advanced countries, closed policies are inappropriate. But neither the USSR or China has the luxury of taking the time to adjust to the world economy *merely* through expanding trade, as many countries did during the 1950s and 1960s, for the trading world is now importantly linked through financial movements, including direct and portfolio investment. They therefore must take a more difficult leap that, if successful, will cause a further restructuring of economic and power relationships among nations.

Last, the attempt to separate national economies by adopting fluctuating or flexible rates has not been successful. The employment and growth policies of each of the major countries has had serious implications for the others, producing a continuous dialogue among them in which each urges others to make greater adjustments—whether they are surplus or deficit countries. Exchange rates have become sticky and "dirty" through the intervention of governments seeking to adjust them to monetary and fiscal policies, to employment and income objectives, or to needed changes in the balance of payments. Even these developing countries that sought to de-link their monetary and fiscal policies from those of advanced countries (through foreign exchange controls and debt financing of development) have found that they cannot simultaneously control the exchanges, limit domestic inflation, and invest borrowed funds wisely for development so as to maintain their credit-worthiness. Consequently, they have not achieved independence from the advanced countries but merely changed the nature of that dependence. Most have now embraced the inflow of direct investment and technology through the transnational companies (TNCs) as a means of stimulating growth, employment, and (hopefully) earning foreign exchange. Trade patterns have changed as a consequence.

The events of the past couple of decades would indicate that the dominance of the world economy over national economies is inexorable and will continue so long as nations seek the benefits of specialization. Further, there will be conflict within it so long as nations seek to change their comparative advantages so as to increase and redirect their production and trade and to raise their share of the total benefits from the world economy.

Despite a concern to remain "independent" or "self-reliant," neither advanced or developing countries, nor the newly industrializing countries, have been able to stem an increasing economic interdependence, which has been brought about not through trade or even the flow of foreign exchange but rather through the *movement of the factors of production*—which classical trade theory assumed would not occur. Trade was seen as a substitute for the movement of factors, whereas trade is now a *result* of the movement of factors.

The spread of the multinational enterprise, in its many manifestations, has carried with it not only capital but also technology, managerial, and marketing skills, new products, and R&D laboratories. Even "land" is effectively made mobile by the ability to move entire plants readily from one location to another without changing organizational arrangements or marketing outlets. To the new ties through the movement of factors must be added the interdependence of the world financial institutions, noted above, and the more recent complex operational ties among independent corporations across national boundaries. Economic integration has occurred mainly through factor movements, with significant volumes of national *manufactured* exports and imports being *within* TNCs (some 50% in the U.S. case).

Consequently, the patterns of trade have been restructured to reflect greater specialization *within* an industry rather than *among* industries internationally. Rather than one country producing wheat or petroleum and selling it for industrial goods, major countries are manufacturing (processing or growing) entire ranges of products, which they are trading with others having similar economic structures. Specialization is occurring at the margin or even infra-marginally (that is, similar products flowing both ways) as a result of increased openness of world markets, followed by complex production and marketing arrangements. The result is a much deeper and more complex interdependence than existed through trade alone.

Significant implications of these events include, first, a greater difficulty in determining the recipient of the costs or benefits as national economies become linked through ownership and organizational ties with many foreign economies (who will benefit from a stimulus to auto demand through lower U.S. interest rates?—the United States or Japan?). Second, substantial shifts in political and strategic interests will occur as financial and industrial institutions become owned and guided more significantly by persons outside of the country. Third, increased openness *should* make the world more closely tied and peaceful with no country dominant and the bipolarity of the world disappearing. Fourth, governments will be able to affect the world economy *only* through quite specific and focused acts, altering their situation only marginally. (No country can avoid playing the game presently, for a policy of opting out or closing the economy is simply too high a cost to pay over the longer run). Fifth, no country is now sufficiently large economically to set the rules of the game or significantly increase its own benefits. Government policies must become similar to the more passive martial arts—giving way and pushing simultaneously in cooperative negotiations.

A final consequence is that there are many more potential partners to play within the international game, and more must be known about them in order to negotiate effectively. This larger number of potential partners increases opportunities for cooperation, but it also implies that *worldwide* agreements will be difficult if not impossible to achieve. It is likely that accommodations will be reached among smaller groups of countries with similar objectives. However, if the world is not to be pulled apart by regional accommodations or specialized arrangements, which close off opportunities to others, there must be a general acceptance of increasing interdependence in the world. This acceptance policywise can be gained only by *greater consideration* being given to *more equitable distribution of benefits from growth in the world economy.* This itself will require development of a closer *community of interests,* which has to date seemed to be virtually impossible to achieve. It *can* be achieved with more specialized arrangements, seeking to reach accommodation on areas of mutual interest among a smaller group of countries—that is, bilateralism and regional agreements among "consenting nations."

REORDERING

From a policy standpoint, what is needed is a means of moving to free trade as soon as practicable under a new "ordering principle." It is evident that nations have considerable reservations about the ordering principle of the market mechanism underlying Bretton Woods and the GATT. These reservations are *not* directed at particular commodities as much as at particular industries, technologies, or even companies—each nation seeking to minimize burdens of adjustment and enhancing its gains. Therefore, it appears a propitious time to move boldly to adopt the advice of free traders from decades ago—remove all barriers and, *if* any "protection" is deemed desirable, let it be forthright and direct, involving whatever incentives or subsidies are deemed necessary, by seeing to it that they are removed as soon as feasible.

The policy implications of this approach are that the U.S. government should take two new initiatives: one, to accept the concern of other nations over their industrial and technological roles (industrial targeting), and propose new institutional techniques to give voice and vent to that concern; and two, to press still harder for removal of all *restrictive* measures impeding *trade.* The result would be to move from *trade restriction* to *industrial promotion*—from protection to restructuring. We should adopt a policy of "structured investment with free trade." This orientation should appeal to a world concerned with accelerating economic growth with equity, for it is expansionistic rather than restrictionist and would allay concerns over the destruction of benefits and burdens.

The first prong of U.S. policy should be a clarion call for *free trade* among the industrial world, with delayed acceptance on the part of the LDCs, *accompanied* by a clear statement accepting the fact that nations are vitally interested in the extent to which they benefit from and participate in industrial advance, particularly in the more technically sophisticated industries. This *call* is not new, but the means of implementation proposed are a new departure.

The policy initiative should be to agree on the rejection of all *restrictive trade* techniques, substituting guidance to direct investment with agreed "performance requirements." The objective should be to *expand* trade, with national participation based on promotion of appropriate (economically efficient, socially desirable, and politically acceptable) industrial structures for each country. Promotional policies should be fostered, permitting agreed selection of and preference to industries and companies under intergovernmental rules. The objective is to give intergovernmental sanction to industrial policies, so as to remove their (national) protectionist bias.

This approach would accept governmental support for *part* of an industry or a *particular* firm, so as to guarantee national participation in the growth of that industry. The techniques acceptable, if properly safeguarded, would be some of those now employed. These would include guarantees of *national* (locally owned and controlled) participation. The U.S. objective should be to admit this claim as a legitimate interest but to keep its impacts circumscribed to precisely that needed to achieve overall objectives, opening investment as much as feasible. How can such agreements be achieved?

It cannot be done on a worldwide basis—there are too many nations—but rather on a bilateral or regional basis. Selected countries should be invited to open negotiations on "structured investment with free trade" in one or more sectors. The "structuring" would be done by asking TNCs in the given sectors to indicate their investment location plans and projected trade patterns if free trade existed, under guidelines of balancing agreed criteria of employment, technology flow, R&D activities, local sourcing, and trade and capital flows. Government would agree on means for inducing changes in these plans so that equitable opportunities for participation existed for each member nation in each sector. Once plans were agreed upon, trade would be unrestricted. Competition among several TNCs would exist, achieving efficiency. Equity would be injected by the initial agreement on patterns of investment, and the resulting interdependence would be acceptable since it had been agreed to by both governments and TNCs.

Assistance would be provided to existing industry to adjust to the freeing of trade— in anticipation of competitive pressures from the new arrangement. *Ex ante* assistance for adjustment to relocation of industry should be given, rather than *ex post* aid, which is protective of inefficiency. Promotion techniques would be adapted to the agreed patterns of investment, and discriminatory trade promotion would be eliminated. The agreements would permit subsidies and incentives to investment by segments of industry and companies, but these should be *overt* and examined annually by a supervisory body.

Besides the techniques of preferential governmental purchasing or direct subsidy of R&D or other expenditures by participating TNCs, governments might offer preferential "buy national" provisions for government purchasing to provide a market initially for local supplies, but this would be phased out under an agreed timetable. The withholding of assistance from other companies or industries would implement an industrial policy decision that marginal units of an industry should be allowed to wither or be absorbed by more efficient elements.

There would be several felicitous results from such a policy approach: the proposal of free trade would accord with the avowed desire of several industries in the United States (autos, steel, pharmaceuticals, electronics, paper, and aluminum) to have sectoral free trade in the world. Few could argue against free trade, if at the same time legitimate national interests were to be safeguarded and greater equity achieved leading to less conflict. The acceptance of the legitimate concern of national governments for participation in international economic development and *mutual* dependance would lead to greater order in the world economy.

Rather than protecting sectors such as textiles, shoes, autos, and others, their international (regional) development would be placed in a context of a full-scale move to free trade under which the various sectors would be given clear signals as to when and how to adjust to greater competition. What would result is a policy of industrial *change,* establishing "free trade corridors" among participating countries, providing regional competition, with assistance being given to establish initial equity in benefits and burdens of adjustments.[1]

With such negotiations, a better understanding would be gained of how to foster industrial development within the LDCs. It would become clearer which of the segments of industry within the advanced industries were likely to fade away, leaving room for the LDCs. Discussions with the LDCs could then shift to the kinds of industrial policies *they* need to promote efficient industry, rather than their seeking preferences in trade for products they are not ready to produce *or* ones that the industrialized countries are not willing to give up, as yet. They could see how to prepare for their own regional associations and for "sectoral free trade" with more advanced countries. Infrastructure would be built for *particular* sectors of agriculture and industry in particular regions of the country to prepare for eventual new investment and competition in trade. As it stands, many countries' industrial policies aim at participation in *every* industrial sector without acceptance of those results by importing countries, who thus set up barriers. Though trade increases, it does so with conflict and restrictions, rather than cooperation and support.

Such regional/sectoral policies would undoubtedly focus not only on *what* industry is developed within a country and *where,* but *who* owns it and controls it. The general revulsion in Canada, Europe, and LDCs against extensive foreign ownership and control of local industry has resulted in restrictions on the *extent* of foreign participation and the *techniques* of that participation. Regional agreements should accept some control over the extent of foreign *entry* into certain industries, over location of the activity, over the constraints imposed by management of the foreign affiliate through the parent company, and imposition of some performance agreements in exchange of more certain degrees of "national treatment."

Such constraints should not be accepted without full discussion of their effect, purpose, and use, and they should be placed under continued surveillance. But it is unrealistic to think that the major countries (or even the minor ones) will accept a policy of nondiscriminatory "right of establishment" and "right of control" on the part of private corporations, whose headquarters and power centers are in another country. To do so is an abdication of essential governmental functions to a (foreign) corporation, whose power is nonetheless real *despite* the frequent assertions that the corporation is not a "power"-oriented entity and can be trusted with wide-ranging decisions on the best use of the world's resources unhindered by governmental constraints. But once the agreement was promulgated and investment occurred, trade should be freed of all re-

---

[1]The idea of "free trade corridors"—zero duties among countries on products of a specific sector—was legislated into the 1962 Trade Expansion Act; but Europe was not then ready to face full-scale competition from the United States in any sector. It continued to prefer to swap apples for oranges, rather than French "Granny Smith" apples for Virginia winesaps. Now, specialization is precisely of this type—*intra*industry, opening the opportunity that should be grasped.

strictions, and it *would* be, for all equity considerations would have been reflected in the investment patterns.

The implications of this approach for foreign investment policies would include the following: first, a cessation of efforts to obtain a Code of Fair Treatment of foreign investment, since that code has been largely based on the concept of nondiscrimination and national treatment. Second, a cessation of efforts to obtain a Code of Good Behavior on the part of foreign investors, since their contributions to national interests will already be under agreement. Third, an effort to acquire full information from business on their treatment in host countries would be necessary to build an understanding of the restructuring of sectors through direct investment. Fourth, with this information, new procedures for surveillance by the member governments should be developed, and agreements eventually hammered out as to the *positive* techniques for industrial promotion as well as those aimed at prevention of undesirable control by foreign interests. With greater experience in the use of such constraints, some will be found to be useless—such as joint ventures in some fields—and others more effective—such as governmental participation in extraction.

The regional agreements relating to foreign direct investment would cover the right of establishment; protection of proprietary rights; acceptable measures of control of quality; regulations on use of intercompany price controls; allocation of intercompany charges and expenses; market allocations; anticompetition, rationalization, and concentration policies; joint venture requirements; restrictions on membership of boards of directors; listing of shares of affiliates or parent companies—all of which remain a concern of governments. But trade would be unrestricted.

Such agreements would go a long way to taking the stigma off of transnationals, for they would then be seen as the *means* of achieving free trade (efficiency) with equity as to benefits and burdens.

One of the most neglected problems in discussions on international trade and production is the role of labor and labor unions. They, particularly, are becoming concerned with the problem of equity and sharing—sharing jobs and employment and equity in wage rates among countries. The unions are becoming quite aware of disparities in wage rates for identical jobs within the affiliates of the same multinational enterprise. They also deplore the migration of industry solely to take advantage of wage differentials, or, alternatively, the use of imports from a foreign subsidiary to break (or weaken) negotiations with the parent. Agreements for "structured investment and free trade" would provide a means of meeting labor's concerns and signaling elements that would need adjustment assistance.

The riposte of the traditional free trader will likely be that the policies proposed here will be a large step toward cartelization of the industrial world. Far from it. Rather, they are a move toward regional interdependence, which opens up competition—similar to that under the U.S.–Canada Auto Agreement. Evidence that this policy direction is not anathema to all free traders is found in the support for this agreement and in the success of the coproduction arrangements under NATO, which included the removal of all barriers to trade in components and final products. Such sectoral arrangements will also be needed to make the recently signed U.S.–Canada Free Trade Agreement effective.

These policies are proposed as a means of reversing the neo-mercantilist position of most governments. They also dovetail with the growing recognition that many social and ecological factors are going to have to be taken into account in the future location and movement of industry. Decisions as to industry location will simply not be made solely on free market criteria, which continue to disregard social and ecological costs and national development interests. But taking these factors into account will introduce governmental or quasi-governmental controls or at least guidelines, which will affect both trade and investment patterns. These complex tradeoffs can best be made bilaterally or regionally *rather* than worldwide, as evidenced by the United Nations conferences on energy, environment, and science and technology, the efforts to develop international "codes," and the inability to achieve a new Bretton Woods.

Full participation of each member nation in the process of any international ordering of industrial development is vital and necessary. It is *only* by a process of making *each* national group feel satisfied with new arrangements that progress will be made toward international integration. And it will be necessary to make adjustment to national interests *if* we are to move decisively to free trade. These adjustments are too complex to make under any worldwide agreement and can best be made in regional groups and with sectoral arrangements. It is toward these that the United States should now turn its attention, selecting its partners carefully.

ENTRY OF CHINA AND THE USSR

In selecting countries as "partners," it will be of the greatest importance in the next decade to make certain that the USSR and China are brought into the world economy as strongly and as far as they will permit. These are three ways of doing this: one is to encourage regional associations of countries around them—as has occurred between Europe and certain African countries and should also occur between the United States and Canada plus some of the Latin American countries. In this mode the USSR would move toward South Asia, and China toward Southeast Asia. Another approach is to establish a strong bilateral tie between the United States and the USSR, and between the United States and China. A third is for the OECD countries to agree on sectoral arrangements to reorder the Northern Hemisphere, including the USSR and China, letting the southern countries decide how they tie into this dominant grouping. Alternatively, these avenues could be pursued simultaneously for different sector.

Both China and the USSR are insisting on guiding and selecting foreign direct (inward) investment, requiring joint ventures, seeking technology inflows, and insisting on exports. The agreements proposed here fit with their concerns and would enhance international interdependence—and cooperation in a more open world economy.

The significance of accommodation with the USSR and China is not only their size and potential contribution to a more efficient world but also that they are so relatively unfamiliar with the workings of free economies that they will need to be brought along with as much goodwill as possible. Each of them, for quite different reasons, has been wary of interdependence or dependence, and a great deal of "good faith" will have to be demonstrated. Equally, of course, the Western countries should expect good faith in return.

Even so, there are enough bases for misunderstanding that the processes of accommodation will be tested again and again. For example, both of these countries appear to have adopted the old developing country insistence on joint ventures or local ownership of foreign-owned affiliates. Given that the enterprises in both countries are presently state-owned, this would create a private-state enterprise, which raises a number of difficulties that need not be faced. The national governments in each case are sufficiently powerful to guide the behavior of wholly owned foreign ventures if they wish—but to do so will require a greater understanding on their part of how the TNCs operate and what their needs are in order to be competitive internationally or efficient domestically. Substantial interchange of information will be necessary, and it is now occurring in a fairly intensive and extensive fashion with China—though the flow is still inadequate.

The gain in bringing these two nations into the world economy is that, of necessity, its reordering will help to establish more cooperative/competitive relationships by helping to resolve the tensions between efficiency and equity the world over. Both the USSR and China have had a more cooperative—though authoritarian—society but both recognize the need for competition to achieve efficiency and higher standards of living. They have sought a more equitable distribution of income—with more-or-less success—and now recognize the necessity for some inequities based on performance and work, rather than on privilege. The presently stated "Socialist" criterion of "to each according to his work" is a familiar classical economic dictum—"to each according to his contribution." We should welcome these new Socialist ideas and work with them, setting ideology aside, as both Deng and Gorbachev are seeking to do in their own countries. Both countries are now willing to accept some of the "pragmatics of the marketplace," but they cannot give up their Socialist orientations or foundations. The United States, on the other hand, has sought a more equitable distribution of income and benefits within its own country, but cannot give up the market signals or classical economic foundations of its system.

As Professors Lodge and Vogel have argued in their recent book, the needs of the new world economy and national competitiveness will lead to more cooperative/communitarian solutions than the more competitive/individualistic solutions, (Lodge and Vogel, 1987). Equity cannot be achieved without an accommodation between individualism and communitarianism, and the opportunity is provided to seek this accommodation on a grand scale through collaboration among the USSR, China and the West. The nettle should be grasped firmly.

From the standpoint of the United States itself, a high priority should be set for initiatives to collaborate with China. There is a long-standing friendship with China not only at the government level but also at the level of people-to-people. This friendly relationship is important to the Chinese as a basis for agreeing on anything, and we should not disregard it or downplay it.

But of even greater importance for successful collaboration is a basic orientation on the part of the United States and China that each has a mission to fulfill in the world. Traditional Chinese philosophy included a world role for China not only as the "middle kingdom" but also as having responsibility for the bringing of order to the world and enhancing its welfare. The history of China itself is that of a struggle for achieving cohesion and order among peoples described by Confucius as "a mountain and loose sand." The Chinese understand the necessity of order and cohesion and the cooperative accommodations required to achieve them. They would like to offer their lessons to the world for consideration.

On its part, the United States was founded as a "City upon a Hill," which was to beam the "light of freedom" to the world. Its "order" was to come from free men and women acting responsibly. This model of freedom and responsibility was to be the basis of worldwide democracy. The United States seems to have forgotten that freedom must be matched by responsibility and needs a larger portion of order to bring that lesson back into focus. The Chinese need a greater portion of freedom so as to permit individual initiative to help raise living standards. We come to the same worldwide responsibility and mission from opposite directions, and an accommodation would provide both of us with needed lessons and strengths.

Many other aspects of our cultures are at opposite poles as well, but it is these opposites that provide a strong attraction. Dichotomies exist in the concepts of community and individualism, of cooperation and competition, in art, in architecture, in language, in philosophy, in religion, in science and medicine, in economics, in political systems, and in concepts of rights and obligations. In addition, there are differences in the concepts of power, of active and passive relationships, in the concepts of time, of history, and of tragedy. We, therefore, have much to learn from each other, for the reconciliation of opposites will lead us to a higher level of evolution.

Within the next few decades, four nations will have a claim to leadership as strong economic entities: the United States, the USSR, China, and Japan. This leaves Europe aside because it still has its own problems of achieving accommodations among its members. One would think initially that it would be advantageous for the United States and Japan to reach accommodations that would help set the stage for the ordering of the new world economy, but there are fundamental reasons why this is exceedingly difficult. Although there exist many similarities between the Chinese and the Japanese so that we face similar differences with each, there are two notable distinctions. First, whereas the Japanese like to base relationships on long-standing relations, they do not have an open attitude to foreigners; that is, friendship is difficult to achieve. The Chinese, conversely, have a saying that "the first visit, you meet a stranger; the second, you meet an old friend." They are much more open and more readily friendly, and Americans are still remembered favorably. Despite the differences in wealth and income, the Chinese do not feel themselves in any way inferior or "second class"; whereas the Japanese consider themselves superior in culture, they feel that the West sees them as "honorary Caucasians." Second, and more importantly, the Japanese have not accepted major responsibility for *world* affairs and will find it exceedingly difficult to do so. They are traditionally and presently willing to accept responsibility only for themselves, remaining highly inward-looking and security conscious, protective, and even isolationist in orientation. A primary objective is to make the world safe for Japan, or to have a world in which Japan is safe. It is not an orientation in which they are *willing* to risk much for world progress and welfare, though the economy and environment is constantly at "at risk" due to buffetings from nature and the world economy.

Similarly, Russia, which has dominated the history of the USSR, has also been isolationist, protective, security conscious, and inward-looking—all for understandable reasons, given the history of invasions into that territory. Also, whereas there is an attitude of joviality at times between Russians and Americans, there is not the same open friendship that one finds with the Chinese. There is, rather, a secretiveness characteristic of the persecuted peasant.

In addition, the United States has nothing to fear from China economically, politically, or militarily. It has much to gain from it culturally—in terms of art, science, and philosophy. Both have much to gain through wider economic relations.

To look in one other direction, the United States has tried over some decades to develop a special relationship with Latin America, only to be rebuffed on a number of occasions, and whereas efforts should be continued to develop closer economic ties in the Western Hemisphere, there does not seem to be at present an opening through which new initiatives could be taken.

The opening does exist with China and success would be cumulative. There are some serious obstacles in easing the state-owned enterprises into a competitive mode and eventually raising them into international competitiveness. There are ways of achieving this through bringing in foreign investors—even with 100% ownership—and providing temporary preference in government purchases to the products and services of the state-owned enterprise (much as the United States provided up to 50% preference for U.S. companies in defense contracts for balance-of-payments purposes). The preference could be as high as 25 or 50%, being brought down to zero over a five-year period, providing time for adjustment. Such a move would stimulate the desire to obtain more effective technology as well as foreign partners. The expansion of such ties would be the basis for a wider accommodation between the two countries, which would help to formulate rules for agreements on international trade, technology transfers, and investment. These must reflect the present *restructuring* of the world economy.

In addition, we need means of *reordering* the world economy so that it is based soundly on the two legs of efficiency *with* equity, on competition *with* cooperation, on individualism *with* community, so that there is a place for all to grow without enduring conflict. The means are available in sectoral agreements, based on regional or bilateral arrangements. These are but the next step to still wider arrangements, *eventually* encompassing the world. But a worldwide accommodation is not feasible presently.

The orientation of this reordering is founded on an understanding that the world is in fact a single entity and that there must be an appropriate place for the "two cultures" of science and art, of intellect and feeling, of rationality and compassion, of material advance and spiritual evolution, and of East and West. The overriding objective should be the creation of a unity with appropriate diversity, in recognition of our common destiny, which can yet be shaped by individual and collective creativity. But we must take partial steps toward the goal.

New opportunities have opened up; it will require a change of perceptions in order to take advantage of them, for we must think differently in seeking new solutions.

References

Drucker, Peter. 1986. The Changing World Economy. *Foreign Affairs,* pp. 768–891.

Lodge, George C., and Ezra F. Vogel. 1987. *Ideology and National Competitiveness.* Cambridge: Harvard University Press.

Chapter 3

THE MECHANICS OF INTERNATIONAL ECONOMIC LOCOMOTION

H. Peter Gray

Given the importance of international transactions to the British economy, it is surprising that Keynes did not pay greater attention to the international sector in *The General Theory* (1936).[1] It is less surprising, given the relative unimportance of the international sector in the postwar U.S. economy, that the formalization of Keynes' model in Cambridge, Massachusetts, was set in a closed economy. As the end of the twentieth century approaches, national economies and financial markets have become much more closely integrated so that some concept of a *global macroeconomy* and of macroeconomic interdependence is now necessary. This interdependence makes possible much closer interrelationships among national economies so that it is now possible for one nation to generate aggregate demand and to absorb output produced in another country on a much larger scale than was previously possible. This process, useful though it is in a Keynesian context because it allows aggregate demand to be matched with saving across national boundaries, carries with it the problem of financing. Problems of financing debt incurred by the generation of aggregate demand can impart an instability to the global macroeconomy and the international financial system. .

The first section of this chapter develops a simple set of global Keynesian identities to create a basic analytic framework for analysis of macroeconomic interdependence in the modern world. In particular, this framework, which draws heavily on a flow-of-funds analysis of international payments (Gray and Gray, 1988/89), permits analysis of the international transmission of aggregate demand through the phenomenon that has come to be known as "locomotion." The second section assesses the limits of such activity imposed by the international balance sheet position of the locomotive economy,

---

[1]Keynes did adumbrate the Keynes Plan in *The Means to Prosperity* (1933) at the same time that he anticipated the basic concepts of *The General Theory*. He was therefore fully aware of many of the international implications of his analysis. It is unfortunate that he never had time to develop it.

i.e., the problems of financing.[2] The third section considers the costs of playing the locomotive. The argument is summarized in the last section.

GLOBAL AGGREGATE DEMAND

Just as in any simple Keynesian model, the equilibrium level of world output, Y_G, is equal to the sum of nayional spending on consumption (C), investment (I), government expenditure on goods and services (G), and current surplus or net exports $(X - M)$ in each nation.[3]

(1) $$Y_G = \Sigma C_i + \Sigma I_i + \Sigma G_i + \Sigma(X - M)_i \ (i = 1, 2, \ldots, G)$$

Because of the symmetric activities of exporting and importing:

(2) $$\Sigma(X - M) \equiv 0$$

Global aggregate demand then comprises:

(3) $$Y_G = \Sigma Y_i = \Sigma C_i + \Sigma I_i + \Sigma G_i$$

Global income or output is the sum of aggregate demand in the G closed economies.[4] What is important is the role of current surpluses $(X - M)$ in the distribution and level of global aggregate demand since this is a source of effective aggregate demand and instability not usually considered. The mechanics of this system are fairly straightforward. Any surplus on current account serves to transfer saving (potential additional absorption and capital formation) from the surplus nation to the deficit nation: it allows the deficit nation to increase its consumption or capital formation beyond what would be possible in a closed economy at a given level of economic activity. This transfer mechanism will enhance global aggregate demand if the surplus country would have produced less if its current surplus were not available, and will, in the absence of a unilateral transfer or aid payment, increase the net worth of the surplus nation vis-a-vis foreigners (the nation's international net worth). At the same time, a current deficit will reduce international net worth (Gray, 1974). Thus a current surplus represents international saving $(S_i \geq 0)$ and a current deficit, international dissaving. International

---

[2]Most macroeconomic analysis focuses on flow variables to the exclusion of balance sheet (or stock) variables; this is a dangerous omission in any study of locomotion.

[3]For simplicity, it is assumed that there is no need to distinguish between transactions for goods and services and transfer payments including dividends and interest. Thus the balance on current account can be represented by $X - M$. Since balances on transfer payments will sum to zero for the world as a whole, this omission of international interest payments has important implications only when the transfers are made by nations with current deficits to those with current surpluses and expand domestic aggregate demand in the surplus countries by less than the net transfer of dividends and interest.

[4]This is, of course, what global income would be in a world of balanced current accounts throughout.

investment $(I_i > 0)$ is the spontaneous or autonomous acquisition of assets abroad by the residents of the nation. International payments (financial flows) are balanced when $S_i = I_i$ and there is no need either for a change in exchange rates or for compensatory capital movements by government. $S_i = I_i = 0$ is merely the special case of balanced trade with no (or balanced) capital movements. Clearly, international investment (and concomitant international saving) plays a positive role in the global economy by allowing saving in one country to be transferred to another in which real rates of return to investment are perceived to be higher.

A nation with a current deficit (international dissaving) is adding to aggregate demand for the "rest of the world" and is stimulating the world economy relative to the global level of aggregate demand compatible with that nation having balanced current account; it is, therefore, a *locomotive economy*. A (mercantilist) nation with a current surplus has output greater than absorption and is detracting from global aggregate demand; it may be described as a "caboose economy" since, in terms of global aggregate demand, it is dead weight.[5] Whereas it is conceivable for a nation to stimulate its own aggregate demand without allowing its current account to sink into (deeper) deficit, and enhancing global aggregate demand without increasing its international dissaving, such an occurrence is improbable and may be neglected. It is assumed that any (policy motivated) increase in aggregate demand will have international locomotive effects.

The transfer of aggregate demand among nations does not necessarily increase global saving and global investment; it merely redistributes a global amount of saving among nations. The nations that generate saving increase their total new worths by capital formation at home and international investment abroad. This international investment may be either real or financial (as distinct from a closed economy model in which the acquisition of financial assets does not constitute aggregate investment).

A locomotive country is necessarily impairing its international net worth and must pay a return on the capital that has been borrowed (real, i.e., foreign direct investment, or financial).

These concepts have been defined in *expost* terms and imply an equilibrium. As in the simple Keynesian model, the social virtue of being an international saver or dissaver depends upon the level of total aggregate demand, and there is no abstract predisposition to think of an international saver as necessarily conducting an antisocial policy.[6] The social value of a surplus or deficit depends upon the level of actual Y_G relative to potential Y_G. This question hinges, in turn, on the level of planned expenditures that may be taken as representing target variables in the standard Tinbergian framework (1970). Target values may be denoted with an asterisk and there is no reason to suppose that these targets, independently arrived at, should obey the global constraint.

$$(4) \qquad\qquad \Sigma(X - M)_i{}^* \neq 0$$

---

[5] A caboose in the United States is the wagon at the end of the train, which houses the conductor; in England, it is called a "guard's van"; and in France, a *fourgon a bagages*.
[6] This leads into complex questions such as what if the dissaver's current deficit is financed on long term at a subsidized rate: value judgments of this kind are probably best avoided.

The sum of the current balances is subject to the constraint that is defined in equation (2): they must sum to zero across the world.[7] Thus if the sum of planned current surpluses and deficits does not equal zero ($\Sigma(X - M)^* > 0$), the international system must adjust and new values of targets must be accepted. There is every reason to expect that the sum of world targets will be positive. In straightforward aggregate demand terms, a country with inadequate domestic investment has the choice of running a government deficit or of incurring debt from foreigners, and the latter, if it can be achieved, is far more appealing. More practically, it is reasonable to expect that the corporate sector recognizes the link between profits. R&D expenditures, and technological leadership (Gray and Milberg, 1988, Section VI) so that governments are always being urged to run a current surplus so that its high-tech sectors may generate sufficient funds to be able to devote as many resources to R&D as expectations warrant and competitive conditions require.

If the sum of the current account targets is positive, then countries will take steps to try and achieve those targets as nearly as possible. In the process, they will need to subordinate their trade policies to the achievement of their macroeconomic targets and the world's trading system will work less smoothly as (covert) increases in established levels of impediments to international trade cause the global economy to function less efficiently. If the sum of the current targets is positive as nations attempt to practice what Robinson (1966) called *The New Mercantilism,* competition for elusive current surpluses may be fierce,[8] and could give a recessionary bias to the global economy.

The world economy will be expected to work most efficiently when macroeconomic targets do not impede the efficiency of the international economy, that is, when the sum of current targets is equal to zero.[9] This happy state of affairs is most likely to be achieved when there is a dominant international power (a hegemon) that will play the role of the *nth* country. This role involves setting as its current target (or its tolerance) the opposite of the sum of the current targets of the other *n-1* countries. In a smoothly working gold standard or under a fixed exchange rate system, the hegemon fills this role. The hegemon is not completely passive in this since it has various options at its disposal to ensure that the other *n-1* countries do not impose excessively on it to its own social cost (Stoga, 1986) and must subject its own economic performance to its international role or else it loses its capacity to be the hegemon. There is nothing that precludes some flexibility of the exchange rate of the hegemon's currency, but this must be limited so that the hegemon's currency (the key currency) remains a reasonable standard of international value.

Short-run pressures on employment levels and the needs of high-tech corporations for an adequate cash flow suggest that the industrialized world as a whole will seek a collective current surplus. An efficient international system will require, then, that the

[7]Of course the free enterprise world is not a closed system in fact since the Eastern Bloc countries can have positive or negative balances on current and capital account. In financial terms, there exist also international financial institutions that may be sources of liquidity.

[8]There is a hair-raising account of the extent to which countries will go in search of a source of additional net exports in a recession in Wellons (1987).

[9]Most countries have a range of targets for the current balance so that if the sum of the expressed targets is positive the inefficiencies will arise only when the sum of the minimum acceptable targets is positive.

Third World runs target deficits equal to the desired surplus of the industrialized countries *and is able to finance them*.

THE BALANCE–SHEET CONSTRAINTS

Locomotive economies add to global aggregate demand at the expense of the steady impairment of their international net worths. This presents no problem for global aggregate demand provided that the locomotive country or bloc continues to be prepared to generate current deficits and to service the accumulating international debt, and provided that it *can finance* those deficits. Failing the ability to finance, a relied-upon source of global aggregate demand can suddenly wither and the global economic sink into a recession with all of the additional, trade policy inefficiencies that are likely to ensue.

When the deficit bloc is the developing countries, the traditional case, the means of finance is usually sovereign debt, countersigned if not incurred by the central government. However, even sovereign governments can exhaust their lines of credit and a shortfall of aggregate demand can suddenly be inflicted on the global macroeconomy. When the locomotive economy is the key currency nation, then the financing of the deficits can be incurred through the private financial sector. In either event, there is the potential for an abrupt decrease in global aggregate demand as financing strains reach their limit: replacement sources of aggregate demand must come from nations with strong creditor financial positions willing to erode those positions by assuming the locomotive role.[10]

There are, then, three possible problems leading to recession that may derive from the global macroeconomy: (1) a global sum of national targets for current surpluses in excess of zero, (2) the exhaustion of a locomotive economy's capacity to continue to play that role, and (3) a reluctance by nations to play the locomotive in time of need.[11]

The possibility that the family of independent national economies will strive for a collective surplus is the crux of the new mercantilism (Robinson, 1966). Cooper (1968) and Williamson (1983) address this problem by having the available planned deficits rationed out among the would-be surplus nations through international negotiation. This is a relatively well-known problem and constitutes the deflationary bias that seems to be inevitable in macroeconomic systems. If the innate desirability of a current surplus is positively related to the likelihood of some adverse shock, as seems reasonable if the surplus is merely an insurance against resource reallocation, then the greater integration of national economies and financial markets suggests that the collective target surplus will increase with integration. In this scenario surpluses are counterproductive

---

[10] As noted below, industrialized countries have not been enthusiastic to do such a thing with the exception of the United States after World War II and during the Reagan administration. The traditional anathema of the industrialized nations can probably be traced to the reasons offered in the text for preferring a current surplus rather than to any fixation with the international net worth as such.

[11] If all nations are in a depression or recession, then locomotion may not be necessary if all nations expand their economies in unison.

and the whole problem recalls the attempt in the Keynes plan to have surplus nations pay interest on their accumulated surpluses.

This is the immediate problem facing the global economy. The traditional deficit nations have ceased to play that role effectively because of the general malaise in Africa, the Third World debt crisis in Latin America, and the tendency in recent years of some Asian newly industrializing countries to accumulate surpluses (e.g., Taiwan and Korea). The bad experiences of international banks has also made locomotive credit more difficult to obtain for developing nations and economic aid is out of fashion. In their place and directly attributable to massive increases in the budgetary deficit of the federal government jumped the United States. This was a happy example of locomotion *par excellence*. The United States played the nth country role and the world economy has thrived during the years 1883 through 1988.[12] Unfortunately, this cannot continue in the absence of some fundamental change in the global financial system.[13] Table 3.1 shows the basic locomotive stimulus provide by the United States from 1983 through 1987 and the way in which the deficits were financed. For the United States to continue to play the locomotive requires that the current indebtedness be funded in some way so that panic withdrawals cannot force the U.S. national and the world financial systems into panic and crisis. It is not sufficient that existing indebtedness be funded but any future current account deficits will also need to be funded. *Only* under such conditions could the United States continue to provide locomotion to the global economy even if it wanted to. However, there are signs that the United States will not be willing to continue in this role for much longer and it is unlikely to want to do so when it discovers the obdurate fact that being a debtor allows other nations to call the economic tune.[14]

Putting aside special cases such as Saudi Arabia, which is running sizeable current deficits in the face of the collapse of oil prices, there seems to be no obvious substitute for the United States as the locomotive economy. During the period 1983 through 1987, Japan and West Germany have been willing to accumulate surpluses and are gradually trying to reduce them. Only if they are prepared to reduce them to zero will this be sufficient and then only if the target current surpluses of other countries are sufficiently small that they can be offset against planned deficits by traditional deficit units. Unfortunately for global aggregate demand, it is quite possible that the United States will strive to reduce its international indebtedness and will want to have positive international saving for a number of years.[15]

---

[12]This role was not wittingly undertaken and may indeed have contributed to a loss of global stability efficiency (capacity to resist adverse shocks; Gray and Gray, 1981) to a degree that offsets its serendipitous locomotive role.

[13]No less an authority than Robert Triffin (1988) describes the current international financial system as the "international financial scandal" because of the huge indebtedness of the U.S. financial system to foreigners. Triffin's piece is concerned with the replacement international financial system; he does not consider the problem of preserving what we have in order for the system to last long enough for a new system to be installed.

[14]Of course, it will be difficult for the creditors to bully the United States since they have large amounts of saving invested in the U.S. economy and since they will lose by economic instability equally as much as the debtor economy. Brazil and Mexico are less fortunate in this regard.

[15]In terms of the stability of the existing financial system, which still relies inordinately on the U.S. dollar, a series of U.S. surpluses are much to be desired.

Table 3.1

A. The International Net Worth of the United States[a] ($ billions at end of year)

	1983	1984	1985	1986	1987*
INW at end of preceding year	137.0	89.6	3.6	−111.9	−269.2
Current account balance	−67.0	−112.5	−122.1	−141.4	−160.7
Adjustments[b]	+19.6	+26.5	+6.6	−15.9	+61.7
INW at end of year	+89.6	3.6	−111.9	−269.2	−368.2

[a]Includes the official U.S. gold stock valued at $42.22 per troy ounce. This valuation results in an underestimate of U.S. international net worth of roughly $100 billion for all end-of-year data. (Gold holdings are valued officially at $11.2 billion.)

[b]Includes the effect of price changes for assets or liabilities and of exchange rate changes. The 1987 data include the upward revaluation of U.S. assets abroad as well as substantial losses in value of U.S. corporate securities held by non-Americans.

B. Outstanding Financial Assets of Non-Americans in U.S. Financial Markets.
(end-of-year data in billions of U.S. dollars)

	1982	1983	1984	1985	1986	1987
Foreign official assets	189.2	194.5	199.0	202.5	241.7	283.1
Foreign private assets	378.1	456.0	527.8	674.1	878.5	990.9
U.S. Treasury securities	425.8	33.9	56.9	83.6	91.5	78.4
Corporate and other bonds	16.8	17.5	32.3	82.5	142.1	171.0
Corporate stocks	76.8	97.3	95.9	124.1	167.4	173.4
Liabilities of nonbank concerns	27.5	26.8	30.5	29.4	26.7	28.8

*Provisional

Source: *Survey of Current Business,* June, 1987, pp. 39–40, 54–55; March, 1988, p. 41; June, 1988.

Locomotion can be the only driving force in the global macroeconomy under particular conditions and these conditions are usually short-lived. In the absence of these conditions, world aggregate demand will approximate the sum of those levels of national aggregate demand that permit balanced current accounts. Locomotion, i.e., major positive international dissaving, can be used only to generate global aggregate demand if there are countries both willing to dissave inter-nationally and *capable of doing so*. Thus locomotive economies must either be nations with large stocks of international assets that can withstand current deficits or the locomotion must be limited to that rate of international dissaving that can be financed as being compatible with economic growth.[16] If international reserves and wealth are centered in countries that are unwilling to play the locomotive, then any global recession/depression will be more difficult to escape from.

---

[16]Here the whole question of the ability to service international debt is involved, but as a first measure it might be reasonable to adopt the principle that the ratio of external debt to GNP or to current revenues should not increase.

COSTS OF LOCOMOTION

Kindleberger (1973) suggests that the severity of the depression of the 1930s was due in large measure to the nonexistence of a *n*th country in the international financial system, i.e., no country was prepared to play the locomotive when that proved necessary. This writer believes that this problem is very important for the stability of the international financial system, but requires the "right" setting before the absence of such a leader nation or hegemon becomes crucial for global prosperity (that is, depression requires a global economy without resilience as well as some trigger mechanism such as an international financial breakdown or crisis). Given that the only nation with any claim or aspiration to playing the role of the *n*th country is currently the largest debtor nation in the world, visions of potential instability cannot be easily pushed aside. If the potential existence of a locomotive is so important, the question of the costs of playing that role becomes a major consideration. It is possible that these costs have increased substantially since the 1930s and even the 1950s and 1960s in large part because of the increased integration of the global economy.

A feature of the modern world is that the industrialized world has been brought much more closely together as a result of the new technologies of communications and data processing. These innovations affect particularly the knowledge-intensive sectors such as finance and banking, management techniques, and technology transfer. The ease with which funds can be moved internationally has contributed to the ability of the United States to finance its locomotive activities. Management techniques and the new wave of technological innovations have made locomotion more costly in terms of its contribution to a failure of industry to maintain its technological competitiveness.

Table 3.1 shows that the United States was able to finance its locomotion by having its private financial sector incur liabilities to nonresidents rather than having the government become obliged to foreigners. This ability to finance international liabilities through the private sector, which probably delayed a full appreciation in the United States of the costs that were being incurred by the locomotive actions of the Reagan administration, was due largely to the strength and sophistication of the U.S. financial sector but also to the development of new communications technology and new financial technologies that (appear to) provide liquidity to foreign holders of dollar assets (Levich, 1987).[17] But these same technologies that have facilitated the procurement of foreign saving also make it easy to withdraw or to attempt to withdraw that foreign saving in the event of a panic or crisis. It is fair to say that this cost of locomotion is not yet fully appreciated by the U.S. electorate or business sector even though the cost of servicing the debt is beginning to gain recognition.

Nor is the effect of locomotion on the competitiveness of home country industries particularly well understood. Branscomb (1988) points out that the scientific base of

---

[17]Guttentag and Herring (1986) point out the fallacy of composition that underlies the belief that any credit system can ensure all asset holders of liquidity in the face of a concerted attempt to obtain that liquidity.

modern industrial technology simplifies both the integration of parts manufactured in different geographic areas and the spread of new technologies to different parts of the world. Markets are becoming more internationally integrated. But the ability to generate technology feeds on past innovations, and any country that loses ground in the technology race will find that its firms have to strive even harder to catch up again (Gray and Milberg, 1988, Section VI). Under a system of flexible exchange rates, the financing of international dissaving is accompanied by a strengthening of the locomotive's currency as the inflow of foreign exchange flows through the foreign exchange market. This, in turn, increases the pressures of foreign competition for the locomotive's firms in both home and foreign markets, erodes market share, and reduces profits. R&D expenditures are positively related to profit rates so that a currency appreciation inevitably puts the locomotive's firms at a technological disadvantage, which will grow because of the inherent dynamics of innovation and with the duration of the overvaluation (Borrus et al., 1986). As this cost of locomotion is more clearly recognized, the willingness of a nation to play the locomotive will decline.

This technological disadvantage that has accrued to U.S. firms has been reinforced by the savage expenditure reductions imposed on the Latin American debtor nations in which U.S. corporations held a leading market position. Together they explain one reason for the slow recovery of the U.S. current balance in the face of quite substantial depreciation of the dollar against the yen and the European currencies. Another reason for this slow reduction in the U.S. current deficit, in addition to the obvious one of increasing interest and dividend payments, is the lack of any significant reduction in the U.S. rate of absorption (in fact, U.S. GNP and consumption have expanded concomitantly with the weakening of the dollar since the fall of 1985).[18]

CONCLUSION

The dramatic switch from a major creditor nation to the leading debtor nation by the United States was brought about by huge deficits on current account (international dissaving). These deficits had the effect of passing the stimulus of the budget deficit of the federal government through to other countries in the global economy so that the United States, unwittingly, sacrificed its creditor position in order to play the locomotive for the world economy. This process has had repercussions on U.S. industry that are not generally appreciated and that represent an identifiable cost for any nation contemplating deliberate assumption of the locomotive role in the future. These costs are likely to prolong the U.S. current account deficit because they make the deficit more difficult to remove. Such costs are also likely to spur the unwillingness of industrialized nations to play the locomotive and, in this way, will tend to increase the "natural" tendency for the bloc of industrialized nations to seek a collective current surplus, thereby enhancing the deflationary bias imposed on the global economy.

---

[18]Traditional balance-of-payments adjustment theory recognizes the dual role of expenditure switches and expenditure reductions. Under flexible rates, the expenditure switch is automatic and de-emphasizes the concurrent need for expenditure reductions (Gray, 1974).

APPENDIX

The ability of Third World nations to serve as locomotives by their willingness to borrow internationally is limited by their ability to increase their indebtedness. The Third World debt crisis of 1982 is a classic example of what happens when Third World countries increase their indebtedness at an unsustainable pace. The excessive indebtedness became a source of embarrassment for international lenders when unforseen events cause a foreign exchange funding crisis. The Third World served as a locomotive area when the OPEC nations became large surplus nations. Together with the industrialized countries that ran current deficits, the Third World countries borrowed large amounts directly and in the Euromarkets. The rate of borrowing was facilitated by bad judgment by the lenders (Guttentag and Herring, 1986) as well as by the borrowers. A rapid increase in the costs of borrowing coupled with a severe recession in the industrialized countries made it impossible for the debtor nations to service their debt. At this time, orthodox wisdom prescribed expenditure reductions in the debtor countries in order that they might generate current surpluses. Thus, whereas the Third World countries played their traditional locomotive role during the 1970s, they played it at a nonsustainable rate in a turbulent environment. The economic costs inflicted on these countries by the subsequent deflationary policies have been enormous and could, unless repealed, threaten existing democratic institutions.

The Latin American debtor countries have been under pressure from private (and official) creditors to service their outstanding debts for some years since the question of their ability to service their commitments first arose in 1982. To this end, the Latin American countries have thrown their economies into severe recessions and have subordinated virtually all of their economic policies to the servicing of their international debt. Even then, they are technically in default. Their efforts to service their debt have transformed a bloc of traditional locomotive economies into caboose economies. In 1988 the collective balance of trade of ten Latin American countries amounted to about $28 billion. Although much of this ostensible international saving will be devoted to interest payments and reduction of principal, this surplus by the bloc constitutes a major reduction in global aggregate demand and must be offset by debt incurrence by some other member of the international system. Because the United States is the dominant supplier of exports to these countries, the effect of the Latin American international saving is to make the problem of elimination of the international deficit of the United States more difficult (alternatively, it automatically enhances the international locomotive effect of the U.S. federal deficit).

References

Borrus, M., L. Tyson, and J. Zysman. 1986. Creating Advantage: How Government Policies Shape International Trade in the Semiconductor Industry, in Paul M. Krugman (ed.): *Strategic Trade Policy and the New International Economics*. Cambridge: MIT Press, p. 93.

Branscomb, Lewis M. 1988. Technological Change and Its International Diffusion, in James H.

Cassing and Steven L. Husted (eds.): *Capital Technology, and Labor in the New Global Economy*. Washington, D.C.: American Enterprise Institute, pp. 107–108.

Cooper, Richard N. 1968. *The Economics of Interdependence: Economic Policy in the Atlantic Community*. New York: McGraw-Hill.

Gray, H. Peter. 1974. *An Aggregate Theory of International Payments Adjustment*. London: Macmillan, pp. 45–48.

Gray, H. Peter, and Jean M. Gray. 1988/89 The International Accounts in a Flow-of-Funds Format. *Journal of Post Keynesian Economics* (Winter), pp. 241–260.

Gray, H. Peter, and J. Milberg. 1988. Discretionary Profits: Concepts and Implications. *Economic Working Paper* No. 45. Dearborn: University of Michigan.

Gray, Jean M., and H. Peter Gray. 1981. The Multinational Bank: A Financial MNC? *Journal of Banking and Finance* 5 (Spring): pp. 55–56.

Guttentag, Jack M., and Richard J. Herring, Disaster Myopia in International Banking. *Princeton Essays in International Finance*, No. 164 (September 1986), p. 13.

Keynes, J. M. 1933. *The Means to Prosperity*. London: Macmillan.

Keynes, J. M. 1936. *The General Theory of Employment, Interest and Money*. London: Macmillan.

Kindleberger, Charles P. 1973. *The World in Depression, 1929–1939*. London: Penguin, p. 292.

Levich, Richard N. 1988. Financial Innovations in International Financial Markets, in Martin Feldstein (ed.): *The United States in the World Economy*. Chicago: University of Chicago Press for the National Bureau of Economic Research, pp. 215–256.

Robinson, Joan. 1966. *The New Mercantilism*. Cambridge: Cambridge University Press.

Stoga, Alan J. 1986. If America Won't Lead. *Foreign Policy*, No. 64 (Fall), pp. 79–97.

Triffin, Robert. 1987. The *IMS* (International Monetary *System. . . .* or *Scandal?*) and the *EMS* (European Monetary *System*) *Banca Nazionale del Lavoro Quarterly Review*, No. 162, pp. 239–261.

Wellons, Philip A. 1987. Banks and Export Credit Wars: Mixed Credits in the Sicartsa Financing, in Rita M. Rodriguez (ed.): *The Export-Import Bank at Fifty*. Lexington, Mass.: Lexington Books, pp. 167–204.

Williamson, John. 1983. *The Open Economy and the World Economy*. New York: Basic Books.

Chapter 4

ENVIRONMENTAL RISKS AND THE BARGAINING POWER OF MULTINATIONAL COMPANIES*

Franklin R. Root

INTRODUCTION

The fundamental proposition of this chapter is that multinational corporations (MNCs) can control to some degree their external environment so as to lessen country and other risks. The degree of control can range from domination over outside actors to agreements involving collaboration or compromise with such actors. We postulate that in most circumstances the MNC must collaborate or compromise with such actors because it does not have sufficient power to dominate them. Because the modality to obtain collaboration or cooperation is negotiation, we can regard risk control by MNCs as mainly *risk negotiation*.

We start by decomposing the MNC's external environment into a *transactional* environment and a *contextual environment*.

TRANSACTIONAL AND CONTEXTUAL ENVIRONMENTS

The *transactional* environment consists of actors with whom the MNC has actual or potential direct relations (transactions), such as customers, host governments, suppliers, competitors, banks, and so on. The transactional environment, therefore, is the set of actual and potential transactions between the MNC and external entities.

In contrast, the *contextual* environment consists of a multiplicity of actors linked by political, economic, technological, socio-cultural, and physical interactions that can constrain the MNC's transactional interactions but do not enter into them. Examples of contextual interactions include the behavior of foreign exchange rates, political revo-

*Reprinted from *The International Trade Journal,* Vol. III, no. 1, fall 1988.

lutions, scientific discovery, the communications infrastructure, and population growth.

A given actor may appear in both the transactional and contextual environments of the MNC. For example, an MNC enters into transactions with the host government on taxation issues. At the same time, that government's relations with other governments can affect the MNC and are therefore part of its contextual environment. Individual private actors in the MNC's transactions environment may also enter the MNC's contextual environment, but to a lesser degree than governments.

Figure 4.1 depicts the transactional and contextual environments of the multinational corporation.

The critical distinction between the two environments is that multinational managers can influence in some degree the behavior of transactional actors, but they cannot affect the behavior of contextual actors. The transactional environment is specific to the individual firm, and it changes over time. When, for example, an MNC grows through geographical and product diversification, it extends its transactional environment by adding new transactions with new or old actors. But the transactional environment is not only a function of the MNC's actions: it also depends on the initiatives of outside actors to interact directly with the MNC, such as governments, competitors, international organizations, and special interest groups.

The transactional environment consists of actors (organizations, groups, and persons) with whom MNC actually or potentially interacts (transacts) in direct ways. The MNC

Figure 4.1. Transactional and contextual environments of the multinational corporation contextual environment.

seeks to strengthen control over its transactional environment to reduce economic and political risks that constrain its exploitation of international business opportunities. The contextual environment consists of a multiplicity of actors linked by political, economic, technological, socio-cultural, and physical interactions that can constrain the MNC's transactional interactions but do not enter into them. This environment *cannot* be controlled by the MNC.

We postulate that MNCs seek to strengthen control over the transactional environment to minimize economic, political, and competitive risk that constrain their exploitation of international business opportunities.[1] To clearly distinguish this proactive mode of controlling environmental risk, we turn to a brief discussion of reactive, active, and proactive modes of response to environmental risk.

REACTIVE, ACTIVE, AND PROACTIVE RESPONSE MODES TO ENVIRONMENTAL CHANGES

Multinational managers may perceive international environmental changes as beyond their ability to anticipate or control. Such managers believe the entire environment of the firm is contextual and so uncertain as to defy any prediction. All managers can do, therefore, is to employ a *reactive response mode* after environmental changes have occurred that constrain MNC performance.

When managers believe that they can anticipate environmental changes but cannot control them in any degree, they use an *active response mode* to environmental changes. Such managers view the entire environment as contextual but predictive to some degree. By responding to anticipated changes, managers hope to limit or avoid constraints on MNC performance.

When managers perceive international environmental changes as controllable in some degree through their own actions, then reactive or active responses give way to *proactive* responses that are aimed at influencing environmental changes in directions that will minimize environmental risks that constrain the exploitation of market opportunities. In effect, these managers decompose the environment into transactional (controllable) and contextual (noncontrollable) environments.

To demonstrate the usefulness of the distinction drawn between transactional and contextual environments for the management of risks by the MNC, we apply it to country risk.

WHAT ARE COUNTRY RISKS?

Country risks express the uncertainties felt by business managers about future government policies and/or political situations in one or more countries that would affect the

---

[1]More generally, managers seek to enhance control over the transactional environment to optimize economic rents. Control is aimed at increasing risk-adjusted economic returns. In this chapter, however, we consider only risks.

safety and profitability of actual or future business ventures.[2] As defined here, therefore, country risk derives from a manager's *subjective uncertainty* about the *future* values of government-policy/political-situation variables that he perceives as *critical* to the performance of a *business venture*.

Country risks may be classified as system risks or policy risks. System risks arise from potential macro changes in the political system, such as revolution, subversion, civil strife, and war. Policy risks arise from a government's potential actions that would change the "rules of the game" for MNCs, such as expropriation, local content requirements, and transfer restrictions. System risks arise from changes in the contextual environment; while some policy risks are contextual, other policy risks arise from changes in an MNC's transactional environment.

In most instances, managers are concerned with policy risks, that is, possible changes in government policies in a foreign host country, although a foreign business venture may also be critically sensitive to government policies in the home country of the parent company.[3] Unless otherwise indicated, however, we take country risks to mean manager's uncertainties relating to the behavior of both transactional and contextual actors in a country that is *foreign* to the parent multinational company. Most commonly, country risks express the managers' uncertainties as to whether or not the present host government or a successor government will arbitrarily change the "rules of the game" so as to cause a loss of earnings or assets of the company's venture in that country.

Country risks may be viewed as expected losses.

Algebraically,

$$E(L_i) = X_i \cdot P(V_i),$$

Where $E(L_i)$ is the *expected loss* to the multinational firm from *event* (i), X_i is the firm's *exposure* to event (i), and $P(V_i)$ is the probability that event (i) will occur over a designated future period.

Event (i) is an event that, if it occurred, would *directly* cause a loss to the MNC by constraining the ownership, control, operations, or earnings convertibility of its foreign venture. The probability estimation of event (i) commonly involves the probability estimation of other events that are considered "precedents" of event (i). In terms of probability theory, therefore, event (i) is usually a compound event.

Exposure to a country risk event is defined as the *maximum* amount that would be lost by the international firm if event (i) were to occur. The firm's exposure is fundamentally the present value of the expected stream of net earnings over the economic life of the venture.[4]

This simple model defines country risk as a *downside* risk. Although it is recognized that environmental changes in a host country could create gains for MNCs, the concern

---

[2]We prefer to use the term *country risk* rather than *political risk* because the latter implies that the causes of the risk are wholly political and therefore outside the concern of economists. Actually, government behavior is motivated by economic as well as political and social factors. Furthermore, the instruments of government policies are commonly economic in nature.

[3]For American companies it is not too much to say that the major source of political risk in business dealings with Communist countries is Washington, D.C.

[4]In practice, firms are inclined to measure exposure in accounting or balance sheet terms.

of managers with country risks is one of potential loss rather than potential gain. Unless otherwise indicated, therefore, we shall regard country risks as downside risks.

To sum up, the expected loss to the MNC from a country risk event is the firm's exposure to that event multiplied by the probability that the event will occur over a designated future period.

RISK–EXPOSURE AND RISK–CONTROL STRATEGIES FOR MANAGING COUNTRY RISKS

The distinction between transactional and contextual environments is the basis for two kinds of MNC strategies for managing country risks.

Risk-exposure strategies lower the economic values exposed to risk in a foreign venture. Such strategies are *active* responses to anticipated risk situations arising from environmental changes that are viewed by managers as uncontrollable by their firm. These strategies, therefore, are addressed to the contextual environment. We can speak of four instruments of risk-exposure strategies: avoidance, insurance, hedging, and retention.

Avoidance is the potential or actual reduction of the MNC's *gross* assets in the host country and ranges from the decision not to invest in a local venture through the reduction of the venture's specific assets (such as cash or inventories) or the sharing of ownership in a joint venture to the liquidation (disinvestment) of the venture.

Insurance is the transfer of risk from the MNC to an outside agency and is most appropriate at the pre-entry phase.[5]

Hedging is the reduction of the MNC's *net* assets in the host country through an increase of local liabilities owed to creditors in the host country.[6]

Retention is the deliberate assumption of exposure to political risk. The MNC can seldom eliminate all of its exposure in the host country through avoidance, insurance, and hedging. If the MNC decides to initiate or continue its foreign venture, therefore, it almost certainly will retain some exposure. However, a distinction should be drawn between a conscious decision to retain a certain exposure as one element of a political risk strategy and an unplanned exposure that results from the absence of a strategy.

In contrast to risk-exposure strategies, *risk-control strategies* of MNCs aim to prevent the occurrence of loss situations by influencing the behavior of host governments, the key transactional actors in the country environment.[7] To do so, MNCs must negotiate with host governments because they seldom have the power to dictate to them. Prag-

---

[5]Insurance against expropriation, inconvertibility, and civil strife, insurrection, and war is available to U.S. MNCs from the Overseas Private Investment Corporation only prior to the decision to invest in a qualified country. Political risk insurance is available from private agencies, such as Lloyd's of London, in later phases of an investment; indeed, private insurance policies usually require annual renewal. Unless the MNC's Early Warning System (EWS) is superior to the EWS, of the private insurance companies, the cost of political risk insurance will be prohibitively high or simply unavailable when a major political crisis is on the horizon.

[6]Hedging may also be used to reduce exposure to foreign exchange risks.

[7]Systemwide political changes, such as those brought about by revolution or war, occur in the contextual environment and lie, therefore, outside the control of the MNC managers.

matically, therefore, controlling political risks may be translated into *negotiating* political risks.[8] Risk-control strategies are proactive responses to anticipated or possible risk situations in the external environment that are viewed as controllable by the firm through negotiations or, very rarely, through dictation. These strategies, therefore, are addressed to the transactional environment.

Figure 4.2 offers a schematic of political risk-exposure and risk-control strategies.

POSTENTRY COUNTRY–RISK MANAGEMENT

International managers may use risk-exposure and risk-control strategies in both the pre-entry and postentry phases of a foreign venture. We offer a brief description of the elements of postentry country-risk management (which has received lesser attention from scholars) before taking a closer look at bargaining leverage.

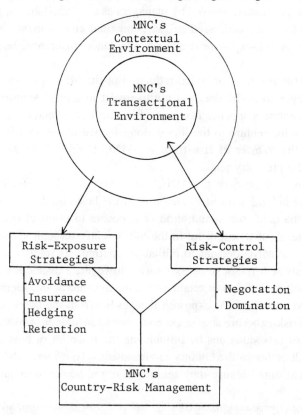

Figure 4.2. Country-risk management: Risk-exposure and risk-control strategies of the multinational corporation.

---

[8]Negotiations with business firms and other private institutions in the host country and elsewhere and negotiations with the home-country government may, at times, supplement or complement negotiations with the host government that are of primary significance in most circumstances.

Postentry risk management begins with the multinational firm's *country-risk strategy* (comprising of a mix of risk-exposure and risk-control strategies) at the start of the venture in the host country. At the very least, this strategy is implied in the design of the venture (its size, ownership, mode of operation, and so on), the "rules of the game" negotiated with the host government, and the investor's assumptions about the future investment climate in the host country. But *implied* strategy is *not* sufficient for country risk management. The MNC needs to have an *explicit* strategy whose assumptions, objectives, and policies are understood by corporate and country managers who are responsible for the viability and profitability of the foreign venture.

An *early warning system* (EWS) continually monitors the host country environment. Its purpose is to alert country and corporate managers to environmental changes that could endanger the foreign venture.

The MNCs *bargaining leverage* with the host government derives from the latter's perception of the foreign venture's social contribution to the host country *and* the indispensability of the multinational firm as the ultimate source of that contribution. *Bargaining leverage is the foundation of risk-control strategies*.

Contingency plans are courses of action prepared in advance to cope with loss situations that cannot be managed under the current country-risk strategy. Contingency plans, therefore, are anticipated responses to *critical discontinuities* in the investment climate, such as revolution or expropriation, that would render the current strategy unworkable. When managers cannot prevent such discontinuities through negotiations with the host government, they need to adopt a contingency plan based on a *new country-risk strategy* with new objectives and a new mix of risk-exposure and risk-control strategies.

MAINTAINING BARGAINING LEVERAGE WITH THE HOST GOVERNMENT

Earlier it was postulated that the MNC and the actors in its transactional environment can influence each other's behavior. The prevailing modality for this two-way influence is *negotiation* because the MNC can seldom completely dominate a transactions actor, or conversely. Some degree of compromise on issues dividing the two parties is necessary if they are to influence each other. However, the more bargaining power the MNC has relative to a transactional actor, the more it can influence that actor's behavior in ways beneficial to the MNC. Our comments here deal with creating and maintaining bargaining power or leverage with the host government—the transactional actor whose behavior is most critical to the country viability of the MNC's venture.

The MNC's bargaining leverage with the host government is greatest *prior* to its entry into the host country. On the one hand, the government wants something the MNC has—technology, access to world markets, management skills, capital, or other proprietary assets—but it cannot compel the MNC's entry that would bring these assets to the host country economy. On the other hand, the MNC wants something the host country has—markets, natural resources, labor, other country-specific assets—but it will not experience a financial loss if it does not enter the country.

However, once the MNC establishes a venture in the host country, it loses some of its bargaining leverage. The host government now has the power to deprive the MNC of the venture's assets through expropriation or limit the venture's profitability through price controls, taxation, local-content requirements, restrictions on repatriation, or in several other ways. In sum, the venture becomes hostage to host government behavior.

The MNC's ability to maintain bargaining leverage with the host government after entry depends on two conditions: (1) the host government's perception that the *social benefits of the MNC's venture continue to exceed its social costs,* and (2) the host government's perception that the *MNC is an indispensable source of net social benefits, a source that would be impossible or costly to replace with a local entity.*

The host government's perception of the net social benefits of an MNC's local venture tends to shift in a negative direction over time. In the early years, the host government may perceive a venture's social benefits as far outweighing its social costs. After all, the MNC is bringing in technology, management, and capital to form a new enterprise while it is taking little or nothing out of the host country. However, once the venture reaches full operation, the inflow of these MNC assets ordinarily slackens off, whereas, at the same time, the MNC starts to repatriate profits. Hence the host government may now perceive the venture as contributing less social benefit and may take actions to halt or reverse this decline, such as higher taxes, withdrawal of incentives, forced sale of some equity to local investors, or even expropriation. The shifting host government perceptions of a foreign venture's social contribution may be conceptualized as the *foreign investment country-risk life cycle.*

How can the MNC sustain the *net social benefits* of its venture as perceived by the government? Fundamentally, by making certain that the policies and operations of its venture support the government's perception of social benefits. But this requires that MNC managers understand what behavior the government views as socially beneficial and what behavior it views as socially costly. It would be rash for MNC managers to assume that the host government evaluates the venture's performance in the same way that they do.[9] However, even when MNC managers understand the government's perception of social benefits, they may be unwilling to adapt the venture's policies and operations to that perception if to do so would lower profitability or otherwise injure the MNC's interests, including its bargaining leverage on the host government. Clever managers look for ways to enhance the perceived social benefits of the venture that do not restrain profits or otherwise injure the MNC's interests. But clever managers also recognize that when perceived social benefits become low, then the venture becomes more vulnerable to adverse government action.

Sustaining the perceived net social benefits of the MNC's venture is necessary but not sufficient to maintain host country viability. This is so because many host govern-

---

[9]In countries where host governments use formal social cost benefit systems to screen the entry of MNC ventures, managers can more easily gain an understanding of the government's "social cost/benefit model" than in countries where MNC ventures are screened on an *ad hoc* basis.

ments, particularly in developing countries, view foreign-owned ventures as undesirable on purely *political* grounds. Hence the presence of foreign investors can be justified only if they are making a positive social contribution *that is beyond the capability of local firms*. To maintain viability in such countries, therefore, the MNC must be viewed by the host government as *indispensable* as a source of social benefits.

How can the MNC maintain or even create political leverage with a host government? Here are some MNC policies that may build leverage:

- Keep local venture dependent on inflows from parent company that would be impossible or difficult to replace, such as technology, technical/management skills, specialized capital equipment, components, materials, and so on.
- Keep control over local venture's access to world markets.
- Establish multiple national production (sourcing) locations for products manufactured by the joint venture.
- Develop transnational alliances whose interests would be injured by the host government's adverse treatment of the venture: consortia with other MNCs, financing arrangements with banks in several countries, long-term, supply contracts with customers in several countries, financing or other arrangements with international institutions, and so on.
- Develop local allies in the host country whose interests would be injured by the host government's adverse treatment of the venture: suppliers, customers, labor unions, distributors, banks, joint venture partners, and so on.
- Lobby the host government through the MNC's own contacts, the foreign business community, and local business organizations.

Not all of these policy measures may be available to an individual MNC. Furthermore, some measures may be undesirable in certain circumstances. For instance, keeping the venture dependent on the MNC may be regarded by some host governments as lowering the venture's net social benefits because it adds to foreign exchange costs (balance of payments effect) or limits the linkages of the venture with indigenous enterprises (economic development effect). In general, the MNC in trying to maintain bargaining leverage must contend with a host government that is trying to make the foreign venture less—no more—dependent on the parent company. MNC policies to maintain bargaining leverage, therefore, may become two-edge swords: a clumsy policy can provoke punitive action by a host government rather than prevent it.

CONCLUDING NOTE

Theories of the multinational enterprise based on monopolistic advantage or transaction costs have ignored the capability of MNCs to minimize risks by controlling to some degree their external environments. Instead, these theories assume a set of *exogenous* environmental, industry, and market factors that together determine MNC behavior. We believe that any such deterministic theories can only be partial explanations of MNC behavior because they fail to take account of the bargaining power ("free will") of MNCs.

In this chapter we offer a conceptual framework for the study of power relations between MNCs and the actors comprising their transactional environments. We are hopeful that this framework will stimulate both theoretical and empirical research that will strengthen our understanding of multinational corporations that together with national governments are the principal actors in the global economy.

Chapter 5

THE THEORY OF INTERNATIONAL PRODUCTION

John H. Dunning

INTRODUCTION

The theory of foreign-owned production seeks to explain the extent and pattern of value-added activities by multinational enterprises (MNEs) outside their national boundaries. MNEs are multiactivity firms that engage in foreign direct investment. Like international trading companies, they undertake cross-border transactions; unlike them, they own and control foreign production facilities. Like multiplant domestic firms, MNEs operate two or more production units, and internalize the transactions between these units. Unlike them, at least one of these production units is located in a foreign country and the markets internalized are transnational rather than domestic.

The theory of foreign-owned production is thus concerned with the *location* of value adding activities and the *ownership* and *organization* of these activities. As such, it draws upon and integrates two strands of economic theory. The first is the theory of international resource allocation based upon the spatial distribution of factor endowments. This theory chiefly addresses itself to the *location* of production. The second is the theory of economic organization, which is essentially concerned with the *ownership* of that production and ways in which the transactions relating to that production (including those that may impinge on its location) are organized.

In traditional, i.e., classical or neoclassical models of trade, which were the dominant paradigms in international economics until the 1950s, only the first issue, viz. the "where" of production was addressed. Questions relating to the ownership and organization of economic activity were ignored. This was because the market was assumed to be a perfect mechanism of exchange and to involve zero transaction costs. Resources were assumed to be immobile across national boundaries but mobile within national boundaries. Firms were assumed to engage in only a single value-added activity. Entrepreneurs were assumed to be profit maximizers. Managerial strategy was assumed to be confined to identifying the optimum level of output and minimizing the costs of producing that output.

However, once one allows for imperfections in goods or factor markets, the possibility of alternative patterns of ownership of firms and/or organizing transactions arises. For example, in place of one firm selling its product through the market to another firm that then adds value to it, the same firm may coordinate both sets of activity, and in so doing, replace the market as a mechanism for transacting the intermediate product. Where at least one of these activities spans national boundaries, foreign production occurs. The factors influencing the modality of organizing cross-border activities are therefore at the heart of the theory of foreign-owned production; indeed, some writers go as far as to assert that it is the only question of interest.

Taking a different starting point, it might equally be asked why, given the ownership of firms and the way in which they organize production and transactions, they should choose to locate at least some of their value-added activities in a foreign country. In this case, the spatial distribution of factor endowments may be as relevant as it is in explaining some kinds of trade. Put another way, the introduction of market imperfections and the multiactivity enterprise not only opens up the possibility of foreign production; it requires a complete reappraisal of the theory of trade. Indeed, some types of international transactions, e.g., intraindustry trade, can be explained only by use of the theory of economic organization.

From the above, it should be evident that any attempt to theorize about the extent and pattern of international production crucially depends on the type of question one wishes to answer. Is it primarily "why do firms own foreign production facilities;" or "why do firms locate their activities in one country rather than another;" or "why does the participation of foreign, relative to indigenous firms, differ between countries and sectors;" or "under what conditions will firms finance their foreign activities in the currencies of their home country rather than in those of another (i.e., engage in foreign direct investment)"? Even a cursory review of the literature on international production[1] suggests that, very often, researchers address themselves to related, but rather different questions.

Similarly, scholars differ in their choice of the unit of analysis, i.e., the variable to be explained. Some authors have essentially taken a macro-economic perspective and concerned themselves with why *countries* engage in foreign direct investment. These economists, e.g., Kojima (1973, 1978, 1982) usually take as their starting point neo-classical-type trade models and extend them to explain the extent and pattern of foreign production. Not surprisingly, they tend to focus on location-specific variables and why firms of particular nationality may have different propensities to engage in trade and production than others. Others, more interested in the behavior of individual enterprise, draw upon the theory of the domestic firm (which seeks to answer very different questions than that of international trade) to explain both the existence and the growth of the MNE. This school of thought, of which Buckley and Casson (1976, 1985), Casson (1987), Hennart (1982, 1985, 1986), Rugman (1986), and Teece (1981, 1985) are leading exponents, looks upon the multinational enterprise as a hierarchy that internalizes the market for cross-border intermediate products, and derives its methodology and

---

[1]For example, as set out by Agarwal (1980), Calvet (1981), Cantwell (1989), Dunning (1973), Grosse (1981). A bibliography of the mainstream writings on the theory of international production is contained in Dunning (1988b).

approach from both the founder of modern transaction cost economics viz. Ronald Coase (1937, 1960) and that of organizational theorists such as Alchian and Demsetz (1972), Herbert Simon (1947, 1955), and Williamson (1975, 1985, 1986).

A third group of economists, more closely allied in background to the second than the first, addresses the question of why firms of one nationality are better able to penetrate foreign markets than indigenous firms located in those markets, and why they wish to *control* value-added activities outside their national boundaries. Stephen Hymer (1960, 1968, 1976) was the progenitor of this type of explanation of foreign production, which he argued could not occur without the investing firms possessing some kind of monopolistic advantages over and above those possessed by their indigenous competitors. In his explanation, he drew not so much on the theory of the firm, but on the theory of industrial organization or market structure, which a few years earlier had been developed to explain the pattern and ownership of U.S. domestic industry by Bain (1956).

In reviewing the literature on the determinants on international production, it is important to distinguish between these approaches, for what may be an exogenous variable in one theory may be endogenous in another. It follows, then, that there is no one correct explanation of international production, only a correct answer to particular questions, each of which may help us to complete a jigsaw of understanding about the pattern ownership and location of firms outside their national boundaries.

Finally, it may be worth pointing out that the nature of value-added activities by MNEs, like that by national firms, is extremely varied. Because of this, both the motives for and determinants of international production will differ. The parameters influencing a UK MNE to invest in a copper mine in New Guinea are unlikely to be the same as those influencing investment by a Japanese color television company in the United States; whereas those determining the pattern of rationalized production in the European Community by a large and geographically diversified U.S. motor vehicles MNE will be quite different from an investment by Korean construction management company in Kuwait.

In summary, we would argue that it is not possible to construct a single operationally testable theory that can explain all forms of foreign-owned production; any more than it is possible to construct a generalized theory to explain all forms of trade, or the behavior of all kinds of firms. It is fully accepted in the literature that interindustry trade needs different explanations than intraindustry trade, and that any theory of the firm critically depends on the assumed motivation of enterprises. At the same time, we would assert that it *is* possible to formulate a general paradigm of international production, which sets out a conceptual framework and seeks to identify clusters of variables relevant to an explanation of all kinds of foreign output. It does not, however, attempt to pinpoint or evaluate the specific parameters relevant to explaining particular types of MNE activities. Within this framework, we believe that most of the partial micro or macro theories of international production can be accommodated, and that, whereas the appropriability and significance of the variables identified by each will differ, they should be more properly viewed as complementary rather than substitutable explanations for the cross border activity of firms.

The next section identifies and briefly reviews a selection of the leading theories of international production that were put forward by economists between 1960 and the mid 1970s. In the last decade, attention has switched to formulating a more general paradigm of foreign owned production. The third section pays especial attention to the eclectic paradigm, which is, perhaps, the most ambitious attempt to integrate each of the main theoretical strands earlier described. This paradigm is then compared and contrasted with two of the more influential contemporary theories of international production viz. the internalization theory of the multinational enterprise, and the macro-economic theory of foreign direct investment set forth by Kojima. The chapter concludes by examining some criticisms of the eclectic paradigm and some possible directions theorizing on international production might take in the 1990s.[2]

THEORIES OF FOREIGN-OWNED PRODUCTION 1960–1976

Prior to the 1960s there was no established theory of foreign production.[3] Attempts to explain the activities of firms outside their national boundaries represented an amalgam of (1) a fairly well formalized theory of (portfolio) capital movements (Iversen, 1935), (2) a number of empirical and largely country-specific studies on the factors influencing the location of foreign direct investment (Barlow, 1953; Dunning, 1958; Southard, 1931; Southard et al., 1936), (3) a recognition by some economists, notably Williams (1929), that the internationalization of some industries required modification to neoclassical theories of trade, and (4) an appreciation that the common ownership of the cross-border activities by firms could not only be considered as a substitute for international cartels and combines (Plummer, 1935), but could be explained, in part at least, by the perceived gains of vertical or horizontal integration (Bye, 1958; Penrose, 1956, 1958). Bye's contribution, which was (and still is) generally neglected by economists was particularly perceptive. It was he who coined the expression "the multiterritorial firm;" and used the case of the international oil industry to demonstrate that "real and financial size enables firms to cross varying thresholds of growth either by extension or integration, and so assure them of a certain bargaining position " (Bye, 1958, p. 161).

The 1960s saw two influential and path-breaking contributions to the theory of foreign production. Each was put forward quite independently of the other and approached its subject matter from a very different perspective. The following paragraphs briefly describe the main features of the two approaches.

The Contribution of Stephen Hymer

The first contribution was that of Stephen Hymer (1960, 1968, 1976), who in a Ph.D. thesis expressed his dissatisfaction with the theory of indirect (or portfolio) capital trans-

---

[2]Throughout this chapter, our emphasis is on economic theories of foreign direct investment and the MNEs, as we perceive these to be of most interest to readers. However, we fully recognize that a full explanation of international production requires an interdisciplinary approach, which is explored in Dunning (1988b, Chapter 12).

[3]Although various economists, from the time of the Mercantilists onward, have had something to say about the subject. A summary of their views are set out in Cantwell et al. (1986) and Dunning (1988b, Chapter 3).

fers to explain the foreign operations of firms. In particular, he identified three reasons for his dissatisfaction. The first was that once risk and uncertainty, volatile exchange rates, and the cost of acquiring information and making transactions were incorporated into classical portfolio theory, many of its predictions, e.g., with respect to movements of money capital in response to interest rate changes, were invalidated. This was because such market imperfections altered the behavioral pattern of firms and, in particular, their strategy in serving foreign markets.

Second, Hymer asserted that foreign direct investment involved the transfer of a package of resources, e.g., technology, management skills, entrepreneurship, etc, and not just that of finance capital, which portfolio theorists such as Iversen (1935) had sought to explain. Firms were motivated to produce abroad by the expectation of earning economic rent on the totality of these resources, including the way in which they were organized. The third, and perhaps most fundamental, characteristic of foreign direct investment was that it involved no change in the ownership of the resources or rights transferred, whereas indirect investment, which was transacted through the market, did involve a change in ownership. In consequence, the organizational modality of both the transaction of the resources, e.g., intermediate products, and the value-added activities linked by these transactions were different. In this connection, it is perhaps worth observing that Hymer was only interested in foreign direct investment is so far as this was the means by which firms were able to control the use of property rights in their foreign subsidiaries.

In his thesis Hymer broached many other issues, which were subsequently taken up more rigorously by other scholars. For example, Aliber (1970, 1971) developed a formal model of foreign direct investment based on the failure of international financial and currency markets to perform efficiently, whereas Hymer's identification of the international firm as a firm that "internalizes or supersedes the market" provided a useful prologue to the theory of internalization as a means for transferring knowledge, business techniques, and skilled personnel (Hymer 1960, pp. 48, 60).[4] However, Hymer's work is best known for initiating an industrial organizational approach to the theory of foreign production. His argument ran as follows. For firms to own and control foreign value adding facilities they must possess some kind of cost or marketing advantages, sufficient to outweigh the disadvantages faced in competing with indigenous firms in the country of production.[5] These advantages, which are assumed to be exclusive to the investing firm (henceforth called *ownership* specific advantages) imply the existence of some kind of structural market imperfection.

In seeking an explanation of these imperfections, Hymer turned to Joe Bain's (1956) classic treatise on the barriers to competition (in domestic markets) and applied the latter's analysis to explain the propensity of firms to undertake foreign production. These were identified by Hymer as *monopolistic* advantages, and in as much as, for at

---

[4]According to some correspondence that the author had with his supervisor (Charles Kindleberger), Hymer did not appear to have read Coase's classic article on the *The Nature of the Firm* (1937) at the time he wrote his thesis. By 1968 he had done so, and had he been disposed to publish his thesis after that date, he would almost certainly have modified some of the judgments he made in his thesis is about the welfare implications foreign direct investment.

[5]These include language barriers, unfamiliarity, and for lack of knowledge about the local economy, business customs, laws, suppliers and industrial relations procedures, and of political and exchange risks.

least some period of time, they are exclusive to the firms possessing them, this is true. But in so far as that ownership advantages may arise from the failure of *markets* to perform efficiently, rather than from the failure of *firms* to operate efficiently or to satisfactorily meet the needs of their consumers, the word *monopolistic* is an inappropriate one, even though the advantage(s) may, but not necessarily will, allow the owning firm to enjoy a temporary economic rent. Hymer then went on to examine the kind of ownership advantages that international firms might possess or acquire; and the kind of industrial sectors and market structures in which foreign direct investment was likely to be concentrated.[6]

Elsewhere in his thesis, Hymer examined other issues germane to foreign production. In particular, like Bye, he was interested in the territorial expansion of firms as a means of exploiting or fostering monopoly power. And although his writings show a clear awareness of the failure of markets to perform efficiently, he always seemed to compare the welfare implications of resource allocation by international hierarchies with those of Pareto optimality offered by a perfect market. In consequence, Hymer overlooked the fact that increased profits from the superior efficiency of foreign firms is not necessarily a social loss if prices are not higher than they would otherwise be (Teece, 1985). The emphasis placed by Hymer on the organization of economic activity by international firms as a means of advancing monopoly power, rather than of reducing costs or improving product quality, also led him to consider the alternatives between engaging in foreign direct investment and licensing in normative terms, rather than by a reasoned analysis of the cost and benefits of these options.

In a later paper, first published in French, Hymer (1968) takes a rather different approach to explaining international production. Here, he seeks—in his own words "to consider things from the firms point of view, . . . and the reasons for it to become multinational as well as the obstacles it may encounter on the way." In developing his analysis, Hymer draws very heavily on the ideas of Coase (1937), whose work he did not acknowledge in his thesis. Hymer applies the analysis of Coase to suggest reasons why firms might wish to engage in cross-border vertical integration. Moreover, although he does not fully develop his argument, Hymer seems to acknowledge that multinational firms may help to improve international resource allocation by circumventing market failure, and to this extent at least his 1968 contribution is a natural point of departure for the rigorous more work of the internalization economists in the following decade.

The Vernon Contribution

If Hymer used industrial and organizational economics to explaining foreign production, Raymond Vernon and his colleagues at Harvard were the first to acknowledge the relevance of some of the newer trade theories put forward in the 1950s and 1960s (as summarized by Hufbauer, 1970, and Stern, 1975) to help explain this phenomenon. In a classic article published in 1966, Vernon used a microeconomic concept—the product

---

[6]See also some earlier empirical studies by Barlow (1953), Dunning (1958), and Southard (1931).

cycle—to help explain a macroeconomic phenomenon—the foreign activities of U.S. MNEs in the postwar period. His starting point was that, in addition to immobile natural endowments and human resources, the ability of countries to engage in trade depended on their capability to upgrade these assets or to create new ones, notably technological capacity. He also assumed that the efficiency of firms in organizing these human and physical assets was country-specific in origin.

Drawing upon some earlier work by Posner (1961), Vernon argued that the competitive or ownership advantages of U.S. firms—and particularly their capacity to innovate new products and processes—was determined by the structure and pattern of U.S. factor endowments and markets. However, it was quite possible that any initial competitive advantage enjoyed by the innovating enterprises creating them might be eroded or eliminated by the superior efficiency of firms in other countries to produce the products based on them. Without explicitly bringing market imperfections into his analysis, Vernon then switched his unit of attention to the firm and particularly the location of its production. Initially, the product (or, more correctly, the value-added activities based on the ownership advantages) was produced for the home market in the home country, near to both the innovatory activities and markets. Subsequently, i.e., at a later stage of the product cycle, because of a favorable combination of innovating and production advantages offered by the United States, it was exported to other countries most similar to the home country in demand patterns and supply capabilities.

Gradually, as the product becomes standardized or mature, the competitive advantage of producing firms changed from those to do with the uniqueness of product *per se* to minimizing the costs of value adding activities, and product differentiation. The pressure to ensure cost efficiency mounts as imitators start making inroads into the market. At the same time, as demand becomes more price elastic, as labor becomes a more important ingredient of costs, and as foreign markets expand, the attractions of siting value-added activities in a foreign rather than a domestic location increase. This might be hastened by barriers to exports, or incentives to local production, or in anticipation of competitors setting up in these markets. Eventually, if conditions in the host country were right, the subsidiary could replace exports from the parent company or even export back to it.

This approach to explaining foreign production was essentially an extension of the neoclassical theory of the spatial distribution of factor endowments to embrace intermediate products; together with an acknowledgement that strategic factors arising from an oligopolistic market structure, in which MNEs were observed to compete, influenced the response of firms to these endowments. It did not, however, address organizational issues. Since the ownership advantages of firms were assumed to be country-specific, little consideration was given to the kind of advantages that arose from firm-specific characteristics. In a later contribution, however, Vernon (1983) did explicitly examine the minimization of organizational risk as a motive and determinant of foreign direct investment.

The product cycle model was introduced in the 1960s to explain a particular type of foreign production by firms of a particular nationality of ownership. It did not explain, nor purport to explain, either resource based or efficiency seeking direct investment.

Like Hymer, Vernon offered a theory that was partial in that it addressed itself only to some of the issues surrounding international production. On the other hand, the product cycle was the first dynamic interpretation of the determinants of and relationship between (some kinds of) trade and foreign production. It also introduced some novel hypotheses regarding demand stimuli, technology leads and lags, and information and communications costs, which have subsequently proved useful tools in the study of foreign production and exchange.

Follow-up Developments

The later 1960s and early 1970s saw various attempts to refine and test the industrial organizational theory of Hymer and the locationally oriented theory of Vernon. Of the former, the work of industrial economists such as Caves (1971, 1974a, b, Horst (1972a, b), Johnson (1970), Magee (1977), and a second generation of researchers such as Calvet (1980), Lall (1979, 1980), Lall and Siddarthan (1982), Owen (1982), and Swedenborg (1979) is particularly worthy of note. Essentially this group of scholars sought to pinpoint *which* ownership-specific variables explained foreign investment. Most concentrated on trying to identify and evaluate the significance of specific intangible assets, e.g., technological capacity, labor skills, product differentiation, marketing skills, and organizational capabilities. Not surprisingly they found that the relevant variables for different industrial sectors were both industry and country specific. Thus, whereas the privileged possession, or access to, technology and human capital explained much of U.S. direct investment in producer goods industries, product differentiation and quality, as proxied by advertising intensity, was revealed as the dominant ownership specific advantage of MNEs in consumer goods industries. The competitive advantages of European and Japanese MNEs were perceived to be different than those of U.S. firms—mainly because the structure of their resource endowments and markets was different (Franko, 1976), whereas the kind of advantages that best explained U.S. outward investment in the 1960s and 1970s failed to explain the pattern of inward investment in the United States in the mid 1970s (Lall and Siddarthan, 1982).

Stephen Magee (1977), in a more detailed examination of technology as an ownership-specific advantage, took a rather different line. He was primarily interested in why the incentive of firms to internalize the market for technology varied over time. He coined the concept of the industry technology cycle, which built upon the Vernon hypothesis that the competitive advantages of firms was likely to change over the life of the product. He argued that firms were unlikely to sell the right to new and idiosyncratic technology for fear that (1) due to information inadequacy, the buying firm was unlikely to pay the selling firm a price, which would yield it at least as much economic rent it could appropriate by using the technology itself, and (2) that the licensee might use the technology to the disadvantage of the licensor. As the technology matured, however, and lost some of its uniqueness, the need to internalize its use evaporated, and the firm switched its modality of transfer from foreign direct investment to licensing.

Around the same time, another group of scholars began to focus more specifically on variables influencing the decision of firms to license their property rights vis a vis engaging in foreign direct investment (Contractor, 1981; Telesio, 1979). However, although these scholars began to identify more carefully the circumstances firms wished to control the use of the technological assets they possessed, they did not really grapple with the more fundamental issue of the organization of transactional relationships as part of a general paradigm of market failure. This task was left to another group of economists (see General Explanations of Foreign Production later in this chapter).

Other researchers—mainly from a business school tradition, and often from Harvard itself—followed the Vernon approach. A monograph summarizing some empirical research on the product cycle appeared in 1972 (Wells, 1972). Work on UK, continental European, and Japanese MNEs closely paralleled that on U.S. MNEs (Franko, 1976; Stopford, 1976; Tsmuri, 1976; Yoshino, 1976). But, perhaps, of greater significance for the development of the theory of foreign production, was a more rigorous attempt to incorporate strategic issues into the theory of international production. These had been implicit in the product cycle model, but it was a group of Vernon's students, viz. Flowers (1976), Graham (1975), and Knickerbocker (1973), who observed that it was not just locational variables that might determine the spatial distribution of economic activity, but the strategies of firms in response to these variables and to the anticipated reaction of their competitors. In a perfectly competitive market situation, strategic behavior (like the firm itself) is a black box. This is simply because the firm has no freedom of action if it is to earn at the least the opportunity costs on its investments. Its maximum and minimum profit positions are one and the same thing. Once, however, markets become imperfect as a result of structural distortions, uncertainty, externalities, or economies of scale, then the options of a firm widen and strategy begins to play an active role in affecting business conduct.

Nowhere is this more clearly seen in an oligopolistic market situation where economists, from Cournot onward, have acknowledged that output and price equilibrium depends on the assumption made by one firm about how its own behavior will affect that of its competitors and how, in turn, this latter behavior will impinge upon its own position. Knickerbocker (1973) argued that, as risk minimizers, oligopolists who wish to avoid destructive competition would normally follow each other into new (e.g., foreign) markets in order to safeguard their own market position. A study of the timing of investment by U.S. MNEs in manufacturing industry seemed to support this proposition (Knickerbocker, 1973). Three years later Flowers (1976) showed that this held for Canadian and European investment in the United States as well as for U.S. investment in Europe, whereas Graham (1975) viewed European investment in the United States as a reaction by European firms to the incursion of their own territories by U.S. MNEs. In particular, Graham hypothesized that a MNE that found its home territory invaded by a foreign MNE would retaliate by invading the foreigner's home turf. A frequently quoted example of this so-called exchange of threats hypothesis is the entrance by Royal Dutch Shell in the United States in the 1900s in response to Standard Oil's entry into Far Eastern markets previously dominated by Shell; but there are many others from such diverse sectors as rubber tires, automobiles, color television, advertizing, and hotels.

In retrospect, the work of these scholars and Vernon himself (1974), who acknowledged that the nature of a firm's foreign investment strategy would depend on its position in the product cycle, was not only path-breaking in that it emphasized the role of a dynamic strategic interaction; but it also pinpointed a particular type of market failure, which was later formalized and incorporated into the organizational theories of the late 1970s.

To summarize, by the mid-1970s the two streams of explaining international production, pioneered by Hymer and Vernon, were beginning to converge, although their focus of interest and the questions they sought to answer were still very different. The industrial organization approach, which was concerned with identifying the main ownership specific advantages of MNEs, was beginning to recognize that the way in which the assets were created, acquired, and organized might itself be an advantage. By the mid-1970s the trade/location approach had also began to acknowledge the role of market structure not only in affecting the ownership of firms, but also the way in which firms chose to organize their cross-border activities. But whereas Hymer viewed foreign direct investment as an aggressive strategy to advance monopoly power, Vernon and his colleagues thought of it more as a defensive strategy, and placed rather greater emphasis on the need of firms to protect their existing market positions.

Other Theoretical Contributions: A Selected View

To complete this short historical review, mention must be made of two other approaches to explaining foreign-owned production, which though outside the mainstream of thinking, when reinterpreted in terms of contemporary theorizing, offered (and still offer) valuable insights into both the location and ownership of international economic activity. Both approaches were developed by financial economists.

The risk diversification hypothesis. The risk diversification hypothesis was put forward by Agmon and Lessard (1977), Lessard (1976, 1982), and Rugman (1975, 1979). Building on some earlier work by Grubel (1968) and Levy and Sarnat (1970), these scholars argued that the multinational enterprise offered individual or institutional equity investors a superior vehicle for geographically diversifying their investment portfolios than did the international equity market. This partly reflected the failure of this market to efficiently evaluate risks or the benefits of risk diversification; and partly the fact that, as compared with their domestic counterparts, MNEs possessed certain nonfinancial advantages that enabled them to cope more effectively with risks associated with international diversified portfolios. Empirical research (Agmon and Lessard, 1977) seems to support the idea that investors *do* recognize the benefits of diversification provided by MNEs. Rugman (1979) also found that the variance of U.S. corporate earnings in the 1960s was inversely related to the ratio of their foreign to domestic operations. However, there remains some doubt as to the extent to which the gains of international diversification are reflected in the cost of equity to, or share prices of, the investing firms.

Rugman and Lessard have further argued that, given that firms deemed it worthwhile to engage in foreign direct investment, the location of the investment would be a function of both the firm's perception of the uncertainties involved and the geographical distribution of its existing assets. In the absence of country-specific hazards, e.g., foreign exchange risk, political and environmental instability, etc., firms would simply equate the returns earned on their assets in different countries at the margin, even if this meant concentrating these assets in a single country. However, as the uncertainty attached to the returns varied with the amount and concentration of assets, this would affect the geographical distribution of their asset portfolio. In a later contribution, Rugman (1980, 1981) acknowledged that the risk diversification hypothesis is a special case of a more general theory of international market failure, based upon the desire and ability of multinationals to minimize cross-border production and transaction costs.

The Aliber theory. Robert Aliber (1970, 1971) took as his starting point the failure of financial markets identified by Hymer in his Ph.D. thesis. However, unlike Hymer, Aliber's investment theory was not concerned with why firms *produce* abroad but why they finance their foreign assets in their domestic currencies. This he explains in terms of the ability of firms from countries with strong currencies to borrow or raise capital in domestic or foreign markets more cheaply than can those from countries with weak currencies, and, because of this, the different rates at which the two groups of firms capitalize their expected income streams. Aliber further argued that structural imperfections in the foreign exchange market allow firms to make foreign exchange gains through the purchase of sales of assets in an undervalued or overvalued currency.

Aliber's theory does not attempt to explain many of the questions tackled by other scholars, and therefore should not be judged on the same criteria. But neither does it have strong claim to a general theory of foreign direct investment. It is difficult to see how it explains the industrial structure of foreign production or the cross-hauling of direct investment between weak and strong currency areas. It does, however, present some interesting ideas about the *timing* of foreign direct investment and particularly that of foreign takeovers, and of fluctuations around a long-term trend. It also offers some reasons as to why countries might shift their international investment status over time.

In many respects, Aliber's theory is better regarded as an extension of portfolio capital theory to incorporate market failure than a theory of foreign direct investment per se. Indeed, his whole thesis rests on the presence and characteristics of imperfections in the capital and/or exchange markets. He argues that such market failure tends to confer advantages on firms whose assets are denominated in certain currencies rather than others, and, as a result, affects the location of where they invest these assets. It is, however, unclear why firms should wish to control these assets; hence, so is the distinction between the motives for direct rather than portfolio investment.[8] Finally, in practice, it is the difference in the nonfinancial assets owned by enterprises that enables

---

[8]In distinguishing between the goals of the portfolio capitalist and the direct investor, Kindleberger (1969) gives the capitalization formula as $C + I/r$ where C is the value of the capital asset, I is the income stream it produces, and r is the return on investment. "The theory asserts that direct investment occurs when the foreign firm can earn a higher I than the local firm whereas ordinary capital movements reflect a lower" (Kindleberger 1969, p. 24.).

them to exploit imperfections in the financial exchange markets. To this extent, Aliber's theory is best regarded as one that is complementary to other explanations of foreign direct investment; albeit, in certain circumstances, it could offer the most satisfactory explanation.[9]

GENERAL EXPLANATIONS OF FOREIGN PRODUCTION

By the mid 1970s, it was becoming clear that none of the theories so far put forward to explain international production could claim to be a general theory or paradigm, and that most were not seeking to explain the same phenomena. Of all the explanations, Hymer's original thesis offered the most promise as a general paradigm, although those parts of it which he pursued with any rigor, and to which later researchers paid the most attention, were primarily concerned with identifying the reasons why some firms, and not others, engaged in foreign production, rather than with the organization and location of cross-border transactions.

In the mid-1970s, three attempts were made to offer more holistic explanations of the foreign activities of firms, which have since attracted a great deal of attention in the literature. Each uses a different unit of analysis; two are quite similar in approach, but the third is very different. These are, respectively, the internalization theory of the MNE, the eclectic paradigm of international production, and the macro-economic theory of foreign direct investment.

The Internalization Theory

The internalization theory is directed to explaining the emergence and growth of the multinational enterprise in terms of the way in which cross-border transactions in intermediate products are organized. It was first put forward in the mid-1970s by a group of Swedish, Canadian, British, and U.S. economists working mainly independently of each other.[10] Its basic hypothesis is that multinational hierarchies represent an alternative mechanism to coordinating related economic activities, and the transactions between them, to that of the market; and that international production is likely to occur whenever the net benefits of an in-house organization of transactions are perceived to exceed those offered by external markets. The prediction of the internalization theory is that given a particular distribution of factor endowments, MNE activity will be positively related to the degree of market failure in the intermediate product markets.

Internalization theory is essentially concerned with identifying the situations in which the markets for intermediate products are likely to be internalized, and hence those in

---

[9]To the best of our knowledge, Aliber has never subjected this theory to rigorous empirical testing. However, an examination of the pattern and timing of British direct investment in the United States over the past decade (at a time in which there have been substantial fluctuations in U.S. and UK interest rates and the \$/£ exchange rate) offers only limited support for his basic hypothesis.

[10]Notably Lundgren (1977) and Swedenborg (1979) of Sweden; MacManus (1972) of Canada; Buckley and Casson (1976, 1985) of the UK; Hennart (1982) of the United States. We have already argued, however, that the germs of this theory appeared in Hymer (1968).

which firms control value adding activities outside their natural boundaries. Like earlier attempts to explain the growth of domestic firms, it seeks to explain both international horizontal and vertical integration of production in terms of the presence or absence of a variety of costs associated wtih market transactions. Certain types of transactions between certain types of buyers and sellers incur higher costs than others. Hierarchial control costs are also industry-, country-, and firm-specific.

Internalization theory may be considered a general theory insofar as it is able to predict the situations in which firms choose to internalize foreign markets. On the other hand, it is less satisfactory in explaining the situations in which firms replace markets by collaborative alliances. In many respects, however, it is better described as a paradigm than a theory, in as much as the kind of market failure that determines one kind of foreign value activity may be quite different from that of another.

For example, in some consumer goods or service industries, the inability of the market to ensure a seller of an intermediate product sufficient control over the quality of the final product, which may bear the seller's name, may be a reason for replacing that market by forward integration. By contrast, backward integration may be motivated by a need to reduce the risk of interrupted suppliers or price hikes, whereas the common governance of multiple activities in dispersed locations may be prompted to the desire to gain economies external to the activities in question but internal to the firm as a whole.

We discuss the concept of market failure in more detail in the next section, which sets out a paradigm that, although accepting completely the logic of the internalization theory, argues that it is not in itself sufficient to explain the totality of the production of a country's own firms outside their national boundaries, or of the production of foreign-owned firms in their midst. This is accepted by at least some of the internalization protagonists. Indeed, both Buckley (1987) and Casson (1987) in separate contributions have acknowledged the need to integrate location-specific variables with internalization variables (which one accepts are not independent of each other) to present a holistic theory of the multinational enterprise. The role of ownership-specific variables as set out by Hymer is rather more contentious. In the static model of internalization, these variables—the outcome of structural market imperfections—are taken to be exogenous. But viewing the growth of the firm as a dynamic process, the legitimacy of this assumption is questionable. For today's "given" factor, e.g., technological capability, is the outcome of past decisions that, at the time they were taken, were endogenous to the firm, i.e., a different decision might have been taken. Here, once again, strategic considerations enter the picture. We give more attention to this point in the final section.

The Eclectic Paradigm

The eclectic paradigm seeks to offer a general framework for determining the extent and pattern of both foreign-owned production undertaken by a country's enterprises and also that of domestic production owned by foreign-based MNEs. It is not a theory of the multinational enterprise per se, as its unit of analysis is the totality of firms engaged in foreign value adding activities. Neither is it a theory of foreign direct investment, as it is concerned with the foreign-owned output of firms rather than the way that output is financed. At the same time, it accepts that the propensity to own income-generating assets may be influenced by financial and/or exchange rate variables. Finally, the eclectic paradigm addresses itself to positive rather than normative issues. It prescribes a conceptual framework for explaining "what is" rather than "what should be," the level and structure of a country's international production, be that of its own firms in other countries or of foreign firms in its midst.

The theory of foreign-owned production stands at the intersection between a macroeconomic theory of international trade and a micro-economic theory of the firm. It is essentially an exercise in macro resource allocation and organizational economics. The eclectic paradigm starts with the acceptance of much of traditional trade theory in explaining the spatial distribution of some kinds of output, which might be termed Heckscher-Ohlin-Sammuelson (H-O-S) output. However, it argues that, to explain the ownership of that output and the spatial distribution of other kinds of output, which require the use of resources that are not equally accessible to all firms, two kinds of market imperfection must be present. The first is that of structural market failure that discriminates between firms (or owners of corporate assets) in their ability to gain and/or sustain control over property rights; the second is that of the failure of intermediate product markets to transact goods and services at a cost less than what a hierarchy might incur by undertaking these transactions itself. The presence of both these imperfections allows firms to be both *active* and *reactive* economic agents, and to influence, as well as respond to, the environment in which they operate.

Such variables as the structure of markets, transaction costs, and the strategy of firms then become important determinants of international economic activity. The firm is not a black box; neither are markets the sole arbiters of transactions. Hierarchies and interfirm cooperative agreements are an integral part in explaining both trade and production. Both the distribution of factor endowments and the modality of economic organization are relevant. This framework is no less applicable of explaining certain kinds of trade, where the advantages of the trading firms are not *country* but *firm*-specific.

It would be possible to reverse this "top-down" approach and consider foreign production from the "bottom-up." In this case, one would start with a theory of the multinational enterprise and then gradually move on to consider the macro resource allocative issues pertinent to the internalization of production by all firms.

The economics of the paradigm. Economic involvement by one country's enterprises in another may be for purposes of supplying either foreign or domestic markets, or both. Production for a particular foreign market may be wholly or partly located in the home country, in the foreign market, in a third country, or in a combination of the three. Similarly, production for the home market may be serviced from a domestic or a foreign location.

The capability of one country's enterprises to supply either a foreign or a domestic market from a foreign production base depends on their possessing certain assets or organizational advantages not available, or not available at the same cost to another country's enterprises. We use assets in the Fisherian sense (Johnson, 1968) to mean resources capable of generating a future income stream to the owners of the assets. These assets include not only tangible assets, such as natural resources, personnel, and capital, but intangible assets, such as technology and information, managerial, marketing skills and entrepreneurial judgment, and access to intermediate and final goods markets. Such assets might be location-specific in their origin and use, but available to all firms. These include not only Ricardian-type endowments, but also the cultural, legal, and institutional environment in which the endowments are used, market structure and government legislation and policies. Alternatively, the assets may be owned by, i.e., be proprietary to, particular enterprises of the home country, but capable of being used with other resources in the home country or elsewhere. Such assets may take the form of a legally protected right or a commercial monopoly, or they may arise from size, diversity, or the technical characteristics of firms, the economies of joint production and/or marketing, and of a successful managerial strategy. In most cases, both location and ownership-specific assets affect the international competitiveness of countries.

For some kinds of trade, it is sufficient for the exporting country to have only a location-specific advantage over the importing country; that is, it is not *necessary* for the exporting firms to enjoy any firm-specific advantages over the indigenous enterprises in the importing country. Much of the trade between industrialized countries (which is of the Ricardian or H-O-S type) is of this kind. Other trade, such as that which mainly takes place between developed industrialized countries, is of high skill intensive or sophisticated consumer goods products, and is based more on the ownership-specific advantages of the exporting firms; but, observe, this presupposes that it is better to use these advantages in combination with location-specific endowments in the exporting rather than in the importing (or in a third) country. Where, however, these latter endowments favor the importing (or a third) country, foreign-owned production will replace trade.

To summarize, the act of foreign production combines the export of intermediate products, requiring inputs in which the home country is relatively well endowed, with the use of resources in which the host country is relatively well endowed. But if this were all there was to it, we would not need a separate theory of international production: an extension of international trade theory to incorporate trade in intermediate products, allowing for the mobility of at least some resources, would be sufficient. On the other hand, attempts to explain patterns and levels of international production without taking account of the distribution of country-specific endowments are like throwing the baby out with the bathwater.

We have argued that the failure of the factor endowment approach to explain completely, or in some cases even partially, international production arises simply because it predicates the existence of perfect markets, both for final and intermediate goods. In neoclassical trade theory, this leads to all sorts of unrealistic assumptions, e.g., atomistic competition, equality of production functions, the absence of risk and uncertainty, and, implicitly at least, that technology is a free and instantaneously transferable good between firms and countries. Since the 1950s, economists have grappled to incorporate market imperfections into trade theory, but, in the main, their attention has been directed to final rather than to intermediate goods markets. Partly because of this, little attention has been paid to the organization of production and transactions across, or indeed within, national boundaries; exceptions include the work of Batra and Ramachandran (1980), Ethier (1986), Helpman (1974), Helpman and Krugman (1985); Horstman and Markusen (1986), and Markusen (1984). In situations involving some locational choice between producing intermediate products at home or overseas, this is assumed to influence the export versus licensing decision on a foreign firm, rather than the export versus foreign production decision.

We have suggested that the lack of concern by trade economists with ownership or governance questions arises because international trade theory—again implicitly rather than explicitly—assumes that all firms are single-activity or product firms. The effect on trade patterns of the vertical integration or horizontal diversification of firms is not discussed in the literature. Since the option of internalizing domestic markets for intermediate products, or buying inputs and selling outputs in the open market within a country, has not generally interested trade economists, it is hardly surprising that they have been little concerned with issues of international production. Yet, the unique characteristic of the MNE is that it is both multiactivity and engages in the internal transfer of intermediate products across national boundaries. Indeed it is the difference between domestic and international market failure that distinguish multinational from uninational multiactivity firms. It is the failure of the market to organize a satisfactory deal between potential contractors and contractees of intermediate products that explains why one or the other should choose the hierarchial rather than the market route for exploiting different factor endowment situations.

Several types of market failure are identified in the literature: Anderson and Gatignon (1986), Buckley and Casson (1976, 1985), Casson (1979, 1982, 1985, 1987), and Teece (1981, 1985). In an assessment of Stephen Hymer's contribution to the theory of MNE, Dunning and Rugman (1985) distinguished between *structural* and *transactional* market failure. The former, which Hymer tended to emphasize, give rise to monopoly rents, which due to entry barriers the constituent firms may seek to increase by way of acquisition and for merger (a form of internalisation).

A no less important, but very different, type of market imperfection reflects inability of the market *qua* market to organize transactions in an optimal way. There are three reasons for this. The first is that buyers and sellers do not enter the market with complete information or perfect certainty about the transactions they are undertaking. Such cognitive imperfections give rise to bounded rationality, opportunism, adverse selection, and information impactness, which are the innate characteristics of some markets (Teece, 1981, 1985). This kind of market failure is particularly likely to be associated with cross-border transactions. The multinational enterprise, if nothing else, engages in foreign production to protect itself against the opportunism of foreign buyers and sellers, and to conteract (and in some cases exploit) political and environmental volatility (Kogut, 1984). Such risks are particularly noteworthy in raw materials and high technology industries that typically incur higher development costs; where there is a danger of disruption of supplies; where there is a likelihood of property rights being dissipated or abused by foreign licenses; and where the threat of the pre-emption of markets or sources of supplies, or an improvement in the competitive position by rival oligopolists, will encourage a follow-my-leader strategy by firms (Vernon, 1983).

The second reason for transactional market failure is that the market cannot take account of the benefits and costs associated with a particular transaction between buyers and sellers that accrue to one or another of the parties but that are external to that transaction. Where products are normally supplied jointly with others, or are derived from a common input or set of inputs, there may be good reason why the different stages of the value-added chain should be coordinated within the same firms. Cross-border transactions may give rise to additional advantages of common governance such as those that exploit the imperfections of international capital and exchange markets and different national fiscal policies.

The third cause of transactional market failure arises wherever the market is insufficiently large to enable firms both to fully captive the economies of size, scope, and coordination, *and* remain perfectly competitive. In other words, there is an inevitable tradeoff between the overall cost efficiency of a firm and its ability to exploit synergistic economies (Galbraith and Kay, 1986), and the elasticity of demand for the individual products it supplies. Such economies may be in production or in purchasing, marketing, research and development, finance, administration, and so on. These latter economies are essentially those that are external to a particular activity, but internal to the total activities of a firm.

These and other market weaknesses cause enterprises, be they uninational or multinational, to diversify their value adding activities—vertically, horizontally, or laterally. They do it partly to reduce the costs of hierarchies and partly to ensure that they gain the maximum economic rent (discounted for risk) from the asset advantages they possess. Again, the only difference between the actions of multinational and uninational production in this respect is the added dimension of market failure when a particular transaction is concluded across the exchanges. Moreover, market failure may vary according to the characteristics of the parties engaging in the exchange; here, too, country-specific factors may enter the equation. Returning to our parallel between firms engaged in international trade and international production, it is quite possible that whereas both may engage in *exactly* the same value-added activities, the former may do so within a single country and export their final product, whereas the latter undertakes at least part of their value-adding activities outside their national boundaries.

The unique characteristic of international production is, then, that it marries the trans-border dimension of value-added activities of firms with the common governance of those activities. Whereas the former draws upon the economies of the spatial distribution of immobile resources and market structures to explain the location of production independently of its ownership, the theory of market failure helps explain the ownership of value adding activity independent of its location. The blending of the two suggests that market imperfections specific to the transaction of intermediate or final goods across national boundaries, together with the desire of firms to locate the production of different stages of the value-added chain in different countries, should be the core ingredients of any generalized paradigm of international production. The precise character and pattern of that production will depend on the configuration of ownership and internalization advantages of firms and the locational advantages of countries; and these, in turn, reflect not only the nature of the activities undertaken, and the countries in which they are undertaken, but also the attributes of firms themselves, vis a vis their competitors, which will determine their strategy in international markets.

A summary of the eclectic paradigm. The principal hypothesis on which the eclectic paradigm of international production is based is that a firm will engage in foreign value adding activities if and when three conditions are satisfied. These are:

1. It possesses net ownership specific advantages vis a vis firms of other nationalities in supplying or wishing to supply particular markets. These ownership advantages largely take the form of the privileged possession of income generating; the efficient management of cross-border risks and the exploitation of the economies of scale or scope. These advantages and the use made of them (see 2 and 3 below) are assumed to increase the wealth creating capacity, and hence the value of the firm intangible assets.[11]
2. Assuming condition 1 is satisfied, it must be more beneficial to the enterprise possessing these advantages to use them (or their output) itself rather than to sell or lease them directly to foreign firms; this it does through an extension of its existing value added chains or the involvement of new ones. These advantages are called market internalization advantages.
3. Assuming conditions 1 and 2 are satisfied, it must be in the global interests of the enterprise to utilize these advantages in conjunction with at least some factor endowments outside its home country; otherwise, foreign markets would be served entirely by exports and domestic markets by domestic production. The distribution of these endowments is assumed to be uneven, and hence according to their location, confer a particular advantage on the countries possessing them over those that do not.

The generalized predictions of the eclectic paradigm are straightforward. The paradigm asserts that, at any given point in time, the more a country's enterprises possess ownership-specific advantages, relative to enterprises of other nationalities, the greater the incentive they have to internalize rather than externalize their use, and the more they find it in their interest to add value to them in a foreign location; the more they (and the country as a whole) are likely to engage in international production. By the same token, a country is likely to attract investment by foreign enterprises when the

---

[11]I am indebted to Mr. M. Itaki, visiting research scholar at the University of Reading, for reminding me that the value of an ownership advantage must be expressed in terms of the capitalization of the income stream generated by such an advantage, and which accrue to the owners of that advantage. The greater that income stream (net of payments made to other factor inputs that helped create that advantage or add value to it), the greater the advantage. I also accept that the ability of the owners of the firm to extract the maximum value added from the various factors inputs it utilizes and the way in which it coordinates these factors, will determine the size of its ownership advantage. For a detailed criticism of the eclectic paradigm, see Itaki (1989).

reverse conditions apply. Similarly the paradigm can be expressed in a dynamic context. Changes in the outward or inward investment position of a particular country can be explained in terms of changes in the ownership and internalization advantages of its enterprises, relative to those of other nationalities and/or changes in its location specific endowments relative to those of other countries, as perceived by its own and foreign enterprises. A good deal of work has been done on identifying the origin and nature of these ownership-locational-internalization (OLI) advantages, and the conditions under which they are most likely to exist.

Table 5.1 offers a classification of some of the more important OLI advantages. Some of these best can help explain the initial act of foreign direct investment; others, and particularly the advantage of common governance accredited to the multinationality of firms, are more relevant to explaining the sequential acts of foreign production (Kogut, 1983, 1987; Kogut and Kulatilaha 1988). Industrial organization theory mainly exlains the nature of some types of ownership-specific advantages and is directly in the Bain tradition. However, those that arise specifically from coordinating properties and the multinationality of the firm stem from the theory of the growth of the firm and from organizational economies. The theory of property rights and economics of transaction costs explain why firms should choose to internalize production based on these advantages. Theories of location and trade explain the factors determining the location of production.

The eclectic paradigm suggests that all forms of foreign production by all countries can be explained by reference to the above conditions. It makes no a priori prediction about which countries, industries, or enterprizes are most likely to engage in foreign direct investment, but it does hypothesize that at least some of the advantages identified in Table 5.1 will *not* be evenly spread across countries, industries, and enterprises. It also accepts that such advantages are not static, and that the strategic response of a firm to any particular configuration of internalization and location advantages may affect the nature and pattern of these advantages at a subsequential period of time.

Although the three strands in the explanation of international production interact with each other, conceptually there is something to be said for considering them separately. Certainly the location and mode of foreign involvement are two quite independent decisions that a firm has to take, even though the final decision on where to locate will itself depend on the nature and characteristics of the ownership advantages possessed by the firm, and the extent to which it perceives that a particular location might help it to internalize intermediate product markets better than another. Take also the distinction between ownership and internalization advantages. Ownership advantages may be internally generated (e.g., through product diversification or innovations) or acquired by enterprises. If acquired, for example, by way of a purchase (be it domestic or foreign) of another enterprise, the presumption is that this will add to the acquiring firm's ownership advantages vis a vis those of its competitors (including those of the acquired firm). Elsewhere (Dunning, 1988a), we have argued that it is useful to distinguish between the *capacity* to organize value adding activities in a particular way, and the decision to opt for one mode of organization rather than another.

We have suggested that the eclectic paradigm offers the basis for a general expla-

Table 4.1

The Eclectic Paradigm of International Production[1]

1. *Ownership-Specific Advantages* (of enterprise of one nationality (or affiliates of same) over those of another)
   a. Property right and/or intangible asset advantages.
      Product innovations, production management, organisational and marketing systems, innovatory capacity: noncodifiable knowledge: "bank" of human capital experience; marketing, finance, knowhow, etc.
   b. Advantages of common governance.
   i. Those that branch plants of established enterprises may enjoy over *de novo* firms.
      Those due mainly to size, product diversity and learning experiences of enterprise, e.g., economies of scope and specialization. Exclusive or favored access to inputs, e.g., labor, natural resources, finance, information. Ability to obtain inputs on favored terms (due, e.g., to size or monopsonistic influence). Exclusive or favored access to product markets. Access to resources of parent company at marginal cost. Synergistic economies (not only in production, but in purchasing, marketing, finance, etc., arrangements).
   ii. Which specifically arise because of multinationality. Multinationality enhances operational flexibility by offering wider opportunities for arbitraging and production shifting. More favored access to and/or better knowledge about international markets, e.g., for information, finance, labor. etc. Ability to take advantage of geographic differences in factor endowments, government intervention, markets etc. Ability to diversify or reduce risks, e.g., in different currency areas and creation of options and/or political and cultural scenarios. Ability to learn from societal differences in organizational and managerial processes and systems. Balancing economies of integration with ability to respond to differences in country specific needs and advantages.
2. *Internalization Incentive Advantages* (i.e., to protect against or exploit market failure)
   Avoidance of search and negotiating costs.
   To avoid costs of moral hazard and adverse selection, and to protect reputation of internalizing firm.
   To avoid cost of broken contracts and ensuing litigation.
   Buyer uncertainty (about nature and value of inputs (e.g., technology) being sold).
   When market does not permit price discrimination.
   Need of seller to protect quality of intermediate or final products.
   To capture economies of interdependent activities (see b. above).
   To compensate for absence of future markets.
   To avoid or exploit government intervention (e.g., quotas, tariffs, price controls, tax differences, etc).
   To control supplies and conditions of sale of inputs (including technology).
   To control market outlets (including those which might be used by competitors).
   To be able to engage in practices, e.g., cross-subsidisation, predatory pricing, leads and lags, transfer pricing, etc. as acompetitive (or anticompetitive) strategy.
3. *Location Specific Variables* (these may favor home or host countries).
   Spatial distribution of natural and created resource endowments and markets.
   Input prices, quality and productivity, e.g., labor, energy, materials, components, semifinished goods.
   International transport and communications costs.
   Investment incentives and disincentives (including performance requirements, etc.)
   Artificial barriers (e.g., import controls) to trade in goods and services.
   Societal and infrastructure provisions (commercial, legal, educational, transport, and communication).
   Cross country ideological, language, cultural, business, political etc. differences.
   Economies of centralisation of R&D production and marketing.
   Economic system and policies of government: the institutional framework for resource allocation.

[1]These variables are culled from a variety of sources, but see especially Dunning (1981, 1988b) and Ghoshal (1987).

nation of international production. We illustrate this point by reference to Table 5.2, which relates the main types of foreign activities by MNEs to the presence or absence of the OLI advantages made for such activities. Such a matrix may be used as a starting point for an examination of both the industrial and geographical composition of foreign production.

In seeking to test the kind of hypotheses implied in Table 5.2, we find it useful to distinguish between three contextual or structural variables that will influence the OLI configuration affecting any particular MNE activity, viz. those that are specific to particular *countries,* to particular types of activities (or industries), and to particular *firms* or *enterprises.* In other words, the propensity of enterprises of a particular nationality to engage in foreign production will vary according to the economic, political, and cultural characteristics of their home countries and the country(ies) in which they propose to invest, the range and type of products (including intermediate products) they intend to produce, and their underlying management and organizational strategies (which inter alia may be affected by their size and attitude to risk diversification). Some of these characteristics are set out in Table 5.3.

Combining the data contained in Tables 5.1 and 5.3, we have the core of the paradigm that offers a conceptual framework for explaining the various types of international production.

The eclectic paradigm and other explanations. What, then, is the positive value of the eclectic paradigm? The paradigm avers that, given the distribution of location-specific endowments, enterprises that have the greatest opportunities for and derive the most from internalizing activities will be the most competitive in foreign markets. Enterprises will engage in the type of internalization most suited to the factor combinations, market situations, and government intervention with which they are faced. For example, our analysis would suggest not only that research intensive industries would tend to be more multinational than other industries, but the incentive for internalization of foreign-based raw materials markets would be greater for enterprises from economies that have few indigenous materials than those that are self-sufficient; that the most efficient MNEs will exploit the most profitable foreign markets; that the participation of foreign affiliates is likely to be greatest in those sectors of host countries where there are substantial economies of *enterprise* size. This paradigm is consistent with Horst's conclusion (1972a) that most of the explanatory variables of foreign direct investment can be captured in the size of enterprise; indeed, one would normally expect size and the propensity to internalize to be very closely correlated, and MNEs to be better equipped to spread risks than national multiproduct firms.

What does the eclectic paradigm predict that the other theories of international production do not? Taking the theories as a group, probably very little, except in so far as the independent variable fail to capture the advantages of internalization. Indeed, it could be argued that this theory is less an alternative theory of international production than one that pinpoints the essential and common characteristics of each of the main line explanations. We believe, however, there are a number of important differences. The eclectic paradigm asserts that it is not the possession of technology per se, which

Table 5.2
Types of International Production: Some Determining Factors

Types of International Production	Ownership Advantages (the "why" of MNC Activity)	Location Advantages (the "where" of Production)	Internalization Advantages (the "how" of Involvement)	Illustration of Types of Activity that Favor MNEs
1 Resource based	Capital, technology, access to markets; complementary assets	Possession of natural resources and related infrastructure	To ensure stability of supplies at right price; control markets obtain technology	Oil, copper, bauxite, bananas pineapples, cocoa, hotels, export processing, labor-intensive products of processes
2 Market based	Capital, technology, information, management and organization skills; surplus R&D and other capacity, economies of scale. Trademarks, goodwill.	Material and labor costs, markets, government policy (e.g., with respect to regulations and to import controls, investment incentives, etc.)	Wish to reduce transaction or information costs, buyer ignorance or uncertainty, etc. to protect property rights and ensure quality control	Computers, pharmaceuticals; motor vehicles, cigarettes, insurance, advertising

3 Rationalized specialization (a) of products (b) of processes	As above, but also access to markets; economies of scope and geographical diversification	(a) Economies of product specialization and concentration (b) Low labor costs, incentives to local production by host governments	(a) As type 2 plus gains from dependent economies of common governance (b) The economies of vertical integration	(a) Motor vehicles, electric appliances, business services, some R&D (b) Consumer electronics, textiles and clothing, cameras, pharmaceuticals
4 Trade and distribution (import and export merchanting)	Market access, products to distribute	Source of inputs and local markets. Need to be near customers. After sales servicing, etc.	Need to protect quality of inputs; need to ensure sales outlets and to avoid underperformance or misrepresentation by agent.	A variety of goods, particularly those requiring contact with subcontractors and final consumers.
5 Miscellaneous	Variety—but include geographical diversification	Markets	Various (see above)	Various kinds (a) Portfolio investment in properties (b) Where spatial linkages essential e.g., airlines and shipping.

Table 5.3

Some Illustrations of How OLI Characteristics May Vary According to Country, Industry, and Firm-Specific Considerations

OLI Structural Variables	Country	Industry	Firm
Ownership	Factor endowments (e.g., resources and skilled labor) and market size and character. Government policy toward innovation, protection of proprietary rights, competition, and industrial structure. Government attitudes toward internationalization of business, and cross-border alliances. The entrepreneurial culture and wealth creating ethos of a country.	Degree of product or process technological intensity; nature of innovations; extent of product differentiation; production economies (e.g., if there are economies of scale): transaction economies (e.g., if there are economies of scope) importance of favored access to inputs and/or markets.	Size, extent of production, process or market diversification; extent to which enterprise is innovative, or marketing-oriented or values security and/or stability, e.g., sources of inputs, market etc.; extent to which there are economies of joint production. Enterpreneurial vision and attitude to risk taking.
Internalization	Government intervention and extent to which policies encourage MNEs to internalize transactions, e.g., transfer pricing; government policy toward mergers; differences in market structures between	Extent to which vertical or horizontal integration is possible/desirable, e.g., need to control sourcing of inputs or markets; extent to which internalizing advantages can be captured in contractual agreement	Organizational and control procedures of enterprise; attitudes to growth and diversification (e.g., the boundaries of a firm's activities); attitudes toward subcontracting-contractual

countries, e.g., with respect to transaction costs, enforcement of contracts, buyer uncertainty etc.; adequacy of technological, educational, communications etc., infrastructure in host countries, and ability to absorb contractual resource transfers.

(cf. early and later stages of product cycle); use made of ownership advantages; cf. IBM with Unilever type operation; extent to which local firms have complementary advantages to those of foreign firms; extent to which opportunities for output specialization and international division of labor exist.

ventures, e.g., licensing franchising, technical assistance agreements etc., extent of which control procedures can be built into contractual agreements

| Location | Physical and psychic distance between countries; government intervention, e.g., tariffs, quotas, taxes, assistance to foreign investors or to own MNEs e.g., Japanese government's financial aid to Japanese firms investing in Southeast Asian labor-intensive industries. | Origin and distribution of inmobile resources; transport costs of intermediate and final goods product; industry specific tariff and nontariff barriers; nature of competition between firms in industry; can functions of activities of industry be split? Significance of "sensitive" locational variables, e.g., tax incentives, energy, and communication costs. | Management strategy towards foreign involvement; age and experience of foreign involvement; (position of enterprise in product cycle etc.); psychic distance variables (culture, language, legal, and commercial framework); attitudes toward centralization of certain functions, e.g., R&D; regional office and market allocation etc.; geographical structure of asset portfolio and attitude to risk diversification. |

gives an enterprise selling goods embodying that technology to foreign markets (irre-spective of where they are produced) an edge over its competitors, but the advantage of internalizing the use of that technology, rather than selling it to a foreign producer for the production of those goods. It is not the orthodox type of monopoly advantages which give the enterprize an edge over its rivals—actual or potential—but the advan-tages that accrue through internalization, for example, transfer price manipulation, se-curity and markets, and control over use of intermediate goods. It is not surplus en-trepreneurial resources *per se* that leads to FDI, but the ability of enterprises to combine these resources with others to take advantage of the economies of production of joint products. It is not the avoidance or reduction of environmental risk as such which in-fluences the location of MNE activity, but the benefits that arise from operating in diverse environments and the spreading of risks.

In other words, without the incentive to internalize the markets for and production of technology, FDI in technology based industries would give way to licensing agree-ments and/or the outright sale of knowledge on a contractual basis. Without the in-centive to internalize markets there would be much less reason to engage in vertical or horizontal integration, and again transactions would take place between independent firms. This it could be argued, is the distinctiveness of the eclectic paradigm.

The Dynamic Theory of International Production

Recent contributions in the literature—as summarized succinctly by Cantwell (1989)—have distinguished between explaining the initial act of foreign direct investment and sequential investment. In a chapter in a book edited by Kindleberger and Audretsch (1983), Kogut persuasively argues that although the possession of superior intangible assets may make possible the initial act of foreign production, once established abroad, the advantages of multinationality *per se*, i.e., those gained from the spreading of en-vironmental risks, and the common goverance of diversified activities in dispersed lo-cations, become more significant. In a later paper (Kogut 1987), he also relates the international strategy of MNEs to the source of their sequential advantages,[12] and to their experiences in coordinating domestic and foreign production. Bartlett and Ghoshal (1988) have also asserted that the diversity of environments exposes the multinational enterprise to multiple stimuli and allows it to develop capabilities and learning oppor-tunities not open to the domestic firm. Though these hypotheses have not been subject to any formal testing, there is considerable casual evidence to suggest that, as markets become globalized, large multinationals increasingly view the geographical dispersion of their assets and the formation of cross-border alliances with foreign firms as a nec-

---

[12]For example, in their exploitation of economies of scale, MNEs are in a better position than uninational firms to practice a balanced strategy of national product segmentation and international aggregation of de-mand; that by a policy of product line broadening and upgrading they are able to benefit from the economies of scope, whereas their ability to update and monitor information, and to acquire their inputs from the cheapest source, helps them further build on their learning advantages and those that arise from the geo-graphical dispersion of plants.

essary strategy to maintain or promote their international competitiveness.

Progress on advancing our understanding about the dynamics of foreign production has been less satisfactory. The literature identifies three main strands. The first is an extension of the Vernon product cycle model that examined the process of internationalization of production. Most of the work so far has been directed to explaining either how the location of value-added activity arising from the ownership-specific advantages of firms or the modes of exploiting these advantages (and especially that of technology) might vary over time. The general proposition is that as a firm becomes more international, it will first replace exports of low value activities by foreign production. This may later be followed by the foreign production of high value activities (Vernon, 1966, 1974). On the other hand, as a firm moves through its technology cycle—from the innovatory to the mature stage—there is less reason to suppose it will need or wish to internalize the markets for that technology; hence foreign-owned production might be expected to be replaced by licensing (Magee, 1977). More recently, economists and business analysts have paid more attention to the nature of ownership advantages (as described above) of multinationals, and the location of different kinds of the activities that create these advantages. In explaining the decentralization of research and development laboratories by multinationals, especially in industrial countries, economists are now arguing that, both for political and economic reasons, multinationals need to establish a innovatory presence in the main technology producing centres, viz. Western Europe, the United States, and Japan.

The second strand looks at the role of strategy as a dynamic force that bridges the internationalization posture of firms at different periods of time. The argument runs as follows. At any given moment of time, a firm is faced with a configuration of OLI variables and strategic objectives, which it will respond to by engaging in a variety of actions, e.g., to do with technology creation, market positioning, the formation of corporate alliances, organizational structure, political lobbying, intrafirm pricing, etc. These actions, together with changes in the value of the exogenous variables it faces, will influence its overall competitive position, and hence its OLI configuration at a subsequent date. The question of what determines the strategy of multinational firms is thus central to an understanding of the dynamics of international production. Here, not only will the kind of firm specific characteristics set out in Table 4.3 be important, but so will how the firm perceives its competitors will react to any change in its own internationalization strategy. Here economic and behavioral theories of the firm interact with each other.[13]

Third, and linked to the other two, have been attempts by economic theorists and political economists to model the extent to which the internationalization of production is linked to the ability of firms to accumulate, integrate, and control ownership-specific advantages across national boundaries. There are a number of variants of this approach; we consider just two. The first is the so-called technological accummulation approach,

---

[13]For a recent attempt to embrace dynamic and organizational factors in extending internalization theory, see an interesting paper by Hill and Kim (1988).

which uses some ideas of Rosenberg (1976, 1982) and suggests that the development of technology within the firm is a cumulative process. The creation of new technology and new technological systems or linkages is to be understood as a time-related series of adjustments and refinements. Each firm, because of differences in its OLI configuration and its strategic response to these variables, will develop a unique and differentiated technological trajectory or path, each step of which needs to be learned and coordinated with that which preceded it. The more complex, incremental, and widely dispersed the technology is, the more the learning process need to be internalized. The path of international production, then, requires an appreciation of the interaction between the various assets over time as well as at a given moment of time.

It is possible to extend this approach to other ownership-specific advantages; and the sequential analysis of Kogut also touches upon this. It is worth observing that there is nothing automatic about a firm increasing the internationalization of its production; only if a multinational believes this to be consistent with its strategic goals will this occur. However, a new generation of political economists have argued that, due primarily to technological development and the lowering of cross-border transport and communication costs, the incentive of firms to conclude collusive agreements to protect or advance their market power is increasing. This is in line with the earlier idea of Hymer that the multinational enterprise is an instrument of monopoly capitalism. The empirical evidence on this question is mixed. While the data show large multinationals are continuing to account for the bulk of foreign production, that cross-border nonequity alliances are growing, and that, in some countries, the presence of foreign affiliates has increased industrial concentration, there appears to be no letting up in the competition for markets by multinationals. Indeed, due to the emergence of new multinationals (especially those of medium size and of Japanese origin) and to the dispersal of production facilities, the evidence suggests multinationals respond to the environment in which they operate at least as much as they try to shape that environment to their own advantage.

A Macro-Economic Approach to Understanding Multinational Activity

Both the internalization and eclectic paradigms of international production are essentially micro-economic or behavioral explanations, in the sense that they attempt to identify and evaluate the variables that determine the foreign activities of particular firms or groups of firms. Using these same data to explain the determinants of a country's propensity to engage in foreign production is legitimate only in so far as the actions of individual producers do not affect the value of the variables that the producers themselves take to be endogenous. After this point, the scholar not only has to move from a partial to general equilibrium perspective. The type of questions he seeks to answer, and, indeed, the unit of analysis itself also change. Instead of trying to explain why firms undertake a particular value-added activity in one country rather than another, the macro economist is more interested in explaining *which* activities of firms are best undertaken in different countries abroad. In the former case, a comparison is made between the absolute costs and benefits of producing in different locations. In the latter, the distribution of value-added activity both within a country and between countries can only be explained in terms of comparative costs and benefits.

With this important distinction between micro and macro explanations of foreign production in mind, let us now consider Kiyoshi Kojima's macro-economic theory of foreign direct investment. This theory is essentially an extension of the neoclassical theory of factor endowments to explain trade in intermediate products, notably technology and management skills. But Kojima is as much interested in normative as in positive issues. A major part of his thesis, set out in Kojima (1973, 1978, 1982) and later revised and extended in Kojima and Ozawa (1984), is that whereas Japanese direct investment is primarily trade oriented and responds to the dictates of the principle of comparative advantage, U.S. direct investment is mainly conducted within an oligopolistic market structure, is antitrade oriented, and operates to the long-term disadvantage of both the donor and recipient countries.

Kojima essentially believes that foreign direct investment should act as an efficient conduit for trading intermediate products, but that the timing and direction of such investment should be determined by market forces rather than by hierarchial control. His prescription is that outward direct investment should be undertaken by firms that produce intermediate products that require resources in which the home country has a comparative advantage, but that generate value-added activities that require resources in which that country is comparatively disadvantaged. By contrast, inward direct investment should import intermediate products that require resources in which the recipient country is disadvantage, but the use of which needs resources in which it has a comparative advantage. To this extent, the Kojima thesis is quite consistent with any macro-economic inferences that might be drawn from the eclectic paradigm—at least in respect of some kinds of foreign direct investment.

The point where Kojima's theory ceases to be satisfactory as a general explanation of foreign production is precisely that at which neoclassical theories fail to explain much of modern trade. That is because neither countenance the possibility of market failure and the fact that firms are both producing and transacting economic agents. This means that they cannot explain the kind of trade flows (including trade in intermediate products) that are based less on the distribution of factor endowments and more on the need to exploit economies of scale, product differentiation, and other manifestations of market failure. Neither can they explain trade in intermediate products based upon the advantages of common governance, which, itself, reflects the inability of the market mechanism to ensure the first-best international allocation of economic activity in situations in which the costs and benefits of transactions extend beyond those who are parties to the exchange; where there is uncertainty of the outcome of such exchanges; and where there is an assymetry of knowledge between buyers and sellers.

To the extent that Kojima uses trade models to explain patterns of foreign direct investment, he follows the Vernon tradition. To the extent that he regards MNEs as creators or sustainers of market imperfections, whose impact on resource allocation must be less beneficial than that predicated by perfect competition, the geneology of this thought can be traced back to Hymer. The result is that whereas he formulates a useful analysis of the cross-border transactions in intermediate products, and correctly identifies some activities of multinationals as being either the result of structural market distortions or as creating such distortions, he ignores the impact of transaction costs on international resource allocation, and hence fails to appreciate that, in conditions of market failure, multinational hierarchies may improve rather than worsen such an allocation. The means by which this is accomplished, which include geographical diversification, the exploitation of the economies of joint supply, better commercial intelligence, and the avoidance of costs of enforcing property rights have been well spelled out by Gray (1982). On such efficiency gains, Kojima is generally silent, and for that reason alone, his cannot be construed as a general theory of foreign production.

FUTURE CHALLENGES FOR THE THEORY OF INTERNATIONAL PRODUCTION

Issues Resolved and Unresolved by Contemporary Theory

In this chapter we have described the evolution of the theory of international production over the past three decades. As of the late 1980s, we have a galaxy of partial theories that purport to explain particular aspects of foreign production, or particular kinds of foreign production, or the behavior of particular types of multinationals. Most of these have been tested—usually by the use of multiple regression techniques, or, in the case of less quantifiable variables, by factor, cluster, or multidiscriminant analysis. Most (for example, as summarized by Clegg, 1987) have attempted to identify the particular OLI variables likely to affect the geographical or industrial distribution of foreign production, or the strategic response of MNEs to these variables. Few have tested the extent to which foreign-owned affiliates actually do record higher profits than their indigenous competitors, or whether they earn higher rates of return than could have been earned had the same activity been undertaken in the home country, although in the 1960s and early 1970s there were attempts to do so from the viewpoint of the efficiency of resource allocation. Stevens (1974) and Caves (1982) offer good summaries of the relevant empirical studies.

In the last decade the focus of attention has been directed to more general—and even interdisciplinary—explanations of international production, of which the eclectic paradigm is the most ambitious. Clearly it is easy to criticize such paradigms; indeed their very strengths—the encompassing of a large set of disparate variables—makes any systematic testing very difficult. But it is worth repeating that the idea of the eclectic paradigm is to produce an analytical framework within which particular theories of foreign production can be evaluated. To this extent, the debate between the view of those who argue that market failure is a necessary and sufficient condition to explain the existence of MNEs and those who assert the eclectic paradigm offers a useful framework for analysing the extent and patterns of foreign production is more meaningful than that between both schools of thought and those who argue for and against generalist explanations.

At the same time, there remain many unresolved issues in international business that require attention. Some contemporary events, e.g., the rapid growth of service MNEs, the emergence of Third World MNEs and the opening up of last East Europe and the Peoples Republic of China to foreign direct investment, we believe require only minor modifications to either the internalization or eclectic paradigms. Similarly, when combined with a theory of strategic behavior, both can satisfactorily embrace many of the issues on nonequity participation (Beamish and Banks, 1987) and even of the determinants of the locus of control *within* firms (Dunning 1988a). But there are other trends in international business that may require a more fundamental appraisal of existing modes of thought. We briefly analyse three of these.[14]

Cooperative Alliances

The blurring of the boundaries of firms brought about by the growth of interfirm collaborative agreements opens up new challenges to the researchers. At one time, the distinction between markets and the hierarchies as modes or organizing transactions seems fairly clear. Nowdays, an increasing proportion of transactions seem to involve the cooperation or affiliation between firms. According to Richardson (1972) cooperation is most likely to appeal to two (or more) firms, rather than a market or a hierarchial relationship, when each engages in complementary but dissimilar activites. Coordination of economic activity by cooperation is preferred to that by hierarchies as it involves lower transaction cost of organizing dissimilar activities, whereas it is preferred to the market because coordination requires not the matching of aggregate supply to aggregate demand (which in the main task of markets) but rather the plans of separate enterprises.

The delineation of the role of the market, hierarchies, and cooperation among hierarchies in terms of the matching of activities to capabilities, rather in terms of products and processes, is only now beginning to receive the attention of economists and business analysts (Contractor and Lorange, 1988). Yet this approach might well be the clue to incorporating networks of interfirm alliances into the received theory of international production. Using Richardson's terminology, if technological advances encourage multinationals to specialize in similar activities across national boundaries, based, for example, on a particular combination of technological and/or managerial capabilities, but that to engage in these activities, these assets need to be combined with a different set of technological and managerial capabilities, then to maximize the value added from the inputs required for these activities, interfirm cooperation may be the preferred organizational form.

---

[14]Other issues that need the attention of the international business scholar are identified by Casson (1986) and Buckley and Casson (1989).

Network Analysis

Whereas most of the analysis of cooperative alliances has centered on the relationship between pairs of firms, i.e., bilateral transactional relationships it is clear that contemporary multinationals are adopting a more multinational or pluralistic approach to their overseas activities. At the same time, the transactional relationships they forge with other firms, e.g., their suppliers and customers, are not independent, hence, it becomes appropriate to consider groups or networks of organizational forms, rather than discrete relationships. Moreover, the form and structure of these networks may well affect the modality of the relationship formed with other firms in the network.

The network approach to theorizing about the foreign activities of multinational firms has recently been developed by a group of Swedish and Japanese scholars. The basic proposition of these scholars is that in order to survive, organizations require resources that can be obtained only by interacting with other organizations that own or control these resources. A network relationship implies that there is some overlap in the transactions of firms within the network. For example, Firm A trades with Firm B, which trades with Firm C, which trades with Firm A. There is a conscious division of work among firms in the network, which means that firms are interdependent of each other. But the activities are coordinated not through the market or by a central hierarchial plan, but by the establishment of a series of relationships established between the members of the network. These networks are assumed to be stable and changing, and the bonds established may vary from the formal to the informal; and protected by a contract or an agreement based on trust and mutual commitment.

The network approach has been used to explain the process of the internationalization of production by Imai (1985) and Johanson and Mattson (1987a,b), and has been contrasted with the internalization model discussed earlier. At the same time, a lot of the work seems to have concerned itself with bilateral relationship (or links in the network) rather than with multilateral relationships (or the network itself). To this extent, the literature on strategic alliances and networks overlaps. But one of the interesting features of at least some of the multinationals of the late 1980s is that their choice of network partners may well be influenced by the relationship between these partners and other forms, which may have a separate relationship—be it one of competition on collaboration—with the first firm. The idea of a galaxy or groupings of firms, each of which is united by complementary activities, to cooperate to promote their individual interests implies that the composition of the galaxy is not independent of the role played by the constituents of other competing galaxies. According to this view, each firm performs a dual role; as a cooperator in the group(s) of which it is a member, but as a competitor in the supply of end products and the demand for factor inputs. To this extent, network analysis would seem to have a lot more to offer than it has so far been able to demonstrate. But it needs to be integrated with work now being done in industrial organization, and especially that in oligopolistic theory and contestable markets.

Finally, mention should be made of the work of Ghoshal and Bartlett (1989) who argue that the multinational enterprise itself should be regarded as a controller of a network of interrelated activities. These interactions may be internal (with in the MNEs) or external (between the MNEs) and other organizations. Ghoshal and Bartlett assert that the extent and form of these link ups will rest on the resource configuration of the MNEs, which in turn will depend on the type of activities and countries in which they are engaged. They further suggest that the allocation of decision taking within MNEs will depend upon the related positions of the headquarters and subsidiaries in the total network of activity.

The Role of Strategic Management

The developments just described suggest the forging of new kinds of cross-border relationships between and within firms. They have been brought about both by the changes in the OLI configuration facing firms, due *inter alia* to technological and organizational changes of the past two decades or more, *and* the strategic response of firms to these changes. The third challenge to the received theory of foreign production derives from the fact that the behaviorial options open to firms in the kind of value-added activities in which they engage, and the organization of such activities have themselves widened. This we suggest is because of the inadequacy of both pure markets and pure hierarchies to offer the optimal solution as to the way in which resources should be organized. On the one hand, we see the majority of industrial activity being dominated by large firms, diversified in their product and geographical structure, but within their main product markets, competing as national or international oligopolists. On the other, because of the growing interdependence among economic functions, rapid technological change and obsolescence, and the growing importance of the economies of scope and of the role of governmental intervention, we observe that, in an increasing number of instances, neither pure markets nor pure hierarchies operating independently can ensure that resources are organized in a way acceptable to the participants. We further observe that not only does market and/or hierarchial failure impinge on the OLI configuration facing firms, it will also affect the strategic response of firms to that configuration. In turn, as have seen, such a response may affect the values of and relationship between the OLI variables in the next period.

The widening strategic options open to firms require a reappraisal of received theory in a number of ways, but basically the challenge to scholars is to switch their mode of thinking away from explaining individual cross-border transactions or acts of foreign production to explaining a system of transactions or acts of foreign production. Both the analysis of markets and hierarchies have tended to focus on particular goods or services transacted or particular decisions taken related to these transactions. But, due to the growing interdependency among factors of production, intermediate products and final goods and services traded, and to the way in which the production of these goods and services are organized among firms, the approach to understanding organization of foreign production needs to be much more pluralistic than it has been in the past. No one model of the multinational enterprise is likely to be adequate. Whatever, the organizational form of any one activity may take, in its strategy toward its foreign value-added activities, the multinational enterprise is likely to use an amalgam of organizational forms—varying among the spectrum from markets, through collaborative agreements, to hierarchies. These will differ among activities, market structure, age and experience of firms, countries of operation, and preception risks involved and strategic objectives.

To summarize, any general paradigm of foreign production must first take account of variables and behavior that can be fully appreciated only by taking an interdisciplinary approach (Dunning 1988b, Chapter 12). Second, it must recognize that because of a multinational engages in many separate but related activities within an uncertain market environment, not only is market failure evident in organizational transactions, but internalizing this market within a single hierarchy may not be the optimum solution either. Transborder interfirm agreements must also be considered a form of foreign production. Hence a theory of foreign production must look at the portfolio of a firms operations and the way it organizes the production of individual products in particular countries. Strategic management is concerned with the ways in which managers act to achieve their objectives in conditions of market failure. It embraces not only decisions as to how resources are acquired, created, and utilized, or the way in which markets are identified or served, but on how the transactions relating to these decisions are organized. Like the choice of what and how to produce, the various strategic strands must be integrated, and it is the totality of strategy rather than its individual components that is wholly within the control of hierarchies.

There are other areas in which own knowledge on the reasons for foreign production leave much to be desired. One is in the dynamics of international production. Here, as an earlier section shows, scholars have yet to tackle the interaction between entrepreneurship, innovation, and the management of human resources—the main engines of business growth—and the way in which the output of these assets affects both the OLI variables earlier identified, and the strategy of firms toward their international operations. Over the last fifty years, tremendous changes have taken place in the extent and pattern of multinational activity. Clearly these changes would not have occurred to the same extent without changes in technological development, in the organization of firms, in population, in social and cultural values, and in the role of governments. Whereas at a given moment it may be correct to analyze the response of firms to these variables, over time, both at a micro and macro level this is unjustifiable. This is now being recognized, as scholars (e.g., Casson, 1988, Cantwell, 1989b; Pavitt, 1987) are giving more attention to issues of innovation and entrepreneurship as they impinge upon the internationalization of business. We believe that if a new breakthrough in our understanding of foreign production occurs, it will be in this direction.

Finally, there needs to be a widening out of trade-related activity to embrace international production, as increasingly the two are interwined. Nowhere in this more clearly seen than in the current round of trade negotiations (the Uruguay round) about the nature of services. In these negotiations, at least one of the major industrial countries (the United States is claiming that the definition of trade ought to include foreign direct investment—as without some physical presence, trade in some services is impossible. Whatever one might think of the logic of this argument, there can be no dispute that the modalities of servicing foreign markets, both with goods and services, are becoming increasingly interdependent.

Research for this chapter was undertaken as part of a larger project on *Multinationals in the World Economy,* and which is being partly funded by the (UK) Economic & Social Research Council.

References

Agarwal, J. P. 1980. Determinants of Foreign Direct Investment. A survey. *Weltwirtschaftliches Archiv, Band* 116, *Heft* 4 739–73.

Agmon, T., and D. Lessard. 1977. Investor Recognition of Corporate International Diversification. *Journal of Finance,* pp. 1049–1055.

Alchian, A., and H. Demsetz. 1972. Production, Information Costs and Economic Organization. *American Economic Review* 62:777–795.

Aliber, R. Z. 1970. A Theory of Foreign Direct Investment, in C. P. Kindleberger, (ed.): *The International Corporation.* Cambridge: MIT Press.

Aliber, R. Z. 1971. The Multinational Enterprise in a Multiple Currency World, in J. H. Dunning (ed.): *The Multinational Enterprise.* London: Allen & Unwin.

Anderson, E., and H. Gatignon. 1986. Modes of Foreign Entry: A Transaction Cost Analysis and Propositions. *Journal of International Business Studies* 17:1–26.

Bartlett, C. A., and S. Ghoshal. 1988. Managing Innovations in the Transnational Corporation, in C. A. Bartlett, Y. Doz, and G. Hedlund, (eds.): *Research on Multinational Management.* London: Addison Wesley.

Bain, J. S. 1956. *Barriers to New Competition.* Cambridge: Harvard University Press.

Barlow, E. R. 1953. *Management of Foreign Manufacturing Subsidiaries.* Cambridge: Harvard University Press.

Batra, R. N., and P. Ramachandran. 1980. Multinational Firms and the Theory of International Trade and Investment. *American Economic Review* 70:278–290.

Beamish, P. and J. C. Banks. 1980. Equity Joint Ventures and the Theory of the Multinational Enterprise. *Journal of International Business Studies* 19:1–16.

Buckley, P. J. 1987. *The Theory of the Multinational Enterprise.* Uppsala: Acta Universitatis Upsaliensis.

Buckley, P. J., and M. C. Casson. 1976. *The Future of the Multinational Enterprise.* London: MacMillan.

Buckley, P. J. and M. C. Casson. 1985. *The Economic Theory of the Multinational Enterprise.* London: Macmillan.

Buckley, P. J., and M. C. Casson. 1989. *Multinational Enterprises and Less Developed Countries: Cultural and Economic Interaction,* University of Reading Discussion Papers in International Investment and Business Studies, No. 126 January.

Bye, M. 1985. Self Financed Multi-Territorial Units and Their Time Horizon. *International Economic Papers.* 8:147–178.

Calvet, A. L. 1980. *Markets and Hierarchies: Towards a Theory of International Business,* Ph.D. thesis, Sloan School of Management, Cambridge, Mass.

Cantwell, J. 1988. *Theories of International Production,* University of Reading, Discussion Papers in International Investment and Business Studies, No. 122, September 1988.

Cantwell, J. 1989. *Technological Innovation and Multinational Corporations.* Oxford: Bane Blackwell.

Cantwell, J., T. A. B. Corley, and J. H. Dunning. 1986. Some Theoretical Antecedents to the Eclectic Paradigm of International Production in P. Hertner and G. Jones (eds.): *Multinationals, Theory and History*. Aldershot: Gower.

Casson, M. C. 1979. *Alternatives to the Multinational Enterprise*. London: Macmillan.

Casson, M. C. 1985. The Theory of Foreign Direct Investment in P. J. Buckley and M. C. Casson (eds.): *The Economic Theory of the Multinational Enterprise*. London: Macmillan.

Casson, M. C. 1986. Recent Trends in International Business: A New Analysis, University of Reading Discussion Papers in International and Business Studies No. 112. Jan. 1988.

Casson, M. C. 1987. *The Firm and the Market*. Oxford: Basil Blackwell.

Casson, M. C. 1988. Enterpreneurship as a Cultural Advantage, University of Reading Discussion Papers in International Investment and Business Studies, No. 124, November.

Caves, R. E. 1971. Industrial Corporations: The Industrial Economics of Foreign Investment. *Economica* 38:1–27.

Caves, R. E. (1974a). Causes of Direct Investment: Foreign Firms' Shares in Canadian and United Kingdom Manufacturing Industries. *Review of Economics and Statistics* 56:272–293.

Caves, R. E. 1974b. Multinational Firms, Competition and Productivity in Host Country Markets. *Economica* 41:176–193.

Clegg, J. 1987. *Multinational Enterprise and World Competition*. London: Macmillan.

Coase, R. H. 1937. The Nature of the Firm. *Economica (New Series)* 4:386–405.

Coase, R. H. 1960. The Problem of Social Cost. *Journal of Law and Economics* 3:1–10.

Contractor, F. J. 1981. *International Technology Licensing*. Lexington, Mass: Lexington Books.

Contractor, F. J. and P. Lorange. 1988. *Cooperative Strategies in International Business*. Lexington, Mass: D. C. Heath.

Dunning, J. H. 1958. *American Investment in British Manufacturing Industry*. London: Allen & Unwin, (reprinted by Arno Press, New York, 1976).

Dunning, J. H. 1973. The Determinants of International Production. *Oxford Economic Papers* 25:289–336.

Dunning, J. H. 1981. *International Production and the Multinational Enterprise*. London: Allen & Unwin.

Dunning, J. H. (1988a). The Eclectic Paradigm of International Production: A Restatement and Some Possible Extensions. *Journal of International Business Studies* 19:1–31.

Dunning, J. H. 1988b. *Explaining International Production,* London: Unwin Hyman.

Dunning, J. H. and A. Rugman. 1985. The Infuence of Hymer's Dissertation on Theory of Foreign Direct Investment. *American Economic Review* 75:228–232.

Ethier, W. J. 1986. Foreign Direct Investment and the Multinational Firm. *Quarterly Journal of Economics* 101:805–833.

Flowers, E. B. 1976. Oligopolistic Reaction in European and Canadian Direct Investment in the US. *Journal of International Business Studies* 7:43–55.

Franko, L. G. 1976. *The European Multinationals* New York: Harper.

Galbraith, C. S., and N. W. Kay. 1986. Towards a Theory of Multinational Enterprise. *Journal of Economic Behaviour and Organisation* 19:3–19.

Ghoshal, S. (1987. Global Strategy: An Organising Framework. *Strategic Management Journal* 8:425–440.

Ghoshal, S., and C. A. Bartlett. 1989. *The Multinational Corporation as a Network Perspective from Inter Organisation Theory*. Mimeo, Fontainbleu and Boston.

Graham, E. M. 1978. Transatlantic Investment by Multinational Firms: A Rivalistic Phenomenon. *Journal of Post Keynesian Economics* 1:82–99.

Graham, E. M. 1985. Intra-Industry Direct Investment, Market Structure, Firm Rivalry and Technological Performance, in A. Erdilek (ed.): *Multinationals as Mutual Invaders*. London: Croom Helm, 67–88.

Gray, H. P. 1982. Towards a Unified Theory of International Trade, International Production and Direct Foreign Investment, in J. Black and J. H. Dunning, (eds.): *International Capital Movements*. London: Macmillan.

Grosse, R. 1981. *The Theory of Foreign Direct Investment*. South Carolina Essays in International Business, No. 3, December.

Grubel, H. 1968. Internationally Diversified Portfolios: Welfare Grains and Capital Flows. *American Economic Review* 58.

Helpman, E. 1984. A Simple Theory of International Trade with Multinational Corporations. *Journal of Political Economy* 92:451–471.

Helpman, E. 1985. Multinational Corporations and International Trade. *Review of Economic Studies* 52:443–457.

Helpman, E., and P. Krugman. 1985. *Market Structure and International Trade*. Cambridge: M.I.T. Press.

Hennart, J. F. 1982. A Theory of Multinational Enterprises. Ann Arbor: University of Michigan Press.

Hennart, J. F. 1986. What Is Internalization? *Weltwirtschaftliches Archiv* 122:791–804.

Hill, C. W., and Kim W. Chan. (1988) Searching for a Dynamic theory of the Multinational Enterprise: A Transaction Cost Model. *Strategic Management Journal* 9:93–104.

Horst, T. 1972a. Firm and Industry Determinants of the Decision to Invest Abroad: An Empirical Study. *Review of Economics and Statistics* 54:258–266.

Horst, T. 1972b. The Industrial Composition of U.S. Exports and Subsidiary Sales to the Canadian Market. *American Economic Review* 62:37–45.

Horstman, I. and J. R. Markusen. 1986. *Licensing v Direct Investment: A Model of Internalization by the Multinational Enterprise*. Mimeo. University of Western Ontario.

Hufbauer, G. C. 1970. The Impact of National Characteristics and Technology on the Commodity Composition of Trade in Manufactured Goods in R. Vernon (ed.): *The Technology Factor in International Trade*. New York: Columbia University Press.

Hymer, S. 1960. *The International Operations of National Firms: A Study of Direct Investment*, Ph.D. thesis, MIT, published by MIT Press under same title in 1976.

Hymer, S. 1968. La grande firme multinetionale. *Revue Economique* 19:949–973.

Imai, K. 1985. *Network Organization and Incremental Innovation in Japan*, Institute of Business Research, Hitosubashi, Discussion Paper No. 122 July.

Itaki, M. 1989. *A Critical Assessment of the Eclectic Theory*. Mimeo. University of Reading.

Iversen, C. 1935. *Aspects of International Capital Movements*. London: Levin and Munksgaard.

Johanson, J., and L. G. Mattson. 1987a. The Internationalization Process of the Firm: A Model of Knowledge Develoment and Increasing Foreign Market Commitments. *Journal of International Business Studies* 8:23–32.

Johanson, J., and L. G. Mattson. 1987b. Internationalization in Industrial Systems: A Network Approach as compared with a Transaction Cost Approach. *International Studies of Management and Organisation* XVII:34–48.

Johnson, J. 1968. *Comparative Cost and Commercial Policy Theory for a Developing Third World Economy*. Stockholm: Almquist and Wiksell.

Johnson, H. 1970. The Efficiency and Welfare Implications of the International Corporation, in C. P. Kindleberger (ed.): *The International Corporation*. Cambridge: MIT Press.

Kindleberger, C. P. 1969. *American Business Abroad*. New Haven: Yale University Press.

Kindleberger, C. P. and D. Audretsch. (eds.) 1983. *The Multinational Corporation in the 1980s*. Cambridge: Cambridge University Press.

Knickerbocker, F. T. 1973. *Oligopolistic Reaction and the Multinational Enterprise*. Cambridge, Mass.: Harvard University Press.

Kogut, B. 1983. Foreign Direct Investment as a Sequential Process, in C. P. Kindleberger and D. Audretsch (eds.): *The Multinational Corporation in the 1980s*. Cambridge, Mass., M.I.T. Press.

Kogut, B. 1985. Designing Global Strategies: Profiting from Operational Flexibility. *Sloan Management Review* Fall, pp. 27–37.

Kogut, B. 1987. *International Sequential Advantages and Network Flexibility*. Mimeo, Stockholm.

Kogut, B. and M. Kulatilaha. 1988. *Multinational Flexibility and the Theory of Foreign Direct Investment*, Reginald H. Jones Center for Management Policy, Strategy and Organization, University of Pennsylvania, July.

Kojima, K. 1973. A Macroeconomic Approach to Foreign Direct Investment. *Hitosubashi Journal of Economics* 14:1–21.

Kojima, K. 1978. *Direct Foreign Investment: A Japanese Model of Multinational Business Operations*. London: Croom Helm.

Kojima, K. 1980. Japanese Direct Foreign Investment in Asian Developing Countries. *Rivista Internationale di Science Economiche e Commerciale* 27:630–640.

Kojima, K. 1982. Macro Economic Versus International Business Approach to Foreign Direct Investment. *Hitosubashi Journal of Economics* 23:1–19.

Kojima, K. and T. Ozawa. 1984. Micro and Macro Economic Models of Foreign Direct Investment: Towards a Synthesis. *Hitosubashi Journal of Economics* 25:1–20.

Krugman, P. 1983. Multinational Enterprise, in C. P. Kindleberger and D. Audretsch (ed): *The Multinational Corporation in the 1980s*. Cambridge: M.I.T. Press.

Lall, S. 1979. Multinationals and Market Structure in an Open Developing Economy. The Case of Malaysia. *Weltwirtschafliches Archiv* 114 (2):325–350.

Lall, S. 1980. Monopolistic Advantages and Foreign Involvement by US Manufacturing Industry. *Oxford Economic Papers* 32:120–122.

Lall, S. and Siddarthan. 1982. The Monopolistic Advantages of Multinationals: Lessons from Foreign Investment in the US. *Economic Journal* 92:668–682.

Lessard, D. 1976. World Country and Industry Relations in Equity Returns: Implications for Risk Reduction through International Diversification. *Financial Anlaysts Journal*, Jan/Feb 2–8.

Lessard, D. 1982. Multinational Diversification and Direct Foreign Investment, in D. K. Eiteman and A. Stonehill (eds.): *Multinational Business Finance*. Reading, Mass: Addison Wesley (also reprinted in 4th edition, 1986).

Levy, H., and M. Sarnat. 1970. International Diversification of Investment Portfolios. *American Economic Review*, September, pp. 668–675.

Lundgren, N. 1977. Comment (on a chapter by J. H. Dunning), in B. Ohlin, P. O. Hesselborn, and P. M. Wijkman, (eds.): *The International Allocation of Economic Activity*. London: Macmillan.

McManus, J. C. 1972. The Theory of the Multinational Firm, in G. Paquet (ed.): *The Multinational Firm and the Nation State*. Toronto: Collier-MacMillan.

Magee, S. P. 1977. Information and the Multinational Corporation: An Appropriability Theory of Foreign Direct Investment, in J. N. Blagwati, (ed.), *The New International Economic Order*. Cambridge: MIT Press.

Markusen, J. R. 1984. Multinational, Multi-Plant Economies and the Gains from Trade. *Journal of International Economics* 16:205–226.

Owen, R. F. 1982. Inter-Industry Determinants of Foreign Direct Investment, in A. Rugman, (ed.): *New Theories of the Multinational Enterprise*. London: Croom Helm.

Pavitt, K. 1987. International Patterns of Technological Accumulation, in N. Hood, and J. E. Vahlne, (eds.): *Strategies in Global Competition*. New York: Wiley.

Penrose, E. T. 1956. Foreign Investment and the Growth of the Firm. *Economic Journal* 66:220–235.

Penrose, E. 1958. *The Theory of the Growth of the Firm*. Oxford: Basil Blackwell, (rev. ed. published 1979).

Plummer, A. 1934. *International Combines in Modern History*. London: Pitman.

Posner, M. V. 1961. International Trade and Technical Change. *Oxford Economic Papers* 13:1961.

Richardson, G. B. 1972. The Organization of Industry. *Economic Journal* 88:883–896.

Rosenberg, N. 1976. *Perspectives on Technology*. Cambridge, Mass.: Cambridge Univesity Press.

Rosenberg, N. ed. 1982. *International Technology Transfer*. New York: Wiley.

Rugman, A. M. 1975. Motives for Foreign Investment: The Markets Imperfections and Risk Diversification Hypothesis. *Journal of World Trade Law* 9:567–573.

Rugman, A. M. (1979). *International Diversification and the Multinational Enterprise*. Lexington, Mass.: Lexington Books.

Rugman, A. M. 1980. Internalization Theory and Corporate International Finance. *California Management Review* XIII:73–79.

Rugman, A. M. 1981. *Inside the Multinationals: The Economics of Internal Markets*. London: Croom Helm.

Rugman, A. M. 1986. New Theories of Multinational Enteprises: An Assessment of Internalization Theory. *Bulletin of Economic Research* 38:101–118.

Simon, H. A. 1947. *Administrative Behaviour*. New York: Macmillan.

Simon, H. A. 1955. A Behavioural Model of Rational Choice. *Quarterly Journal of Economics* 69:99–118.

Southard, F. A. Jr. (1931. *American Industry in Europe*. Boston: Houghton Mifflin.

Southard, F. A. Jr., and H. Marshall and K. W. Taylor. 1936. *Canadian-American Industry*. New Haven: Yale University Press.

Stern, R. M. 1975. Testing Trade Theories in P. B. Kenen (ed.): *International Trade and Finance*. Cambridge: Cambridge University Press.

Stevens, G. V. 1974. The Determinants of Investment, in H. H. Dunning, (ed.): *Economic Analysis and the Multinational Enterprise,* London: Allen and Unwin.

Stopford, J. M. 1976. Changing Perspective of Investment by British Manufacturing Multinationals. *Journal of International Business Studies* 7:15–28.

Swedenborg, B. 1979. *The Multinational Operations of Swedish Firms: An Analysis of Determinants and Effects*. Stockholm: Almquist and Wiksell.

Teece, D. J. 1981. The Multinational Enterprise: Market Failure and Market Power Considerations. *Sloan Management Review*, Spring, pp. 3–17.

Teece, D. J. 1985. Transaction Cost Economics and the Multinational Enterprise: An Assessment. *Journal of Economic Behaviour and Organisation*. 7:21–45.

Telesio, P. 1979. *Technology Licensing and Multinational Enterprise*. New York: Praeger.

Tsmuri, Y. 1976. *The Japanese are Coming: A Multinational Interaction of Firms and Politics*. Cambridge, Mass: Ballinger.

Vernon, R. 1966. International Investment and International Trade in the Product Cycle. *Quarterly Journal of Economics* 80:90–207.

Vernon, R. 1974. The Location of Economic Activity, in J. H. Dunning, (ed.): *Economic Analysis and the Multinational Enterprise*. London: Allen & Unwin.

Vernon, R. 1983. Organizational and Institutional Responses to International Risk, in R. J. Herring, (ed.): *Managing International Risk*. Cambridge: Cambridge University Press.

Wells, L. (ed.) 1972. *The Product Life Cycle and International Trade*. Cambridge, Mass.: Harvard University Press.

Williams, J. H. 1929. The Theory of International Trade Reconsidered. *Economic Journal* 39:195–209.

Williamson, O. E. 1975. *Markets and Hierarchies: Analysis and Antitrust Implications*. New York: Free Press.

Williamson, O. E. 1985. *The Economic Institutions of Capitalism*. New York: Free Press.

Williamson, O. E. 1986. *Economic Organisation*. Brighton: Wheatsheaf Books.

Yoshino, M. Y. 1976. *Japan's Multinational Enterprises*. Cambridge: Harvard University Press.

countries with a combined foreign debt of close to one-half of one trillion dollars—or several times their combined GNP. Their failure to find a manageable solution will not only seriously jeopardize the global banking system, but it has the potential of doing likewise to the international trade system. In Chapter 8, Khosrow Fatemi analyzes one of the more promising and least harmful approaches to this problem: swapping foreign debt for equity ownership in productive facilities in debtor nations. Fatemi discusses the debt capitalization programs adopted by several countries and analyzes the benefits and costs of these programs to all the parties concerned: the international banks, the host countries, and the MNCs that take over assets in the debtor countries.

The contention of this chapter is that contrary to public belief, international banks are not losing any of their original loans. Even when discounting some LDC notes at 50% or more, the banks are recovering all of their original loan plus some interest, the rate for which will be much lower than market rates and will depend on a series of factors discussed in the chapter. Also contrary to public belief, the debtor nations are not gaining debt relief at no cost. Debt-equity conversion results in the infusion of hundreds of millions of dollars in local currencies in inflation-prone economies, often contributing to triple-digit inflation as witnessed in Brazil, Mexico, and Argentina. Such problems notwithstanding, Fatemi concludes that debt-equity swaps are the most promising of all the solutions developed in recent years to remedy the debt problem of the LDCs. In fact, debt-equity swaps may be the only hope for these countries to regain normalcy in their economies and become active participants in the international trade system.

In Chapter 9, James M. Lutz analyzes the shifting comparative advantage among different developing countries and its impact on international trade. He maintains that the newly industrialized countries (NICs) became important participants in international trade by specializing in the production of labor-intensive manufactured goods. They capitalized on a shifting comparative advantage away from industrial countries and toward NICs. Lutz then raises the question of whether or not a new shift—this time away from the NICs and toward other LDCs—has already begun. The significance of this hypothesis is that accepting it would suggest that international trade has a major role to play in the industrialization process in the developing countries. To test his hypothesis, Lutz develops a correlation model using selected three-digit categories of SITC (Standard Industrial Trade Classification) codes for sixteen different countries for the two periods of 1968–1976 and 1976–1982. Testing the hypothesis by applying his model, Lutz reaches the conclusion that there is little evidence for the presence of a process of ongoing shifts in comparative advantage from NICs to other LDCs.

Chapter 6

PREFERENTIAL VS. TARIFF LIBERALIZATION: EFFECTS OF THE TOKYO ROUND ON LDC EXPORTS

Craig MacPhee

INTRODUCTION

The seventh and longest round of GATT trade negotiations concluded on April 12, 1979 with agreements on tariff concessions, some nontariff measures, and changes in the legal framework of international trade. Implementation of the accords by certain countries began January 1, 1980 and continued through 1987. Although it is too soon to estimate the effects of the Tokyo Round expost, this chapter attempts to resolve some of the controversy about its predicted effects on exports from less-developed countries (LDCs). The continuing differences over this question are reflected in LDCs concerns about the current Uruguay Round of multilateral trade negotiations, which commenced in 1987. A better understanding of potential LDC gains and losses might lead to improvement in north-south economic relations.

OBJECTIVES AND RESULTS OF THE NEGOTIATIONS

There have been several different evaluations of the Tokyo Round, but seldom have the accords been judged with reference to (1) the specific objectives established by GATT signatories in the Tokyo Declaration of September, 1973, or (2) the goals which the LDCs, wished to pursue in the negotiations as enumerated at the Fourth United Nations Conference on Trade and Development (UNCTAD IV).[1] The Tokyo Decla-

---

[1]Balassa (1980) has generally praised the accords, writing that ". . . the benefits derived from the general provisions of the codes, from special and differential treatment and from participation in dispute settlements and surveillance procedures point to the desirability for the developing countries to subscribe to the codes on nontariff measures" (p. 112). Winham (1980) reports mixed results: On the one hand, "the MTN Agree-

ration (reprinted in GATT, 1979) established the objectives of "ever-greater" trade lib-eralization "as rapidly as possible" through "general application" of tariff-cutting for-mulae and reduction or elimination of nontariff measures. LDCs' expectations for the negotiations were undoubtedly raised by the admission of all countries as participants, even those that were not contracting parties of the GATT. The Tokyo Declaration spec-ified that the negotiations should aim to secure additional benefits for the international trade of LDCs, and that the more-developed countries (MDCs) did not expect full rec-iprocity from LDC in the negotiations. The ministerial meeting in Tokyo also recog-nized the importance of the application of differential measures to LDCs in ways that would provide special and more favorable treatment for them in the negotiations. They also recognized the importance of treating tropical products as a special and priority sector and the importance of maintaining and improving the generalized system of pref-erences (GSP).

At UNCTAD IV, the LDCs indicated the specific areas of major importance to them and the concessions they wanted in the tariff negotiations. They called for the binding of commitments and concessions in their favor; the inclusion of all LDC as beneficiaries in the GSP; advance implementations of concessions in their favor; special priority in the scope, content, and depth of tariff concessions for tropical products requested by LDCs on a nonreciprocal basis; and, as appropriate, on a preferential basis. In addition, the LDCs requested deeper-than-formula tariff cuts for products of interest to them that were not covered by the GSP; the binding in GATT of preferential tariff margins; and effective compensation in the event of the erosion of preferential tariff margins resulting from MFN tariff cuts.[2]

The Tokyo Round accords fell short of the Declaration's ambitious goals. Eighteen MDCs cut industrial tariffs by only two percentage points based on an import weighted average. Percentage reductions in industrial tariffs by the major traders (EC: 27%; Ja-pan: 28%; and the United States: 31%) were about half the size of the reduction au-thorized by the U.S. Congress at the beginning of the negotiations. Many industrial items were excepted from tariff cuts and tariffs were lowered on only one-quarter of current agricultural trade (GATT, 1979).

The negotiations also departed from the expectations of the LDCs in a number of areas. As in the past, trilateral rather than full multilateral discussions formed the basis of the accords, and LDCs complained that they were not given the opportunity for meaningful participation. The United States also insisted on more reciprocity from the LDCs in the negotiations. LDCs' frustration was compounded by a Big Three (U.S., EC, and Japan) decision in mid-1977 to postpone consideration of differential and more favorable treatment for LDC until agreements were reached on other matters.

---

ment is generally regarded as being the most comprehensive and far-reaching results achieved in trade negotiations since the creation of the General Agreement on Tariffs and Trade (GATT) in 1947" (p. 379). But, on the other hand, "The most important aspect of the codes is the extent to which they constitute the beginning—and not a final step—toward a more open national economy. . . . The codes will reduce trade protectionism but they will probably be oversold if assessed only on this criterion" (p. 380). Kelkar (1980) believes that the Tokyo Round failed to improve GATT Articles VI and XVI on dumping and subsidies enough for LDCs to subscribe to the code. Two studies provide quantitative estimates: U.S. Department of Labor (1979) and Deardorff and Stern (1979). Both of these studies, however, ignore tariff preferences and probable trade diversion effects.

[2]The LDC positions are summarized in UNCTAD (1977 I).

Some special measures in favor of LDCs were eventually agreed upon, but in general they exempted LDC signatories from full implementation of the provisions to liberalize nontariff measures.[3] MDCs concessions on tropical products were given early priority as promised and entered into effect in 1977, but these tariffs were reduced by much less than the average industrial tariff, and the tropical product concessions applied to a much shorter list of items than that requested by the LDCs.

With respect to other MDCs tariff reductions, the LDCs did not receive advance implementation or bound concessions (except for LDC members of the GATT). They also received below-average tariff cuts on all products whether or not covered by the GSP. This occurred, in part, because the Big Three agreed on a harmonizing formula to cut most tariffs, and MFN tariffs on GSP-covered products were generally lower than average to begin with. As for high-tariff products that are either not covered by the GSP or subject to quantitative limitations on preferential treatment, they were often excepted from the formula or from any tariff cuts whatsoever and thereby incurred relatively small average reductions as well. Tariff escalation, which creates higher rates of effective protection, actually increased in relative terms as a result of the Tokyo Round in so far as products of interest to LDCs are concerned. Import-weighted tariffs on semimanufactures were about four times the level of raw material duty rates before, but over six times higher after (GATT, 1979).

As a result of the Tokyo Round, an enabling clause was added to Article XXXVI of the GATT that gives more formal and permanent status to preferential treatment for LDC exports. Aside from some tropical product concessions consisting of additions to the lists of GSP-covered products, however, the negotiations produced no other improvements in the GSP: no binding of preferential margins, no extension of the GSP to all LDCs, and no compensation to LDCs for erosion of preferential tariff margins.

CONTROVERSY OVER TARIFF PREFERENCE

Failure to improve or even maintain the GSP in the Tokyo Round stemmed mainly from U.S. insistence that LDCs had more to gain from MFN tariff cuts by MDCs than they would lose form the erosion of preferences. The U.S. position was supported by several studies. Finger concluded his 1976 analysis of Kennedy Round tariff concessions by stating:

> The findings also suggest that in pushing for tariff preferences the developing countries may be seeking an advantage they do not need. It seems likely that they would benefit from a general (MFN) reduction of trade barriers, and it is possible that the establishment of precedent of separate treatment of developing countries may not be in their long-run interest.

A Brookings Institution study, which served as a guide to negotiators long before publication, analyzed the impact of various MFN tariff-cutting formulae without allow-

---

[3]For a lengthier review of the Tokyo Round Codes, see Ginman, et al. (1980); additional analysis may be found in Kelkar (1980) and O'Leary (1980).

ance for the LDC tariff preferences on the grounds that "The preference systems are so fettered by restrictions that essentially they already are fully exploited, or exhausted, by the LDCs" (Cline et al., 1978).

Finally, widely publicized estimates by Baldwin and Murray (1977) predicted that the LDCs exports gain for 50% MFN tariff cuts would exceed the loss from the erosion of GSP margins by twelve times, because not all LDCs were GSP beneficiaries, not all products were covered by the GSP, and not all imports from LDCs received unlimited preferential treatment.

These studies won some support for the U.S. position, but the overwhelming majority of LDCs remained unconvinced and refused to sign the Tokyo Round accords.[4] In support of the LDCs view, a 1980 UNCTAD study concluded that Tokyo Round concessions would lower potential LDC export expansion by as much as $1 billion annually. The losses from MFN tariff cuts were 2.6 times the gains in the case where the Multi Fiber Arrangement limiting textile imports was taken into account.

Continued LDC doubts about the Tokyo Round mean that the reconciliation of the conflicting tariff analyses has some policy significance as well as a Hegelian appeal to *academe*. This chapter approaches a synthesis by placing a new focus on three inadequately developed aspects of previous research on the tariff question. These are: (1) the basis on which the LDCs evaluated the Tokyo Round tariff negotiations, (2) the implications of assumptions about product substitution in the trade forecasting model, and (3) the completeness, accuracy, and timeliness of the data. Following a review of these topics, the chapter presents new estimates of the trade effects of the Tokyo Round tariff concessions and compares them with the benefits of improvements in the GSP. As in other studies the analysis is confined to industrial products in CCCN Chapters 25–99, since nontariff measures rather than tariff concessions tend to dominate agricultural trade.

LDC CHOICES

The LDC perspective on the Tokyo Round was complex. They did not simply weigh the losses from erosion of current preferential margins against the gains for tariff cuts on trade subject to MFN treatment. Instead, they wanted consideration of a number of alternatives. These included improvements in the GSP such as increasing product coverage, abandoning limitations on preferential treatment, liberalizing rules of origin, extending preferences to all LDCs, binding preferential tariff margins, excepting GSP-covered products from formula tariff cuts or delaying such reductions. They also advocated MFN tariff cutting techniques that would minimize or delay the erosion of preferences.

Most studies have neglected the LDCs' view of the negotiations. Although Baldwin and Murray (1977) did compare the costs and benefits of the Tokyo Round under improved GSP schemes, they de-emphasized the LDCs' approach, because they regarded

---

[4]Ginman et al. (1980) cite the failure to research agreement on safeguards as the primary cause of LDC dissatisfaction with the Tokyo Round.

any improvement in the GSP as unlikely.[5] This assessment reflects their belief that most previous improvements in the GSP have been "cosmetic." GSP beneficiaries, however, may have regarded further improvements as more likely. In fact, there had been substantial changes for the better. GSP product coverage had expanded significantly between 1972 and 1977. The EC, for instance, increased the value of its coverage of agricultural products twentyfold and nearly doubled the size of preferential tariff margins. Partly reflecting improvements such as these, the group of eleven non-Socialist (Australia, Austria, Canada, EC members, Finland, Japan, New Zealand, Norway, Sweden, Switzerland, and the United States) GSP schemes implemented in 1972 raised their product coverage as a percent of dutiable imports by over one-fourth (from 23 to 29%) in their first three years of operation. By 1984 this proportion had risen to 48%.[6]

Ceiling limitations, which are effective in only three (albeit the largest) of the fourteen schemes in force, also had been liberalized. In 1975 the EC reduced the number of products subject to the most rigorously enforced ceilings by 75%, and in the subsequent two years, imports actually receiving preferential treatment rose by nearly two-thirds. The EC also abandoned the system of global limitations on preferential imports in 1981, retaining only its ceilings on individual beneficiaries. Japan reduced the number of products subject to the most rigid control from 95 in 1971 to 41 in 1976 and made extra increases in its ceilings beyond the regular annual increases in 1977, 1981, and 1984. (Yamazawa, 1988). This liberalization allowed the share of covered imports actually receiving preferences to grow from 31% in 1971 to 71% in 1984. Many donor countries extended unlimited duty-free treatment to the least-developed countries. Thus the LDCs' expectations for further improvement in the GSP, as promised in the Tokyo Declaration, were realistic in view of the GSP's history.

Not only were the LDCs disaffected by the lack of GSP improvements in the Tokyo Round accords, but they have been further discouraged by subsequent moves to restrict preferences. The EC restricted textile imports from 21 beneficiaries under bilateral tariff quotas commencing in 1981. Fifty other product groups were made subject to more stringent surveillance and specific ceilings in 1981. One-quarter of the so-called sensitive products in the EC scheme actually had their ceilings lowered in 1981. The United States also lowered its ceilings (called competitive need criteria) in 1987 or 290 products whenever imported from nine beneficiaries. Furthermore, the U.S. "graduated" four major GSP suppliers (Hong Kong, Republic of Korea, Singapore, and Taiwan) from its list of beneficiaries in 1989.

SUBSTITUTABILITY OF MDC AND LDC PROCUCTS

Although the UNCTAD and Baldwin-Murray prediction of the Tokyo Round trade effects are strikingly different, they are based on the same traditional partial-equilibrium

---

[5]Baldwin and Murray (1977) eschew a straightforward comparison of the benefits of an improved GSP with the benefits of MFN tariff reductions in favor of a presentation in terms of trade benefit streams over time. They consider several alternative durations for the GSP but indefinitely long MFN concessions. According to their results, only a permanent and unrestricted GSP generates benefits in excess of the Tokyo Round over time.

[6]Details on improvements in the GSP may be found in UNCTAD (1973).

model of trade creation and diversion. The model employs price elasticities of import demand to predict the trade creation effect of changes in the prices of imports relative to the prices of domestic production, and cross elasticities to predict the trade diversion effect of changes in relative prices among govern suppliers of imported products.

The model assumes product differentiation among foreign and domestic suppliers, iso-elastic import demand function, infinite supply elasticities, and no changes in income, exchange rates, or pre-duty prices. The import demand equation gives both the trade creation and trade diversion effects of a preferential tariff cut (dt) on the value of imports (M) of a product produced by beneficiaries (indicated by the subscript 1):

(1) $$dM_1 = M_1 \frac{dt}{1 + t} (\eta_1 - \epsilon_{12})$$

where $n_1 < 0$ is the price elasticity of import demand and $\epsilon_{12} > 0$ is the cross elasticity applicable to changes in the relative price of products (1) and (2), a similar product produced by nonbeneficiary foreign suppliers. In the case of MFN tariff cuts, this relative price change is zero rather than $dt/1 + t$ so that the import expansion is due solely to trade creation:

(2) $$dM_1 = M_1 \frac{dt}{1 + t} \eta_1.$$

The main point of contention is over the size of the trade diversion effects. In contrast to UNCTAD, Baldwin and Murray (1977) estimate them to be very small so that the loss of competitive advantage for the LDCs due to MFN tariff cuts is negligible in comparison to the gains in trade creation from MFN tariff cuts on the products not receiving preferential treatment. Whereas there has been some criticism of the UNCTAD methodology, however, there has been no attempt to examine the root of the controversy, namely the different values assigned to ϵ_{12}.[7]

There are many readily available, econometric estimates of (η) for use in equations (1) and (2). Cross elasticities in this sort of study, however, are usually given assumed values for lack of good empirical estimates. Instead of making completely arbitrary assumptions about specific values of (ϵ), however, Baldwin and Murray adopted an estimation method that supposedly reflected more general and reasonable assumptions. They assumed that:

> the substitutability between a developing country product and a similar product produced in non-beneficiary countries would be similar to the substituability between a developing country product and a similar product produced in the donor country. This latter substitutability has already been shown to be trade creation (TC_1) and can be rewritten, as before,

---

[7]Balassa (1980) criticizes the UNCTAD (1980) study for "failing to allow for limitations imposed on imports from developing countries under GSP," although it does so. He also points out that application of the cross elasticity to imports from nonbeneficiaries (M_2) enlarges the trade diversion estimate because M_2 greatly exceeds M_1 (imports from beneficiaries). He does not explain, however, why the elasticity should be applied to one instead of the other, as explained below. See footnote 11.

as a share of domestic production. . . . Thus, trade diversion (TD_1) becomes trade creation weighted by the ratio of imports from non-beneficiaries (M_2) to domestic production (M_3).[8]

Thus the value of ϵ_{12} implied by the Baldwin and Murray formulation is

(3) $$\epsilon_{12} = -\eta_1(M_2/M_3)$$

Since their cross elasticity is undefined whenever there is no domestic production of a similar good (indicated by the subscript 3), in that case Baldwin and Murray simply assume equality of trade creation and diversion so that $\epsilon_{12} = -\eta_1$.

The UNCTAD study also assumes "equal substitutability," but without full explanation the authors interpret this to mean that nonbeneficiaty products will be displaced by beneficiary products on a one-for-one basis and that

$$\eta_1 = \eta_2.[9]$$

The implicit value for the UNCTAD cross elasticity is

(4) $$\epsilon_{12} = -\eta_1 M_2/M_1$$

There are, however, basic problems with both of these approaches. Neither is grounded

---

[8]Baldwin and Murray (1977), p. 33 (symbols added). To find the value of 12 implicit in their analysis, set their equation for trade diversion equal to the traditional equation. Their equation is:

(8.1) $$TD_1 = TC_1(M_2/M_3)$$

Note that the subscripts 1, 2, and 3 stand for similar products from beneficiary, foreign nonbeneficiary, and domestic suppliers, respectively. Substitution of the traditional trade creation expression in equation (2) yields:

(8.2) $$TD_1 = M_1 \frac{dt}{1+t} \eta_1(M_2/M_3)$$

The trade diversion component of equation (1) may be written:

(8.3) $$TD = M_1 \frac{dt}{1+t} \epsilon_{12}$$

Setting equations (8-2) and (8-3) equal to each other yields equation (3).

[9]The UNCTAD (1980) study assumes that "the degree of substitutability between domestic products of a preference-giving country and imported products is the same, whether the source of imports is a GSP beneficiary or a non-beneficiary country. This rationale permits the use of the same elasticities of import demand in respect of a given preference-giving country to estimate both the trade creation and trade diversion effects." For some unexplained reason, however, the import demand elasticity (ϵ_1) is applied to nonbeneficiary imports (M_2) to yield the following estimate of trade diversion:

(9.1) $$TD_1 = M_2 \frac{dt}{1+t} \eta_1$$

Setting equation (9-1) equal to the traditional formulation in equation (8-3) reveals the value assigned to the cross elasticity by UNCTAD.

on the most widely accepted economic theory of buyer behavior. In fact, the methods employed in both studies are inconsistent with that theory, and needlessly so since the theory itself can be used to derive specific values for ( ) under the same assumption of equal substitutability.

An apparently much neglected study by Clague (1972) demonstrated that the assumption of equal substitutability can be defined logically in terms of substitution elasticities ($s_{12} = s_{13}$). The effects of such an assumption can be seen by formally deriving the import demand equation (1) from a well-behaved, separable utility function, which represents the preferences of the mass of consumers in the importing country for the three similar products (1, 2, 3) and all others (indicated by the subscript 4). In this case, the relationship between ϵ_{12} and η_1 can be written in the following way:[10]

(5) $$\epsilon_{12} = h_2[\eta_1 - \eta_{14}]/h_3$$

where $_{14}$ is the absolute value of the domestic elasticity of demand for product (1) and h_2 and h_3 are respectively the shares of nonbeneficiary and domestic production in the total consumption of all goods in the importing country.

It is also possible to use the theory to derive an appropriate value for $_{12}$ in the case of zero domestic production, rather than relying on arbitrary approximations. Whenever $h_3 = 0$, the value of the cross elasticity will be:

(6) $$\epsilon_{12} = h_2(s_{12} + \eta_{14})/(h_1 + h_2)$$

---

[10]Clague (1972) derives the following demand equation for the beneficiary product (1):

(10.1) $$dM_1 = \frac{M_1T_1[-h_2s_{12} - h_3s_{13} - h_1h_4s_{14} - (h_1 + h_2 + h_3)h_1s_1]}{[h_1 + h_2 + h_3]}$$

where $T_1 = dt/1 + t$ = the relative price change due to the preferential tariff reduction of dt_1, all other prices and tariffs constant; $h_i(i = 1, 2, 3, 4) = M_i/M_1 + M_2 + M_3M_4)$ = the share of any product in total expenditures on all products by the importing country in question: $s_{ij}(i, j = 1, 2, 3, 4; i\#j)$ = the elasticity of substitution between i and j where $s14(i = 1, 2, 3)$ = a constant, indicating equal substitutability of products (1, 2, 3) for all other products (4); s_1 = the income elasticity of demand for product (1), assumed to be the same for products (1, 2, 3).
In the case of an identical MFN tariff cut where $T_1 = T_2$ and there is no change in relative price among foreign suppliers, the trade creation would be:

(10.2) $$dM_1 = \frac{M_1T_1[-h_3s_{13} - (h_1 + h_2)h_4s_{14} - (h_1 + h_2 + h_3)(h_1 + h_2)s_1]}{[h_1 + h_2 + h_3]}$$

The bracketed expressions in equations (10.1) and (10.2) define $(n_1 - _{12})$ and n_1 respectively from equations (1) and (2). Therefore, the difference between them will yield the relationship between the cross elasticity and other parameters:

(10.3) $$\epsilon_{12} = h_2(s_{12} - n_{14})/(h_1 + h_2 + h_3)$$

where $n_{14} = h_4s_{14} + (h_1 + h_2 + h_3)s_1$, the absolute value of the elasticity of demand for the aggregate of products (1, 2, 3) since all s_{13} are equal.
In the case of equal substitution elasticities ($s_{12} = s_{13}$), it is possible to derive the relationship between ϵ_{12} and n_1 by transforming equation (10-2) in the following way: Substitute s_{12} for s_{13}, divide both sides by M_1T_1, subtract n_{14} from both sides, and multiply both sides by h_2/h_3. This calculation yields the cross elasticity under the assumption of equal substitutability as shown in equation (5) of the text.

Equation (5) enables us to see the difficulties created by the use of ad hoc methods. First, it is obvious that empiricists should not assume values for ϵ_{12} independently of η_1 if they regard the assumption of equal substitutability as plausible. Second, it can be seen that the implicit Baldwin and Murray formula (equation 3), represents the highest possible estimate of ϵ_{12} consistent with the economic theory rather than the underestimate suggested by UNCTAD. The Baldwin-Murray estimate is obtained only by the implicit assumption of a zero elasticity of domestic demand for the product group, for this is the only nontrivial way of getting to equation (3) from equation (5). It is also clear from equations (4) and (5) that the UNCTAD cross elasticity would equal the value consistent with the underlying model only in the unlikely event of a zero domestic demand elasticity and equality of market shares for beneficiaries and domestic producers. Since imports from nonbeneficiaries and domestic production usually exceed imports from beneficiaries, these conditions are not likely to hold in reality and the UNCTAD estimates of trade diversion are probably exaggerated. The extent to which the Baldwin-Murray and UNCTAD estimates are distorted by these inconsistencies is the subject of another study (MacPhee, 1987).

In contrast to earlier work, the present study offers estimates of trade effects that are consistent with economic theory. The predictive model employs import demand price elasticities from the Brookings study, domestic price elasticities from UNCTAD (1974), Houthakker (1965), Houthakker and Taylor (1965), and Philips (1974), and import shares from UNCTAD (1976) to estimate the cross elasticities with equation (5). These were calculated for seventeen comprehensive categories of industrial products in the case of each of the Big Three import markets for GSP products and for total industrial imports for other cases in which less detailed information was available. The elasticities combined with import values and import-weighted tariff averages for each trade category from UNCTAD computer tapes were then employed in equations (1) and (2) to generate post-Tokyo Round predictions.

DATA PROBLEMS

It should go without saying that the ideal short-run analysis of preferential and MFN tariff cuts should reflect the impact of all actual changes in duties for all industrial products currently exported from all LDC beneficiaries. Scarce data obviate the ideal, but this study attempts to make some substantial improvements on previous work.

Baldwin and Murray (1977) included Spain, Greece, and other countries that are not beneficiaries in most GSP schemes among their undefined LDCs. They also treated several current beneficiaries as excluded from the U.S. GSP scheme. Both the Baldwin-Murray and UNCTAD studies ignored even better EC preferences for African, Caribbean, and Pacific (ACP) countries and overseas territories under the Lome' Convention and for certain Mediterranean countries under various bilateral agreements. Both studies also neglected other GSP schemes that have far fewer limitations on preferential treatment. Baldwin and Murray estimated that many more products would be excluded from preferences by limitations than turns out to be the case, in part because they based their overall trade estimates on a sample of major products that more frequently encounter restrictions. Finally, Baldwin and Murray worked with 1971 trade data, a preliminary version of the United States GSP scheme, and an assumed 50% MFN tariff cut, across-the-board except for textiles, shoes, and petroleum.

This study, on the other hand, covers the actual 1976 versions of all preferential arrangements for LDCs. It employs more current (1986) import values as well as the actual pre-and post-Tokyo Round tariff averages for all manufactured products except petroleum. Rather than *assuming* that certain import products were subject to limitations on preferential treatment like Baldwin and Murray, this study computers the effects of only those limitations which were actually applied. Having surveyed these improvements in perspective, model, and data, let us turn to the results.[11]

TRADE BENEFITS OF PREFERENCES FOR LDCs

Inspection of the left-hand column in Table 6.1 reveals that studies that confine themselves to the impact of the Tokyo Round on the Big Three GSP schemes actually ignore about one-third of preferential imports from LDCs. Moreover, the other preferential systems are virtually free of limitations on preferential treatment, although product coverage of the other GSP schemes is relatively low in comparison to that of the EC and Japanese preferential regimes. The Big Three GSP schemes cover only 61% of dutiable, manufactured imports from beneficiaries, and less than two-thirds of the imports of covered products could expand on a preferential basis because of quantity or value limitations. Despite improvements in the GSP, these proportions are less than those estimated by Baldwin and Murray because they ignored imports of textiles, shoes, and some other import-sensitive items that have been denied preferential treatment one way or another.

Following the procedure described above, the trade effects of LDC preferences were estimated under three alternatives: (1) the existing preferential arrangements that in some cases are restrictive with respect to product coverage and limitation, (2) the same preferential arrangements in the absence of limitations, and (3) unlimited preferences extended to all industrial products except petroleum. The estimates are presented in Table 6.1.

Estimated trade expansion from existing preferential arrangements is $8,045 million,

---

[11]No study including the present one attempts to account for rules of origin, which, according to Baldwin and Murray (1977), "frequently result in a de facto elimination of preferences for particular products" (p. 31). In fact, preferences are denied for this reason far less often than is suggested by their examples. For instance, they cite the U.S. law that specifies that direct domestic processing costs plus locally produced materials and components must exceed 35% of export value, and they claim that this rule will deny preferences even to goods wholly produced in a beneficiary country. In fact, U.S. Customs has issued regulations that state that wholly produced goods will be presumed to meet the 35% rule, and there have been no challenges of this ruling. In addition, the U.S. Customs has liberally interpreted the definition of domestic materials and components to include foreign materials and components that are substantially transformed in the production process. See UNCTAD (1977 II).

or 14% of 1986 preferential imports.[12] With the highest import demand elasticity and second-highest average tariff among the Big Three, the U.S. imports from beneficiaries grow the most (18%). The relatively small expansion in imports under other GSP schemes (10%) and under the EC special preferences (8–9%) is similarly explained by lower elasticities and lower MFN tariffs, which more than offset freer access under these arrangements.

The findings in Table 6.1 also measure burden sharing, the somewhat ambiguous but nevertheless perennial subject of governmental consultations among the MDCs. Let us define burden sharing as the amount by which each MDC has contributed to increased LDC exports. In absolute terms the U.S. preferences generate the largest expansion ($4,332 million) and the EC and Japan are far behind with $2,221 million and $855 million, respectively. It must be remembered as well that some EC Mediterranean preferences in 1976 were extended to borderline LDCs such as Spain. Greece has been excluded from all calculations because of its accession to the EC in 1981, but Spain remains because its accession did not begin until 1986 and it is not included in EC import data in that year.

A better measure of burden sharing compares the degree to which each MDC increased its total imports from LDCs as a result of preferences, and this measurement can be obtained by dividing the top right-hand column by the bottom left-hand column in Table 6.1. Now a different picture emerges, which suggests that the MDCs have roughly equalized the "burdens." Japan leads the way with increases of 6.7%, whereas the EC and the United States follow closely with 5.8 and 6.0 percent, respectively.

Trade diversion was responsible for 12% of the estimated trade expansion under existing preferential trade arrangements. This result is consistent with other empirical studies of the trade effects of integration, but it is much lower than the UNCTAD estimate that trade diversion is three times larger than trade creation (Kreinin, 1972). This difference is due to the fact that the UNCTAD study ignores the domestic price elasticities and overestimates the cross-price elasticities when it uses the ratio M_2/M_1 instead of M_2/M_3 and M_3 greatly exceeds M_1. More remarkable is the Baldwin-Murray estimate that trade diversion contributes to only 12% of the total expansion, when it was shown above that their technique produces larger estimates than the method employed here. Moreover, the findings differ by importing country. Their ratios of trade diversion to total expansion for Japan and the EC are one-fourth as large as those in Table 6.1, whereas their estimates for the United States are over twice as large. Apparently, the U.S. anomaly occurs because their study used preliminary product coverage data, which included many products now ineligible for preferences. Since more imports of these items came from other MDCs, the appropriate cross elasticity becomes smaller when the products were excluded from coverage. In the case of the EC and Japan, liberali-

---

[12]The trade creation is less than two-thirds of the relative size of the Baldwin-Murray estimates. The differences are at least partly explained by my use of the Brooking's elasticities, which average −1.4 for the Big three in contrast to −1.97 from the Buckler-Almond estimates used by Baldwin and Murray. The rest of the difference may be reconciled by MFN tariffs, which were higher in 1971 or which were higher for the Baldwin-Murray product sample.

Table 6.1
Trade Benefits of Preferences for LDC without Tokyo Round Tariff Cuts
(1986 annual trade flows in millions of U.S. dollars)

	Preferential Imports of Manufactures[1]	Preferential Trade Expansion		
		Trade Creation	Trade Diversion	Total
With actual product coverage and limitations:				
US GSP	24614	4037	295	4332
EEC GSP	5837	525	263	788
ACP[2]	1069	78	12	90
MED[2]	14271	1170	171	1341
OST[4]	31	2	0	2
Japan GSP	5413	790	65	855
Other GSP[5]	6300	479	158	637
TOTAL	57535	7081	964	8045
With actual product coverage but not limitations:				
US GSP	33017	5217	363	5580
EEC GSP	22053	2514	507	3021
ACP	1069	78	12	90
MED	14563	1194	189	1383
OST	31	2	0	2
Japan GSP	9211	1382	120	1502
Other GSP	9304	707	233	904
TOTAL	89248	11094	1424	12815
With complete product coverage and no limitations:				
US GSP	71827	16377	646	17023
EEC GSP	22922	2636	550	3186
ACP	1069	78	12	90
MED	14563	1194	189	1383
OST	31	2	0	2
Japan GSP	12830	3156	244	3400
Other GSP	14719	1178	368	1546
TOTAL	137961	24621	2009	26630

[1]Preferential imports were estimated by the author on the basis of 1986 trade data in UNCTAD (1989) and pre-Tokyo Round (1976) versions of the schemes.
[2]Signatories of the Lome Convention.
[3]Mediterranean countries with bilateral arrangements with the EEC: Algeria, Cyprus, Egypt, Israel, Jordan, Lebanon, Malta, Morocco, Spain, Syria, Tunisia, and Turkey.
[4]Overseas territories of the EEC.
[5]Includes the schemes of Australia, Austria, Canada, Finland, Hungary, New Zealand, Norway, Sweden, and Switzerland.

zation of limitations on preferential treatment has mainly benefited products for which other MDCs are more important suppliers, with opposite consequences for the cross-elasticity estimates. Similarly, trade diversion in favor of ACP and Mediterranean beneficiaries of EC preferences is smaller, because those countries are the major suppliers of those products that they export to the EC.

If the limitations on GSP and EC-Mediterranean preferential trade did not exist, trade expansion would be 61%. This is more than the 50% increase estimated by Baldwin and Murray for 1971 mainly because the EC imposed more limitations on textiles when it included more of these products in its scheme. As an indication of the relatively liberal U.S. limitations, trade expansion would be only 29% larger without the so-called competitive need exclusions, but the elimination of EC and Japanese limitations would boost imports from GSP beneficiaries by 283 and 76%, respectively. Of course, limitations under other preferential arrangements are nil.

If all the preferential schemes offered across-the-board coverage on an unlimited basis, trade expansion would triple. Most of this expansion would occur under the U.S. GSP, because it now has the narrowest list of eligible products. Only 46% of dutiable industrial imports from beneficiaries are covered by the American scheme, whereas the others cover 80% of the average. Japanese trade expansion also would increase significantly with across-the-board coverage. This would occur because Japan is a relatively large importer of industrial raw materials from LDCs and these are virtually the only products excluded from the Japanese scheme.

To summarize, the present estimates of benefits from GSP *improvement* are much higher than the Baldwin-Murray findings. Two factors reconcile the discrepancies: (1) they used *proposed* American product coverage, which was much broader than *actual,* and (2) they ignored shoes, textiles, and some other products excluded from several GSP schemes.

IMPACT OF MFN TARIFF REDUCTIONS

The LDCs' attitude toward the Tokyo Round tariff negotiations stemmed from the belief that reductions in MFN duties would adversely affect their exports. Smaller margins of tariff preferences would reduce the competitive advantage over MFN suppliers and shrink the trade diversion element of the preference-induced trade expansion in Table 6.1. Of course, the LDCs would also stand to gain from MFN reductions in two important ways.

First, many GSP products are subjected to limitations on preferential treatment, which as we have seen reduce potential trade expansion by roughly one-third. If MFN tariff reductions on these products were unlimited, then the full trade creation effect could be realized. Second, many important LDC products are excluded from the GSP, and if MFN tariff cuts were implemented on these items, LDC exports would receive another boost. This analysis must be tempered, however, by the fact that most products are excluded from preferential treatment for the same reasons that they are excluded from MFN trade liberalization. Protectionism leads to smaller MFN tariff cuts on items that are also denied GSP access, and many of the same items are restricted by safeguards, quotas, voluntary export restraints, and orderly marketing arrangements.[13] Thus the across-the-board approach of Baldwin and Murray could have seriously overestimated the benefits as well as the costs of the Tokyo Round. The following analysis is

---

[13]UNCTAD (1980) estimates that the Multi-Fibre Arrangement alone would prevent $1 billion in potential trade creation in textiles from Tokyo Round tariff cuts.

based on the actual MFN duty reductions, although no attempt has been made to estimate the impact of nontariff measures.

Part I of Table 6.2 shows both costs and benefits of the Tokyo Round for the LDCs
enjoying limited preferences. The cost consist of the reductions in the trade diverted to
beneficiaries due to the erosion of their preferential margins, which amount to $553
million or about one-half of the trade diversion. The benefits accrue from the MFN
trade creation on products that are either excluded from preferences entirely or subjected
to limitations and they amount to $2,586 million in terms of 1986 trade flows.

In contrast to the UNCTAD study, which shows costs exceeding benefits by 2.5
times, this study comes up with results that are coincidentally close to those of Baldwin

Table 6.2

Costs and Benefits of MFN Tariff Reductions and GSP Improvements for Beneficiaries of
Preferences (1986 annual trade flows in millions of U.S. dollars)

	U.S. (GSP)	ED			Japan GSP	Other GSP	Total
		GSP	ACP	MED			
I.							
Cost due toerosion of preferential margins	(224)	(183)	(2)	(41)	(25)	(58)	(533)
Benefit from absence of limitations on MFN cuts	513	423	0	2	148	78	1164
Benefit from broader product coverage of MFN	830	34	0	0	492	66	1422
Net gain (loss) from MFN tariff reductions	1119	274	(2)	(39)	615	86	2053
II.							
Benefit from elemination of preference limitations	1248	2233	0	42	647	303	4473
Benefit from expanded product coverage for preferences	11443	165	0	0	1898	606	14112
Total gain from improvements in preferences	12691	2398		42	2545	909	18585

Source: See text.

and Murray. Benefits exceed cost by about five times for beneficiaries. It is interesting to note, however, that the results differ by preferential arrangement, with beneficiaries of the Lome' Convention, and Mediterranean agreements losing from the multilateral trade negotiation. Since the ACP and Mediterranean countries account for a majority of LDCs and since the EC is their most important customer, it is easy to see their concerns about the erosion of preferences.

Whereas overall benefits exceed costs of the Tokyo Round for beneficiaries of MDCs preferences, this is not the evaluation relevant to LDCs that sought improvements in preferences. Instead, the benefits of unlimited preferential treatment for all LDC products (Part II of Table 6.2) should be compared with the benefits of the MFN tariff reductions. The results show clearly why LDC preferred improvements in the GSP to MFN cuts. Elimination of only one-half of the limitations on preferential treatment, or expansion of product coverage by only 14% would have produced net gains equal to those derived from the Tokyo Round. If the LDCs were to receive unrestricted duty-free access to the MDCs' markets, the gains would have exceeded those of the Tokyo Round by nine times. Thus the size of the purse would seem to justify gambling for GSP improvement even though the odds were against that outcome. Certainly, the failure to obtain such improvements helps to explain the frustration of the LDCs in the aftermath of the Tokyo Round and their reluctance to participate in another series of multilateral trade negotiations.

CONCLUSION

This study addresses the question of the extent to which the LDCs have benefited from the Tokyo Round tariff concessions. It attempts to correct many of the factual and conceptual problems in previous analyses. The calculations indicate that minor GSP improvements would have been superior to or have compensated for MFN tariff cuts. Of course, the cost-benefit ratios probably differ among the LDCs, depending on the extent to which their industrial products receive preferential treatment. The analysis must also be qualified on grounds that it ignores agricultural and petroleum products, rules of origin, the duration of tariff reductions, and the trade effects of nontariff measures.

The findings of the study do not mean that the LDCs should have adopted negative stance in the tariff negotiations. Instead, they imply a strategy of pressing for differential treatment, trying to get products benefiting from preferences exempted from the general tariff cuts, advocating deep MFN tariff cuts for products not likely to receive preferential treatment, pushing for removal of nontariff barriers, and requesting improvements in the GSP.

The elements of this strategy are not new and its benefits for the LDCs were obvious. The LDCs' goal of maintaining preferential tariff margins, however, was in direct conflict with the goal of across-the-board liberalization of trade among the MDCs on an MFN basis. This trade still accounts for an overwhelming share of world imports of industrial products, and it is this trade that would be adversely affected by the trade diversion effects of improved preferences. Thus the fate of the LDCs in the Tokyo Round may have been disappointing, but it certainly was not unexpected.

References

Balassa, Bela. 1980. The Tokyo Round and the Developing Countries. *Journal of World Trade Law* 15,(2): 93–118.

Baldwin, R., and T. Murray. 1977. MFN Tariff Reductions and Developing Country Trade Benefits under the GSP. *Economic Journal* 8: 30–46.

Clague, C. 1971. Tariff Preferences and Separate Utility. *American Economic Review, Papers and Proceedings,* pp. 188–194.

Clague, C. 1972. The Trade Effects of Tariff Preferences. *Southern Economic Journal* 38: 379–389.

Cline, W. R., N. Kawanabe, T. O. M. Kronsjo, and T. Williams. 1978. *Trade Negotiations in the Tokyo Round: A Quantitative Assessment.* Washington, D.C.: Brookings Institution.

Deardorff, A. V., and R. M. Stern. 1979. An Economic Analysis of the Effects of the Tokyo Round of Multilateral Trade Negotiations on the United States and the Other Major Industrialized Counties, *MTN Studies No. 5,* Committee on Finance, United States Senate, June.

Finger, J. M. 1976. Effects of the Kennedy Round Concessions. *The Economic Journal* 38: 87–95.

GATT. 1974. *Basic Instruments and Selected Documents, Twentieth Supplement,* Geneva.

GATT. 1979. *The Tokyo Round of Multilateral Trade Negotiations.* Geneva.

Ginman, P. J., T. A. Pugel, and I. Walter. 1980. Mixed Blessings for the Third World in Codes on Non-Tariff Measures. *The World Economy* 3(2).

Ginman, P. J., T. A. Pugel, and I. Walter. 1980. Tokyo Round Tariff Concessions and Exports from Developing Countries. *Trade and Development,* No. 2, autumn.

Hellinger, G. K. 1980. The New Industrial Protectionism and the Developing Countries. *The Atlantic Papers,* No. 39, April.

Houthakker, H. S. 1965. New Evidence on Demand Elasticities. *Econometrica* 33(2): 277–288.

Houthakker, H. S., and L. D. Taylor. 1972. *Consumer Demand in the United States 1929–1970,* (2nd ed. Cambridge: Harvard University Press, pp. 60–144, 158–160.

Kelkar, V. L. 1980. GATT, Export Subsidies and Developing Countries. *Journal of World Trade Law* 14(4).

Kreinin, M. E. 1972. Effects of the EEC on Imports of Manufacturers. *Economic Journal,* September.

MacPhee, C. R. 1987. The Consistency of Partial Equilibrium Estimates of Trade Creation and Diversion. *Weltwirtschaftliches Archive,* March.

O'Leary, J. P. 1980. After the Tokyo Round: Protectionism of Collective Economic Security? *Orbis,* Spring pp. 129–141.

Philips, R. 1974. *Applied Consumption Analysis.* Amsterdam: North Holland, p. 195.

Philips. 1973. *Operation and Effects of the Generalized System of Preferences: Selected Studies Submitted to the Special Committee on Preferences and Subsequent Documents with the Same Title* (E.73.II.D.16, E.75.II.D.9, E.78.II.D.2, E.85.II.D.15), Geneva: United Nations.

UNCTAD. 1974. *Survey of Commodity Demand and Supply Elasticities.* Geneva: United Nations. March.

UNCTAD. 1976. *Handbook of International Trade and Development Statistics*, TD/STAT.6. Geneva: United Nations.

UNCTAD. 1977. *Other Questions Related to the Operation of the Generalized System of Preferences: The Generalized System of Preferences and the Multilateral Trade Negotiations* (TD/B/C.5/52). Geneva: United Nations.

UNCTAD. 1977. *United States Rule of Origin and Relevant Procedure: Report by the UNCTAD Secretariat* (TD/B/C.5/WG(VI)/3). Geneva: United Nations.

UNCTAD. 1979. *Operation and Effects of the Generalized System of Preferences* (TD/B/C.5/61). New York: United Nations.

UNCTAD. 1989. Review of the Implementation, Maintenance, Improvement and Utilization of the Generalized System of Preferences: Twelfth General Report on the Implementation of the Generalized System of Preferences (TD/B/C.5/122. Geneva: United Nations.

UNCTAD. 1980. *Specific Matters Arising from the Resolutions, Recommendation, and Other Decisions Adopted by the Conference at its Fifth Session Requiring Attention or Action by the Board at Its Twentieth Session: Assessment of the Results of the Multilateral Trade Negotiations. Part II: Implications of the Tokyo Round Tariff Reductions, for the Trade of Developing countries* (TD/B/778/Add.1). Geneva: United Nations.

U.S. Department of Labor. 1979. Trade and Employment Effects of Tariff Reductions Agreed to in the MTN, Bureau of International Labor Affairs, Washington, D.C., June 15, *Technical Appendix A,* p. 2.

Winham, G. R. 1980. Robert Strauss, the MFN and the Control of Factions. *Journal of World Trade Law,* September–October.

Yamazawa, Ippei. 1988. Effects of the Generalized System of Preferences on Japan's Imports from Developing Countries, UNCTAD/ST/MD/31. United Nations: Geneva.

Chapter 7

SAFEGUARDS AND THE DEVELOPING COUNTRIES' INTERESTS IN THE URUGUAY ROUND

K. A. Koekkoek

INTRODUCTION

Most commercial agreements contain at least one safeguard clause that makes it possible for the participating countries to withdraw from commitments they entered into or depart from agreed rules in exceptional circumstances. Such clauses should thus not be seen as allowing exceptions to the rule, but as escape clauses. They apply only if circumstances arise that are fundamentally different from those prevailing at the time the commitments were entered into and that could not have been anticipated at that time.

The General Agreement on Tariffs and Trade (GATT) also contains safeguard clauses. The clause that has been the subject of discussion for several years in Article XIX, entitled "Emergency Action on Imports of Particular Products." The problems relating to this clause form the crux of this chapter. The many aspects of safeguards are dealt with in detail below; for the purpose of this introduction it will suffice to indicate the essence of the problem. This consists of two elements. First, the nature of safeguard clauses, as described above, means that they must not be too easily applicable. One element of the problem thus concerns the conditions under which Article XIX may be applied. Second, GATT obligations are characterized by the application of the most-favored-nation clause. This means that no trading partner may be treated more favorably than any other when measures are taken to liberalize trade. This principle is referred to in the converse case, when trade restrictions are imposed, as nondiscrimination. In the case of safeguards under Article XIX, this means that if the conditions for action are satisfied, such action may not be directed against individual trading partners. In other words, safeguards may not be applied selectively.

As a result of the difficulty in applying Article XIX and the nonselective character of the clause, safeguards are often introduced outside the scope of the article. The GATT contracting parties tried in the Tokyo Round to resolve this conflict between theory and practice, but without success. This was partly the result of strong opposition from the developing countries, objecting in particular to the selectivity aspect, an element that the EC, on the other hand, strongly favored. Both parties indicated they would prefer to settle the problem of safeguards as a priority in the new GATT round.

This chapter begins by looking at the present situation with regard to Article XIX and the objections to it. This is followed by a discussion of the application of safeguards in practice, that is, the application of nontariff barriers or "gray zone" measures. The effects of bilateral measures on trade and prosperity are examined with particular emphasis on the consequences for the developing countries. Then a number of considerations are presented that are relevant to any settlement of the problem of safeguards. After that, two possible solutions to the discrepancy between theory and practice are presented in order of preference. Finally, recent developments regarding the negotiations on safeguards in the Uruguay Round are discussed, including the results in the midterm review.

SITUATION WITH REGARD TO ARTICLE XIX OF THE GATT

Governments cannot resort to Article XIX without due cause.[1] A number of conditions must first be satisfied regarding the origin, nature, and consequences of the injury.

The following cumulative conditions apply with regard to the origin. The injury must result from a tariff reduction and more specifically from the tariff reduction that the importing country wishes to repeal. Moreover, the injury must result from circumstances that were not foreseen at the time that the concession with respect to the tariff was made. Finally, the injury must be caused by an increase in imports relative to domestic sales of the product. In other words, there does not necessarily have to be an absolute increase in imports. The relative price of imports compared to similar domestic products is also irrelevant.

As to the nature of the injury, it is stated that Article XIX applies only in the event of serious injury, but this is not defined. This applies both to actual injury and to the threat of injury. As far as the consequences are concerned, this should be taken to refer to injury or threat of injury to existing producers and not to potential newcomers to the market.

It is not necessarily the case that the country that wishes to introduce a safeguard must show that these conditions are met. In some cases when Article XIX has been applied, exporting countries have been asked to show that these conditions were not satisfied. In other words the burden of proof was transferred.

Article XIX implies that measures should be taken in respect to one or a few products only. The measures may in practice remain in operation for an unlimited period of time. The nature of the measures to be taken is not specified. Although the article refers explicitly to the withdrawal of tariff concessions, experience has shown that other measures, in particular quantitative restrictions, are also allowed. Finally, any measure taken is subject to the principle of nondiscrimination between trading partners.

---

[1]This section is partly based on Merciai (1981).

In order to protect the interests of the trading partners affected—or likely to be affected—by a safeguard measure, the measure must be reported to GATT. Multilateral talks can then be held on the measure(s), which in principle can lead to compensation for the countries affected. If no agreement is reached between the parties, the trading partners affected may retaliate against an arbitrarily selected product. In view of the need to provide compensation and the risk of retaliation by other states if compensation is not provided, countries will not likely invoke Article XIX. Nevertheless, in the 1970s there was a sharp increase in the number of times Article XIX was invoked, and in more and more cases countries had recourse to introducing quotas instead of raising tariffs.

The nondiscriminatory nature of these measures makes them a rather unsuitable method of negating the considerable comparative advantage that developing countries often enjoy in their most competitive industries. In other words, it is not the most but the less competitive trading partners that are most affected by global measures of this sort. These therefore demand compensation, too. If the case involves major trading partners, it is obvious that the demands for compensation that may be expected will place a constraint on the number of times Article XIX is invoked.

Nevertheless, in order to achieve the import reduction they want, countries are more and more frequently resorting to bilateral arrangements outside the scope of Article XIX, the so-called gray zone measures. Some well-known examples are the restraint on exports of Japanese cars to the United States and the arrangement on steel between the United States and the EC. Recently the semiconductor arrangement between the United States and Japan has been added to this catalogue. But besides these and other arrangements between the major trading powers, there are numerous examples in trade between these trading blocs and other countries, such as, the arrangement in footwear trade between Britain and South Korea. The importance of these measures in international trade is dealt with below. Because these measures are technically voluntary, they do not contravene the letter of the GATT. However, they are undoubtedly contrary to the spirit of the GATT because of the selectivity achieved. In contrast to Article XIX these measures are subject to no disciplinary controls.

GRAY ZONE MEASURES

Effects

The gray zone can, and indeed does, encompass a broad range of instruments, and in practice it is impossible to define the boundary between safeguard and protection. Before looking at certain measures frequently applied, a few general remarks are in order on the purpose and operations of these measures. The aim of this sort of measures is to strengthen the competitive position of domestic industry by providing protection. This may be achieved in two ways. First, the authorities may push up the price of imports, either directly by increasing tariffs, or indirectly by placing restrictions on foreign supply. Domestic industry, which sells at the price set by imports, then profits from the higher price. Alternatively, instead of pushing up the price of foreign supplies, the authorities can try to reduce the costs for the domestic producer, thereby venturing into the realm of subsidies.

Clearly, the different measures will have different effects and the costs and benefits for the various parties involved will also vary. We now consider the effects of certain measures that impose quantitative restrictions, first because they are frequently applied, and second because they particularly lend themselves to selective application.

Two types of quantitative restrictions are distinguished in this section: bilateral quotas and voluntary export restraints. The consequences of bilateral quotas, that is, quotas in respect to a single trading partner, may be summarized as follows. In the first instance, there are the direct effects. Restrictions on the supply from one source lead to a higher price than would be the case without the restriction. Feenstra (1984) shows that the restraint on Japanese car exports to the United States led to an 8.4% increase in import prices, of which two-thirds was attributable to quality improvements and one-third was a de facto price increase. This being the case, the other foreign suppliers and domestic producers both profited from the price rise. It is the consumer that pays. The trading partner affected by the bilateral quota suffers because of the reduction in its volume of trade. The margin that opens up between the export price of the affected trading partner and the new price, after the introduction of the quota, benefits the party that obtains the right to import under the quota. The idea behind this is that the party that has the right to import is in the strongest position to appropriate this rent, although, of course, a certain sharing of this rent between exporters and importers may occur, depending on other aspects of their market power. One might argue here that there is an inherent bias toward rent transfer to exporters, as this type of measure is mostly taken against very competitive suppliers, selling a commercially attractive product.

The indirect effects of the introduction of a bilateral quota derive from the tendency of the countries affected to minimize the impact of the quota. They will, for example, unload their export surplus—and with it the potential problem—on other markets. Within the quota, they will try to maximize the value per given volume. In other words they will try to upgrade their export package and in time, and this may occur in the short term, switch to exporting more advanced goods aimed at the upper end of the market for that particular product. One example is the above mentioned quality improvement in cars reported in Feenstra (1984). Another example can be found in Pearson (1983). He shows that upgrading of exports of footwear from Korea and Taiwan took place following the 1977–1981 restraint on their footwear exports to the United States. The problem for the domestic producer seeking protection thus assumes a different form, but it is not always solved.

This type of protectionism has two harmful effects. First, of course, there are the direct effects in the exporting country, associated with a reduced volume of trade, that is, less foreign currency—depending on the elasticity of import demand and amount of rent transfer—less employment, less income, and the related multiplier effects in the economy. These have an impact in two particularly vulnerable areas of the economic development of the developing countries: First, the balance of payments and the employment situation—because exports from developing countries often consist of labor-intensive products. Second, and perhaps even more important, there may be an indirect effect that stems from the nature of this new type of protectionism, that is, from the fact that it is unpredictable, lacks transparency, is relatively easy to apply, can be introduced on an ad hoc basis, and affects developing countries disproportionately. It may lead to developing countries being, to put it mildly, less inclined to gear their economies to the world market (McNamara, 1979). Although it is being impressed upon them from all sides—the World Bank and the IMF included—that it is in their own interest to do precisely that. Of course, this effect can hardly be quantified. But without comparing the 1930s in all respects with the 1980s, countries then also eventually turned inward, as a consequence of chaotic international economic relations that included rampant protectionism. The harmful consequences of not gearing their economies to the world market, particularly in the case of the rather more industrialized developing countries, are well known.

The consequences of voluntary export restraints are largely similar to those of bilateral quotas described above, with one significant difference: the implementation of voluntary export restraints is in the hands of the exporters. An indication for this is that for textile and clothing products there is a market for quota rights in major textile exporting developing countries, Hongkong, Taiwan. (For examples, see Wolf, 1983, and Hamilton, 1985). This enables them to derive benefit from the price margin mentioned above. An income transfer thus occurs from domestic consumers to foreign producers, In other words, the detrimental effect of the restriction for exporters is partially compensated for by a higher price. The volume of trade is, however, restricted, and the volume-related effects in the exporting country, for example, the impact on employment, remain the same as under a quota system. The higher price acts as a measure of compensation. The result is a sort of cartel. This may be further enhanced because voluntary export restraints may also be agreed at the level of industrial sectors, without government intervention.

The conclusion in both cases of selective restrictions must be that they are inefficient. That is to say, they make little contribution to solving the problem, which is the loss of competitiveness of domestic industry. The problem may be partly shifted elsewhere, to other countries and other products, thereby reinforcing the tendency for these types of measures to proliferate. Actually the most straightfoward examples of all of these effects can be found in the Multi Fibre Arrangement. The MFA started out as a short-term arrangement regarding trade in cotton textiles in 1961. Recently, MFA IV has been established, covering many more countries and a substantially larger number of products than its predecessor. And the end is not yet in sight. Whereas these measures may give domestic producers a breathing space and a chance to adjust, these industries will not have a strong incentive to do so if there are no controls on, for example, the duration of the measures and the way they operate.

Application

It was noted in the introduction that the developing countries fear they will suffer the most if selectivity in safeguards is formalized. Is this fear well-founded? It is obviously impossible here to give a complete survey of the literature on this subject. Most of the work in this area takes the form of case studies on trade measures and the associated effects on trade and welfare.[2] In the context of the present problem, however, it is more interesting to examine whether there is any evidence of bias in the application of non-tariff measures as a whole to particular categories of goods and/or trading partners.

For this purpose, the results of two recent studies that attempt to analyze the totality of measures are used. One study is by the Development Research Department of the World Bank (Noguès et al., 1985), which sets out to measure the extent of nontariff barriers (NTBs) in two ways. The first way is by the number of goods to which NTBs apply as a percentage of the total number of goods traded. This produces the frequency ratio that reflects the importance of NTBs in terms of the number of goods affected. The second measure concentrates on the quantity of trade to which NTBs apply as a proportion of a country's total trade. This gives the coverage ratio, that is, the importance of NTBs in terms of the quantity of trade that they affect. Both measures were applied to the imports of sixteen industrial countries in 1981. These countries accounted for 60% of world imports and 70% of imports from developing countries. The application of the two measures to individual categories of goods revealed that NTBs are applied more than average to imports of agricultural products, textiles, iron and steel, vehicles, and fuels (Noguès et al., 1985, p. 15, Table A). In addition to imports classified by product category, the two measures were also applied to imports classified according to geographical origin, that is, according to whether they came from industrial or developing countries. This revealed that imports from developing countries were subject to NTBs to a greater extent than those from industrial countries. The coverage ratio for imports from developing countries was 34.3%, compared to 21.0% for imports from industrial countries. The frequency ratios were 18.6% and 8.0%, respectively (Hoguès et al., 1985, p. 25, Table D). Voluntary export restraints in particular are applied to a much greater extent to imports from developing countries than to those from industrial countries, the coverage ratios being 12.1% and 3.9%, respectively. (Notuès et al., 1985, p. 25, Table 6C). The authors conclude that "three different measures indicate that NTBs are significantly more prevalent on imports from developing countries than from industrial countries."[3]

The second study is by Ray and Marvel (1984). They set out to determine what factors dictate the structure of the industrialized countries' protection against imports. The countries studied include the EC member states, the United States, and Japan. The conclusion, which is of relevance to the problem under consideration, is that "While it has been clear for some time that innovations in protectionism have been predominantly in the form of NTBs, this study has been able to demonstrate that those innovations in the industrialized nations have been directed predominantly against consumer goods, agricultural manufactures, and textiles, products of particular significance to the developing countries" (Ray and Marvel, 1984).[4]

---

[2]For an extensive description of trade measures taken by the major trading blocs in respect to vulnerable product categories, and the effects thereof, see IMF (1985).

[3]The third measure referred to is a variant on the coverage ratio described above.

[4]A recent study, UNCTAD (1988), leads to much the same conclusion, especially regarding manufactured imports from developing countries. Table I.6 in that study shows that in 1988 the import coverage ratio for nontariff barriers on imports from developing countries into industrialized countries was 29.7%. The comparable ratio for imports from other industrialized countries was 19.5%.

Nontariff barriers in general, and voluntary export restraints in particular, are thus predominantly directed against the developing countries. The fear of developing countries that they will be the prime targets if selectivity in trade policy is formally allowed is thus a justified one.

Together these considerations and observations lead to the following summary conclusions. First, selective measures are an inefficient form of safeguard or protection. They remove the stimulus to restructure sunset industries. They are also an expensive form of protection. This point is not developed above, but examples may be found, among other sources, in OECD (1984). Pearson (1983) calculates that for one particular type of footwear exported under the VER with Taiwan in the period 1977–1981, the national annual welfare cost per job protected for the United States amounted to about $22,000, whereas an MFN tariff, with the same employment and production consequences, would have led to a national annual welfare loss per job protected of $3,200. Voluntary export restraints are more expensive than bilateral quotas for the country seeking protection because of the income transfer to foreign countries that is inherent in them. This transfer makes such restrictions less unattractive to the countries affected.

Second, selective measures have an inherent tendency to proliferate. The clearest example of this is, of course, the Multi-Fibre Arrangement, but it is equally true of shoes and steel, for example. Third, selectivity in trade policy measures means that countries other than the target ones are exempted; they are "innocent bystanders." This has a sympathetic ring, but in fact it means that domestic consumers pay not only for the protection of their country's domestic producers, but also for the protection of foreign trading partners.

Finally, gray zone measures tend to affect developing countries comparatively more. This stands to reason in that the comparative disadvantage in the traditional sectors is particularly pronounced vis-à-vis the developing countries. It can also be explained by the weak negotiating position of developing countries. These measures thus hit the most efficient producers. Comparative disadvantage is difficult to remedy by means of either a tariff measure or a global quota. It is claimed that selectivity penalizes only the "worst offender," but this is too static a view of the situation. An "innocent bystander" can quickly be transformed into a leading offender, particularly if it is a developing country that is busy setting up an export industry.

PRINCIPLES FOR A SOLUTION TO THE SAFEGUARD PROBLEM

The problem in regard to Article XIX may be summarized as follows. Safeguards may not be applied selectively. The introduction of safeguards requires compensation to be given to the affected trading partners. If no compensation is provided, these partners are entitled to retaliatory measures. The cumulative result is that the application of safeguards in accordance with Article XIX is not a straightforward matter. For this reason safeguards are often introduced outside the scope of Article XIX, that is, selectively, without compensation and thus with relative ease.

The gap between practice and theory has its origin in the many global economic problems that emerged in the 1970s. The speed of the changes—one has only to think of the rise of the NICs and their successors—combined with the slow pace of adjustment in many rich countries has led to a defensive reaction in the latter. This has manifested itself in all kinds of trade policy measures, supplemented with huge subsidies, to preserve their positions. These defensive measures were not effective enough, and partly for this reason greater weight has been given to a more offensive approach since the beginning of the 1980s. This has meant that instead of placing all of the emphasis on defending their existing positions, many countries have started to look for new ones that are in keeping with their level of development, their resources, and the general comparative advantages they enjoy (OECD, 1983).

The aim of a settlement of the safeguard problem must be to make Article XIX more easily applicable. This may be achieved by excluding compensation and/or retaliation from the regulation. This will significantly reduce the tendency to selectivity in safeguards. Accordingly, the principles governing any settlement of the safeguard problem must be based on the following considerations. First, safeguards may be applied in the event of rapid, unforeseen changes in the market for a specific product. Where such safeguards involve changes in the supply side—for example, the rapid emergence of developing countries as competitors in various sectors—the assumption must be that these are the result of genuine comparative advantages and should, therefore, not be frustrated.[5] Moreover, the guiding principle must be that the purpose of safeguards is to give domestic industry a chance to adjust. In other words the conditions under which safeguards may be applied must promote this adjustment.

Third, the adjustment must be as efficient and swift as possible, that is, with a minimum of costs (loss of welfare). The costs of safeguards must weigh as little as possible on the trading partners, given that in cases where comparative advantage is changing, the crux of the problem lies in the failure of domestic producers to adjust. Fourth, any new, improved arrangement for the conditions under which safeguards may be applied must contain provisions that will ensure that safeguards are not used more frequently than they already are at present, both in accordance with GATT and via gray zone measures. Care must also be taken to ensure that if a new safeguard system is created, illegal or semilegal practices do not once again emerge. For this reason evasion of any new code of safeguards must be penalized in one way or other.

Finally, the special position of developing countries must also find expression in any new safeguard system. In extremes the possibility of applying safeguards against developing countries could be ruled out. In view of the other considerations discussed above, this would not be efficient. The special position of developing countries should find expression in the provision of compensation.

POSSIBLE SOLUTIONS TO THE SAFEGUARD PROBLEM

It is clear from the considerations outlined above that the solution for industries that have found themselves in difficulty, or are likely to do so as a result of changing pat-

---

[5]There are other more suitable means of defending industry against practices such as dumping and export subsidies that contravene GATT. Issues regarding the "correct" use of the procedures involved in these cases are not discussed here, but these are also very relevant to the problem of safeguards in the widest sense.

terns of international competition, must be sought in positive adjustment. Two alternatives for achieving this purpose, (A) and (B), are outlined below. Alternative (A) is preferable in that it does not provide for the possibility of selective safeguards, whereas alternative (B) does. In order to balance to some extent its drawbacks, the regulation has been tightened up in various places as compared to option (A). Of course there are many possible variations regarding the details of each alternative, but these are not discussed here.

Alternative (A) contains the following aspects. Conditions for application would be (1) the existence of serious injury or a risk thereof, (2) the injury must be demonstrably caused by imports, and, (3) there must be a sudden, unforeseen change in imports. These conditions require no explanation given that they are consistent with the conditions that currently apply.

The preferred instrument would be subsidies to the industry in question, possibly in conjunction with nondiscriminatory protection at the border. Subsidies are used here to mean any form of financial aid in the context of a restructuring plan for the industry in question. Subsidies entail the lowest costs for the national economy of all possible instruments.[6] Border protection may be a necessary complement in practice but should in principle be nondiscriminatory. The possibility of positive discrimination for developing countries should not be excluded. If border protection takes the form of a global quota, this should be administered by the countries whose export openings are being restricted. The importing countries should only be allowed to verify.

Before implementing the safeguard measure several requirements would have to be complied with. The importing country must demonstrate that the conditions for application have been satisfied. There must be a restructuring plan for the sector in question that must involve adjustments toward new (or expected future) comparative advantage. There must be a maximum period during which the subsidy may be provided, for example, two years. The same should apply for the border protection. The subsidy should gradually decrease over this period. In the case of border protection the gradual reduction might take the form of either decreasing tariffs or increasing quotas.

These points, together with the visibility of the subsidy instrument, all have the effect of putting pressure on the affected industry to adjust. In general there would be no provision for compensation or retaliation. If the conditions are satisfied, compensation will not be necessary and retaliation will not be allowed. Only in cases where border protection would affect a major export product of the developing countries should some form of equivalent compensation be found.

For monitoring purposes an independent multilateral commission would have to be installed to be supplemented in the case of each safeguard by experts on the industry

---

[6]There are several reasons why subsidies, rather than quotas or VERs or tariffs, are not used more often for this purpose right now. First they constitute a drain on the government budget; there is competition for these funds from other parts of government. Moreover they have to be allocated every year anew. In other words they have a high political visibility. The other measures, on the other hand, may even contribute to the government budget; their costs are not very visible for the average citizen and renewal every year is either unnecessary or has a much lower public profile.

in question. Each safeguard action would have to be transmitted to this commission, partly with a view to ensuring the transparency of the procedure. The commission would be responsible for assessing the action in the light of the conditions specified earlier. The commission's decision should be binding.

Finally, the possibility of sanctions, financial and/or publicity, would have to be included. If countries introduce safeguard measures outside the scope of the official safeguard system, retaliation should be allowed. Retaliation is often not a real possibility for weaker trading partners; therefore it should be possible to enforce compensation for the affected countries by law. Publicity could be used as a sanction by making the measure widely known, particularly in the country in which it originates. The financial consequences for all parties—consumers, producers, domestic and foreign, and taxpayers—should be explicitly discussed.

These points mean that it would be easier to introduce safeguard measures than it is under the present Article XIX and that the emphasis would be clearly placed on adjustment.

If the absence of selectivity is seen as an insuperable obstacle, the system proposed could be partially modified as outlined below to create an alternative, which is clearly a second best.

The conditions for application would be the same as under (A), with the understanding that the injury must be demonstrably caused by imports from the country against which measures are being considered.

In this case the instrument would be subsidy in conjunction with border protection, with the possibility of the latter being selective. If selective protection consists of a quota, this should be administered by the country whose volume of exports is being restricted. The quota should also provide for a certain minimum, for example, the average volume of imports over the previous two years. Selective safeguards would not be allowed against a developing country that is heavily dependent on the product in question.

As additional condition for implementation, it would be stipulated that a safeguard may not be applied again against the affected country in respect to the same product within a limited number of years.

Again compensation or retaliation would in general not be provided for, unless selective protection is aimed at a developing country. In this case a type of equivalent compensation would have to be found.

The other aspects of this alternative would be the same as under (A). The status of existing safeguards that are not GATT-conforming, and are affected by the introduction of a new safeguard system, has not yet been considered. Two possibilities may be distinguished, at opposite ends of the spectrum. The first would be to bring non-GATT-conforming safeguards immediately into line with the new system. The second would be to exclude from the system all non-GATT-conforming safeguards that precede the introduction of the new safeguard code. A third option would be to introduce a transitional arrangement whereby all measures taken before a certain date would in the first instance remain untouched. Within a period to be decided, they would then either have to be terminated or brought into line with the GATT code.

RECENT DEVELOPMENTS

In September 1986 the Uruguay Round of trade negotiations started. Safeguards are one of the important items on the agenda. The objective of the Uruguay Round in respect to safeguards is to bring theory and practice more in line with each other. The following text, GATT (1986), serves as the basis for that:

    (i) A comprehensive agreement on safeguards is of particular importance to the strengthening of the GATT system and to progress in the MTNs.
   (ii) The agreement on safeguards:
- shall be based on the basic principles of the General Agreement
- shall contain, *inter alia,* the following elements: transparency, coverage, objective criteria for action including the concept of serious injury or the threat thereof, temporary nature, degressivity and structural adjustment, compensation and retaliation, notifications, consultation, multilateral surveillance and dispute settlement; and
- shall clarify and reinforce the disciplines of the General Agreement and should apply to all contracting parties.

The most striking thing in this text is the reference to "the basic principles of the General Agreement," not to the MFN principle as such. This is all the more remarkable because among the elements, mentioned under the second indent, one may find another principle, "transparency," mentioned explicitly. It could, of course, not be expected that the proponents of selectivity would give up their goal at the start of the negotiations. Nevertheless it is revealing that apparently the reference to basic GATT principles is sufficient for them to keep this option open.

Selectivity, then, is the crucial issue regarding a new safeguard agreement. And it is clear that developing countries are resisting its inclusion, as one may find in the position of, inter alia, Brazil (SUNS, 1987) and India (SUNS 1988), with broad support from other developing countries. But not only developing countries take this position, witness the view of a mixed group of countries, consisting of Australia, Hong Kong, Korea, New Zealand, and Singapore (Financial Times, 1987).

The position of the United States and of the EC is less clear. In the Tokyo Round, the United States was opposed to the introduction of selectivity. Now it has not yet indicated its position, but does not seem to be as firmly opposed as in the past (Brief, 1988).

The EC, the main proponent of selectivity in the Tokyo Round, has not yet officially taken position in the current round. There may be several reasons for this. Doubts may have arisen as to the merits of selectivity. More than in the 1970s, it has become itself the victim of selective protectionism. On the other hand, since the end of the Tokyo Round three southern European countries have acceded to the EC. On average these are more inclined to protectionism in general and more vulnerable to developing country competition. Nevertheless, by not staking out its position formally as yet, the EC makes it clear that the forces in favor of selectivity are relatively not as strong as in the past.

Often a link is suggested between solving the textile and clothing problem—another contentious issue in the Uruguay Round—and the safeguard dilemma. Presumably this refers to the need of developed countries to be able to use sufficient safeguard protection in a more liberalized textile and clothing environment. In this case, though, there is a clear danger to the system as a whole. If a new safeguard agreement were to be set up with the textile and clothing issue in mind, the risk is that it would be more favorable to importers than strictly necessary if considered in its own right. All the same it would have general applicability. It would thereby legally spread restrictiveness associated with the textile and clothing problem to all other areas of international trade presently coming under GATT. It would be much better if the issues of safeguards and the MFA could be kept apart. Insofar as phasing out of the MFA would require a safeguard backup, the latter should be linked only to this phasing out. This would imply having, for the time being, two different safeguard systems for the same sort of purpose in two different sectors, but it would be much better than having the presumably more restrictive one apply generally.

In December 1988 there was a midterm review of the negotiations in Montreal. Its purpose was to to take stock and to get a political impetus for the negotiations. Agriculture proved to be the stumbling block, allowing developing countries to take advantage and hold up results in some other areas, safeguards as well. Extension of the midterm review to April 1989 led to a successful conclusion. The following text serves as the basis of the negotiations for the remainder of the Uruguay round, GATT (1989):

> Ministers stress the importance of concluding a comprehensive agreement on safeguards based on the basic principles of the General Agreement which would aim to re-establish multilateral control over safeguards, *inter alia,* by eliminating measures which escape such control. Ministers recognize that such an agreement is vital to the strengthening of the GATT system and to progress in the Multilateral Trade Negotiations. Accordingly, they: (a) take note of the in-depth examination of the specific elements which has contributed to a better understanding of the whole issue; (b) recognize that, because of the interrelationships between the elements, substantive agreement cannot be reached on individual elements in isolation; (c) recognize that safeguard measures are by definition of limited duration; (d) in the light of the decision of the Negotiating Group, authorize its Chairman, with the assistance of the secretariat and in consultation with delegations, to draw up a draft text of a comprehensive agreement as a basis for negotiation, without prejudice to the right of participants to put forward their own texts and proposals, preferably before the end of April 1989; and (e) agree to begin negotiations on the basis of the draft text by June 1989 at the latest.

This text gives rise to the following comments. First, there is an explicit indication of the aim to eliminate measures that at present escape multilateral control. Of course, these cannot just be eliminated. An agreement on safeguards must make these measures either superfluous or "infeasible." Second, safeguard measures are acknowledged to be of limited duration, something that is right now not necessarily the case. Third, there is an explicit objective to negotiate on the basis of a concrete text, to start by mid-1989 at the latest. This is a very laudable aim, but in the light of earlier references to the importance of achieving early results regarding safeguards, some doubts are justified, especially in view of the link with textiles for which no early results can be expected at all.

SUMMARY

The problem in regard to the safeguard clause (Article XIX) may be summarized as follows. Article XIX implies that safeguards—the protection of the domestic market in unforeseen circumstances—cannot be introduced easily or on a discriminatory basis. As a result of worldwide economic problems since the mid-1970s, Article XIX has been evaded to an increasing extent, with the help of gray zone measures. These are particularly aimed at the developing countries.

In view of the discrepancy between theory and practice in this area, the industrialized countries are advocating a modification of the existing safeguard system, with the EC in particular pressing for the possibility of the introduction of selective, that is, discriminatory safeguards. It is not in the interests of the developing countries that this possibility be formalized.

A settlement of the safeguard problem should be one in which the emphasis is placed on adjustment within the country that requests the safeguard, and that excludes selectivity in protection at the border. The system could be easier to apply than the present one because compensation and/or retaliation would not in general be built into the arrangement. If selectivity were to be introduced into the system, it would have to be more difficult to apply the provision.

In both cases the special position of the developing countries would have to be taken into account in the system, for example, by insisting upon compensation for countries under conditions to be specified.

Recent developments in the Uruguay Round of trade negotiations do not give rise to high expectations in regard of a solution of the safeguard problem. On the contrary, until April 1989 the main controversial issue—selectivity—has not been debated between the main protagonists at all.

References

Brief van de Staatssecretaris van Economische Zaken. 1988. Kamerstuk 20.200, Hfdst. XIII, nr. 101, The Hague, May 31, p. 4.

Feenstra, Robert C. 1984. Voluntary Export Restraint in U.S. Autos, 1980–1981: Quality, Employment and Welfare Effects, in R. E. Baldwin, and A. O. Krueger, (eds.): *The Structure and Evolution of Recent U.S. Trade Policy*. Chicago: University of Chicago Press.

Financial Times. 1987. Pacific Rim Nations Urge Action on GATT Safeguards Provision, May 29.

GATT. MIN (86)/W/19, September 20.

GATT. 1989. Safeguards, MTR-text, April 8, mimeo.

Hamilton, Carl. 1985. Economic Aspects of Voluntary Export Restraints, in David Greenaway (ed.): *Current Issues in International Trade*. London: MacMillan, pp. 99–117.

IMF. 1985. Trade Policy Issues and Developments, Occasional Paper No. 38, Washington D.C.

McNamara, R. S., 1979. Address to the United Nations Conference on Trade and Development, Manila.

Merciai, P. 1981. Safeguard Measures in GATT. *Journal of World Trade Law* 15(1): 41–66.

Noguès, J. J., Olechowski, A., and Winters, L. A. 1985. The Extent of Non-Tariff Barriers to Industrial Countries' Imports. World Bank mimeograph.

OECD. 1983. Positive Adjustment Policies, Paris.

OECD. 1984. Competition and Trade Policies; their Interaction, Paris.

SUNS, Special United Nations Service. 1987. Regular Publication of the International Foundation for Development Alternatives: Elements for Safeguards Agreements Outlined in GATT, Nyon, June 2.

SUNS, Special United Nations Service. 1988. Regular Publication of the International Foundation for Development Alternatives: US will not Negotiate Dismantling MFA in Uruguay Round, Nyon, May 7.

Pearson, C. 1983. *Emergency Protection in the Footwear Industry*, Thames Essay No. 36. London: Trade Policy Research Centre.

Ray, E. J., and H. P. Marvel. 1984. The Pattern of Protection in the Industrialized World. *Review of Economics and Statistics*, LXVI, (3): 452–458.

UNCTAD. 1988. Protectionism and Structural Adjustment, document TD/B/1196/Add.1, December 29, Geneva.

Wolf, M. 1983. Managed Trade in Practice: Implications of the Textile Arrangements, in Cline, W. R., (ed.): *Trade Policy in the 1980s*. Washington D.C.: Institute for International Economics.

Chapter 8

A COST-BENEFIT ANALYSIS OF DEBT-EQUITY SWAPS*

Khosrow Fatemi

INTRODUCTION

In April 1986 the Mexican government, under considerable pressure from both Mexican and international financial sources, announced a new program to alleviate the burden of the country's $100 billion foreign debt. Mexico thus became a new addition to a growing list of developing countries that have adopted debt capitalization as a means of solving their foreign debt problem.

A debt capitalization program (DCP), or a debt-equity swap (DES), is defined here as a negotiated agreement whereby a public sector external debt of a developing country is converted into—swapped with—local currency denominated assets at discounted rates. These new assets can be used to purchase stocks in existing facilities, or can be used to expand a company's operations in the country. They can also be in the form of portfolio investment or foreign direct investment, and can be held by the foreign bank holding the original debt or be transferred to other entities.

Considering the large number of banks involved in different DESs in several countries, it is difficult to compile exact figures on DES arrangements. It is, however, estimated that in 1985 approximately $5 billion in LDC debt was converted into about $2 billion in equity ownership by banks and other multinational enterprises. The number increased in both 1986 and 1987, reaching $8 billion by the latter year.

The purpose of this chapter is to provide an analysis of the debt capitalization program both conceptually and as implemented in recent years. This introductory section is followed by an historical perspective of the DES in recent years.

*Also published in Bernard Katz, and Rosie Bukics, eds., *The Handbook of International Financial Management,* (Chicago: Probus Publishing Co., 1990).

HISTORY

The first reference to the concept of capitalization of a sovereign debt can be traced back to the mid-1970s and the Turkish economic revitalization program. This program included a provision under which a certain portion of Turkey's external debt would be converted to equity ownership in existing economic facilities by foreign companies. At the time of its first introduction, this proposal predated the global debt crisis and consequently received little attention, and less action, by the parties concerned. A decade later, in a world now deeply concerned with the debt crisis, a similar proposal by Chile received global attention and swift implementation.

The Chilean proposal introduced in early 1985 included a series of new regulations under which investors could buy Chilean pesos for investment purposes by exchanging them for existing external public debt at highly discounted rates. The program's success has been phenomenal. In its first three years, Chile's DESs have enabled the country to retire $2–3 billion, or about 10% of its total foreign debt. In fact, the Chilean model has been so effective that many other countries have copied it.

Even before Chile's reintroduction of DES in early 1985, banks holding LDC notes were swapping them—not for equity but for debt in other LDCs. This debt-debt swap started shortly after the beginning of the debt crisis and was founded on three different approaches that creditor banks used in dealing with their debtor nations: diversification, consolidation, and, whenever possible, liquidation.

Diversification. This seemed to be the logical approach for many banks with large exposures in one or more developing countries. Rather than risking a bankruptcy-threatening default in one country, the bank would swap part of its exposure with another bank with a similar dilemma in another country. For example, Citibank would exchange a $200 million Mexican debt with Chase Manhattan's $200 million Brazilian debt (assuming here that Mexico and Brazil presented similar risks).

Consolidation. Many banks soon came to the realization that they have long-term strategic interests in a few countries and cannot simply "swap" their way out of trouble there. Consequently these banks decided to consolidate their exposure in a few countries in which they have such interests and liquidate their exposures in other countries, essentially committing themselves to the economic recovery of the former.

Liquidation. This is the approach used by the banks with small exposures in the developing countries. Rather than getting entangled in rescheduling schemes, often requiring additional commitment, these banks would liquidate their exposures, write off their loss, and eliminate the burden of continued risk.

Whichever the approach the banks adopted, the use of DES expanded rapidly, from $5 billion in its first year to an estimated $7–8 billion in 1987. By mid-1988 several countries had introduced various versions of DES and many more were expected to join the list (see Table 8.1) Initially, the banks' participation in DES arrangements was primarily by European and regional U.S. banks, with money-center American banks

Table 8.1
Debt-Equity Swaps

Country	Program inception/status	Secondary market price ranges %	Total debt ($bn)	Conversion ceiling (annual)	Privatization program
Argentina	Jan 1987	45–58	50	$400 mn	Yes
Brazil	Nov 1984	61–63	107	Pending	Incipient
Chile	May 1985	67–69	19	$480–720	Intensive
Ecuador	Feb 1987	45–47	7	None	Incipient
Mexico	Apr 1986	53–95	100	$1.8 bn	Incipient
Philippines	Aug 1986	67–70	26	$100–$150 (mn)	Active[1]
Nigeria	Apr 1984	25–31	22	None	Incipient
Venezuela	Apr 1987	69–71	32	None	None

[1]Active sale of nonperforming assets.
Source: Summarized from Steven M. Rubin, *Guide to Debt-Equity Swaps, Special Report No. 1104* (London: Economist Publications Ltd., 1988), pp. 100–101.

being conspicuously absent. The large-scale entry of money-center U.S. banks came in May 1987 when Citibank announced that it was increasing its loan-loss reserves for its LDC debt by some $3 billion. To a casual observer, this may have indicated a prelude to a future decision by Citibank to write off $3 billion from its LDC loan portfolio. More likely, it was a first step by Citibank to liquidate $6–8 billion of its LDC debt through DES. If implemented, this would reduce Citibank's total LDC debt by approximately 50% (from $14.0 to $7.0 billion).

The real impact of the Citibank action—and the subsequent similar steps by other major banks—was the boost it gave to the development of an active secondary market for DES.

There are three different broad categories of debt capitalization schemes. All the programs that have been implemented thus far are different versions of these three categories. The categories differ from each other only in regard to the number of parties involved in a swap.

Four-Party Swap

A typical four-party DES involves the following interlocking steps (see Fig. 8.1):

1. A multinational bank holding a $100 million public sector debt of a developing country (LDC-A) exchanges it with a multinational company (MNC-B) interested in making a new investment, or expanding its existing portfolio in that country. The bank receives a discounted price (55 million in dollars in the example illustrated in Fig. 8.1).

2. MNC-B then transfers the loan, now countersigned to it, to the host government, at a price lower than the face value of the original debt, but higher than the amount paid by the company to the bank in step A above. Additionally, and significantly, the government's payment will not be in dollars, rather in the currency of LDC-A (equivalent of $75 million in local currency is the example used here).

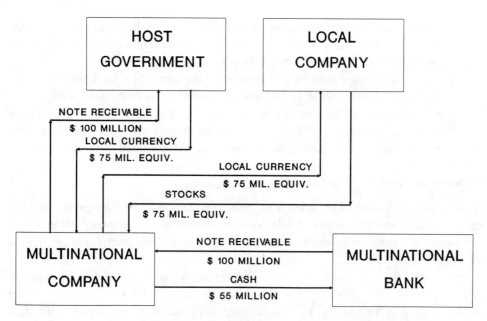

Figure 8.1. Four-party debt-equity swap.

3. The multinational company now uses the local currency to buy stocks in a local company (among those approved by the government for this purpose), or to build a new plant (again, only in approved industries), or otherwise expand its operations. The criteria used by many countries to include an industry in an "approved list" include:

a. Those industries or companies that are among those that the government considers part of—at least supportive of—its overall development plan.

b. Those industries or companies that have export potentials, and therefore by having a multinational firm as a partner enhances their chances of increasing their efforts.

Additionally, the approved list specifically excludes certain key industries such as energy and communications.

It should be noted that the above steps are *ad referenda* and must all take place before any of the three transactions are finalized.

It should also be noted that the companies whose stocks are transacted under step 3 could be state-owned (among them previously nationalized enterprises) or they can be privately held companies. In the first instance the DES will result in at least partial privatization of the firm. In the latter case, the multinational company will have to negotiate with the current owners of the stocks as to the price and other conditions. Needless to say, no privatization will result from such a transfer of ownership.

Three-Party Swap

If a bank decides also to play the role of an investor, then the functions of the bank and the multinational company are combined into one and the swap will have three parties (see Fig. 8.2).

The steps involved in a three-party DES are:

1. The multinational bank exchanges its $100 million public sector debt with the government of the host country for a discounted value in *local currency* (equivalent of $75 million in the example illustrated in Fig. 8.2).
2. The bank can then use its local currency to buy stocks in a local company. Depending on the size of the investment in comparison with the total value of the local company, this purchase of stocks may be for portfolio purposes or entitle the bank to some managerial control. As in the case of a four-party swap, the list of the companies of which the stocks can be bought is limited by the government.

Two-Party Swap

A two-party DES takes place when a multinational bank and the host government directly exchange the government's debt for some stocks in a state-owned company. A two-party DES is easier to negotiate because it involves fewer parties and the debt is discounted only once.

The important characteristic of a two-party swap is that it will definitely result in privatization of a state-owned company. Also, a two-party DES will not add to the stock of capital in the country. In contrast, the local proceeds of a four-party DES may be used to build new buildings and plants, thus adding to the country's stock of capital.

BENEFITS AND COSTS TO CONTRACTING PARTIES

A typical debt capitalization program involves two–three contracting parties:

1. The government of the host developing country.
2. The foreign bank holding the original receivable.

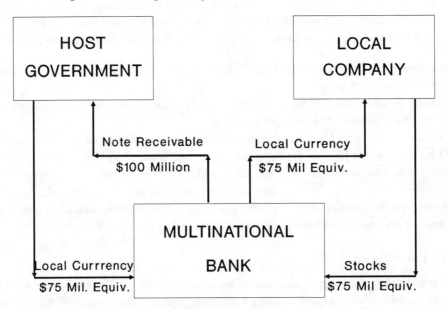

Figure 8.2. Three-party debt-equity swap.

3. Depending on the type of DES, a multinational company with interest in investing in the host LDC.

As in any contractual agreement, the consummation of the agreement depends on the satisfaction of all the parties involved. The benefits and costs of a DES can be categorized in the groups discussed below.

The Host Developing Country

The benefits. It can be argued that the host LDC is the major—in some cases, the only—beneficiary of a DES. According to this argument the host LDC's benefits include the following.

1. Reduction of foreign debt. One of the most serious economic problems of the LDCs in recent years has been their external financial obligations of over $1.0 trillion. (For a listing of the foreign debt of the fifteen largest debtor nations, see Fig. 8.3.) At current interest rates, this requires annual interest payments of over $100 billion by a group of countries short in foreign currencies. A major benefit of DES to any developing country is that it reduces the country's debt servicing payments, allowing the country to allocate the hard-earned and scarce hard currency to development projects. An important part of this benefit is that the host LDC pays only a fraction of its debt but receives full credit. The discount rates vary from time to time, depending on the country, but have averaged around 50%. This indicates that to pay off a $100 million foreign debt, the debtor country would pay only $50 million.

2. Payment of foreign debt in local currency. Additionally, the discounted debt is paid in local—and not foreign—currency, resulting in further savings of foreign

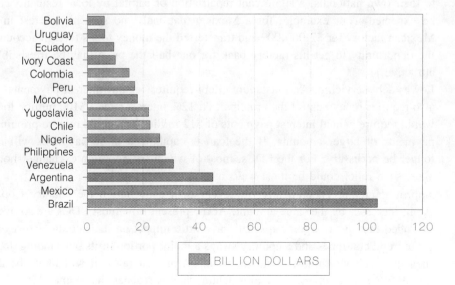

Figure 8.3. External debt; fifteen largest debtor nations.

currencies for the host LDCs. The $100 million foreign debt in the above example is retired by paying the equivalent of $50 million in the host LDC's local currency, which the government can generate—even print—more readily than any convertible currency.

3. Attraction of new investment in desired industries. The local currency received by a multinational company in a DES can only be used for investment purposes in selected industries and enterprises of the host nation. Accordingly, each debt cancellation results in additional foreign investment in the country. This investment can be guided into desired—for example, exports-generating—industries, thus further increasing the investment benefits of the swap. Additionally, the reduced cost of investment for the MNC can attract new and marginal investment to many LDCs. This reduced cost in effect increases the potential rate of return on investment, thus making marginal projects more attractive. A probably unacceptable expected rate of return of 15% on a $20 million investment would increase to an acceptable 24% if the project's cost can be reduced to $12.5 million through a DES with the host government.

4. Privatization. Another important advantage of this type of foreign direct investment is that it results in greater privatization of industrial facilities in the developing countries. Considering the inefficiency of state-owned enterprises, particularly in the LDCs, this privatization cannot help but increase productivity, and if channeled properly could result in a vitalized private sector in these countries.

5. Repatriation of capital. Most debtor nations' attempts to revitalize their economies have been severely hampered by the flight of capital from those countries. In Mexico's case, for example, the burden of its foreign debt would be drastically reduced if the estimated $20–30 billion of Mexican capital held by Mexican residents abroad would be returned home. For the countries that have opened DESs to their own nationals, a significant repatriation of capital by local residents can be expected. (For example, for a Mexican national who sold his interest in a Mexican factory for $2,000,000 and transferred the money to his foreign account, the opportunity to get his factory back for one-half the price may be irresistibly attractive.)

6. Lower debt servicing. An outstanding debt requires regular interest payments. It also requires repayment of the principal. At 12% interest rate, a $100 million loan would require annual interest payments of $12 million and could require principal payments of larger amounts. If the loan is capitalized these payments will no longer be necessary. For the LDCs, most of which have foreign exchange shortages, such relief could be most welcome.

7. Improved credit. Theoretically, for every debt cancellation the country's open credit increases by the same amount. At the present time most LDCs are so overextended that even large swaps will have little impact on their credit. However, if the trend continues and a country swaps a major portion of its outstanding debt, then its credit worthiness could improve. At present rates, it will likely be the mid-1990s before any of the major debtor nations reaches that point.

The costs. The above advantages of DES to the host countries notwithstanding, debt capitalization programs do have their costs, among them:

1. Reduction of foreign debt? Many private economists, particularly among the academicians in the debtor nations argue—somewhat convincingly—that these countries are simply not in a position to pay back their external debt, and such liabilities would have to be written off in one form or another. Converting them to equity ownership increases the likelihood of payment, and in fact *increases* the burden of the LDCs. In many cases this may be based on a valid premise. A country whose debt servicing is a major part of its total foreign exchange earnings must either sacrifice all development aspirations and cut imports of essentials— food, medicine, and spare parts, among others—or default. The choice seems rather obvious. From this perspective, DESs only convert a "nonpayable" present liability to a "probably payable" future commitment. To many critics of DESs, this is not much of a bargain for the debtor nations.

2. Payment of foreign debt in local currency. This obvious benefit of paying off foreign debt using domestic currency drastically loses its appeal when the inflationary impact of such arrangements is added to the equation. The retirement of a $200 million foreign debt, discounted at 40%, will result in an addition of $120 million in local currency to the host country's money supply—*without a matching increase in the production side of the economy*. Even the staunchest supporters of DES agree on its inflationary impact. Their defense lies usually in the control of the liquidity in the host countries. In other words, this argument maintains that the sudden injection of million of dollars in local currency should be negated by other measures to control inflation.

3. Attraction of new investment. There is little doubt that DES attracts capital investment to the host country. There is, however, an unanswered question: how much of this new capital is additional capital? That is, how much of the new capital would not have been invested without a DES? It can be argued that most MNCs that participate in a DES arrangement are already committed to invest in the host country and the DES only makes their investment that much cheaper. Accordingly, DESs bring little or no additional investment and only make it cheaper for foreign MNCs to invest in the host LDCs. It can be concluded that the degree of success of any DES program is a function of additionality. But additionality is difficult to measure and varies from country to country and even in the same country from situation to situation. Furthermore, large investment projects cannot be planned and implemented quickly simply because a debt-equity swap becomes available. For example, automobile manufacturing multinationals were a party to about 50% of the debt capitalization schemes approved by Mexico in 1986. It is doubtful that any of these investment projects were initiated because of the availability of DES arrangements. Some, in fact, had been planned several years before Mexico announced its DES program.

4. Flight capital. The downside of the flight capital argument, that is, that DES

generates repatriation of capital by local residents, is that this characteristic also provides a great opportunity for an enterprising arbitrageur. This is particularly true in cases like Mexico where foreign exchange controls are lax to nonexistent. At current rates, a Mexican resident with assets abroad can convert those into Mexican pesos at substantial discounts, then reconvert them into dollars at close to their full face value. For example, currently a Mexican public sector debt can be bought at 45–50% discounts in the secondary markets. An arbitrageur can purchase $2 million Mexican public sector debt for $1–1.1 million. Even if the government requires a 10% discount (fee), $1.8 million worth of Mexican pesos can be bought for $1.1 million. If the pesos can then be reconverted into dollars, this transaction represents a $7–800,000 arbitrage profit. Such a transaction is generally known as round-tripping or bicycling. It would serve the purpose of reducing the country's external debt, but the payment—albeit lower than the face value of the original debt—will in effect be in a convertible currency purchased in the black market. (One redeeming benefit may be that it rapidly depletes the black market supply and makes it too expensive for most users.) Round-tripping can also take place through overinvoicing imports and underinvoicing exports. This way traders will use legitimate trade as a means of facilitating capital flight.

5. Lower debt servicing. There is no doubt that any cancelled or swapped debt will result in lower interest payments. However, swapped debts are replaced by equity ownership and the latter entitles the new owner to dividend payments that probably will be higher than interest payments. This is nothing more than a switch in the type of payments—from interest to dividend. More realistically, fixed or almost fixed interest payments are replaced with fluctuating and, therefore, higher dividend payments. (Dividend payments reflect the business risk that the owner undertakes and are therefore higher than interest payments that have more limited risks.) Neither the increased amount nor the increased fluctuations serves the interests of the host LDCs.

The Banks

The benefits. Superficially, the banks may seem to be the sole loser of a DES. Further examination, however, points to the contrary. Specifically, the advantages of DES for banks include:

1. Recovering potentially lost receivables. Even though banks sell their receivables at highly discounted rates, they still recover most of their money. Considering that the probable alternative would be default, partial recovery become even more attractive. It should be remembered that multinational banks are the most guilty partner in the creation of the debt crisis, and in essence they should pay for it. It was their clumsiness and lack of adequate control in granting these loans that precipitated the crisis. Therefore, it does not seem inappropriate for the banks to bear part of the burden. Nevertheless, in almost all instances banks are recovering

their original loans and the discounted rates generally are smaller than the interest they have earned on these loans. In effect, they have given sovereign loans at very low interest rates to LDC host governments.

The majority of the loans date back to the 1970s but certainly no later than 1982. These loans generated interest at rates of one or more points over the prime rate in the United States and over LIBOR (London Inter-Bank Overnight Rate) in Europe. In all cases, a loan given in 1981 or before and swapped in 1987 or later would have generated more interest (either paid or converted into principal through rescheduling) than the discount rate at the time it was swapped. For example, a $50 million loan granted in 1980 and swapped in 1987 (for simplicity, the two dates are assumed to be January 1, 1980 and December 31, 1987, respectively) would have generated 3.83% in interest (assuming interest payments were paid regularly) or 3.04% (if all interest was converted into principal), see Table 8.2.

Since actual figures are not available on individual loans, it is impossible to estimate the exact effective interest rates applicable to each country and to each loan. It is, however, unlikely that any bank has lost, or will lose, any of its original capital. The degree of recovery of interest will vary from situation to situation and will depend on:

When the loan was granted.

The nominal rate of interest charged.

Table 8.2
Calculation of Effective Interest Rate[1]

	Scenario A[2]		Scenario B[3]	
Year	Prime Rate	Interest Payments	Yearly	Year-End Value
1980	15.27	8.10	8.14	58.14
1981	18.87	9.94	11.55	69.69
1982	14.86	7.93	11.05	89.77
1983	10.79	5.40	9.52	90.26
1984	12.04	6.52	11.77	102.03
1985	9.93	5.46	11.15	113.18
1986	8.35	4.68	10.58	123.76
1987	8.21	4.60	11.40	135.16
Total		53.17		
Principal (Disc'd at 45%)		27.50		74.34
Total Payment under DES		80.67		74.34
Effective Interest Rate		3.83%		3.04%

[1]In scenario A this is calculated by adding total interest payments to the discounted value of the original loan. The face value of the loan is subtracted from the total and the result is divided by the number of years the loan was outstanding (8). In Scenario B the face of the original loan is subtracted from the discounted value and the reminder divided by eight.
[2]Scenario A. Interest payments made regularly (interest charged at prime +1%).
[3]Scenario B. No interest payments were made (interest accrued at prime +1%).
Source: *International Financial Statistics* (various issues, line 60 pp.).

If any of the principal was repaid.

When interest payments were stopped.

When the swap took place.

2. Exposure diversification and asset collateralization. This is used particularly in the case of two-way swaps when a bank converts its receivable into an equity ownership. This action benefits the bank in two ways. First, its exposure is diversified within the host LDC. Second, the loan is in effect collateralized with stocks in, for example, a manufacturing plant or a hotel. These changes, particularly in instances when the ownership is of a facility with foreign exchange earnings potential, greatly enhance the probability of the bank recovering its original loan and sometimes with high returns. Ownership may also entitle the bank to some managerial control in the firm, further increasing its chances of regaining its original loan.

The costs. Costs to the banks include:

1. Discounting of receivables. The major drawback of a DES for the banks is that they have to heavily discount part of their assets. For the banks with large sovereign exposures, this could mean a long period of operational losses or limited profits. For example, if a bank with a $3 billion exposure in LDCs swaps one-half of its total exposure at 40% discount in three years, it would have to write off $200 million in bad—unrecoverable—debts per year. Unless the bank has developed a special reserve for this purpose, such payments will have to come from its profit. This is another reason why Citibank's $3 billion reserve was so important. It enhanced the bank's ability to swap its foreign debt. In fact, because of this action, Citibank is now in a position to swap at least $6 billion of its LDC debt without adversely affecting its profitability.

2. Involuntary conversion into investment banking. Two-way swaps have the effect of converting commercial banks into investment banks. Whereas in the long run and under right circumstances this may be a right step, blanket capitalization of a bank's foreign debt cannot help but damage its operations. These investments are not for their profitability or feasibility, rather to avoid facing default in major loans. At best, this is the wrong reason for making an investment decision. (The recent trend has been toward more four-party swaps, thus eliminating this disadvantage.)

It should be noted that since financially a DES is a zero-sum proposition, one party's gain must come at another party's expense. If a bank receives $55 million for a $100 million debt (the example portrayed in Fig. 8.1), it means a "loss" of $45 million. The bank may have a reserve to write off the loss, but nevertheless its profitability is adversely affected, in this example by $45 million. If the bank is in the 50% tax bracket, this loss is evenly distributed between its shareholders and, through the government, the tax paying public. In this example, $22.5 of the total loss is borne by the government in the form of reduced taxes.

It should also be noted that a portion of the $45 million write-off is accrued to the MNC, resulting in higher profits and tax payments. Assuming that the bank and the company are of the same nationality and the MNC is also in the 50% tax bracket, part of the loss in tax revenues ($10 million in the above example) will be regained through higher taxes by the company, making the net loss to the home government of the multinational bank $12.5 million, or 12.5% of the total value of the swapped debt. If these ratios hold true for all capitalized debt during the 1985–1988 period, the home governments of multinational banks have lost $1.5–2.0 billion in tax revenues, of which at least $1.0 billion was by the United States government.

Multinational Companies

MNCs can be described as innocent bystanders in this game, willing to help the banks and host LDCs solve their problem. Alternatively they can be portrayed as vultures waiting for a bank to face a default, then jump in and buy the receivable at heavily discounted rates. In either case they are hardly in a position to lose. As good samaritans or opportunists, they will become a party to a swap only if it benefits them, and this cannot be a losing proposition.

Multinational companies' purchase of bank receivables occur in two situations: preplanned investment and marginal investment.

Preplanned investment. American automobile manufacturers had decided to expand their production facilities in Mexico long before Mexico announced its debt capitalization scheme in 1986. Their investment decision was based in part on the attractiveness of the inexpensive Mexican labor and in part on their ability to re-export their finished product to the United States duty-free. (This is the result of U.S. Customs regulations 806 and 807, which allow the re-importation of foreign-assembled American parts into the United States paying minimal tariffs only on the value-added portion.)

In the case of U.S. automobile manufacturers, their ability to obtain Mexican pesos at discounted rates meant that the peso cost of their Mexican investment was 40–50% less than they had anticipated, making an already profitable venture even more so.

Marginal investment. Take the situation of MNC-A with an interest to invest in LDC-B. The company's minimum acceptable rate of return is 20%. The cost of the proposed investment project would be evenly divided between equipment and machinery—to be spent in the United States and in U.S. dollars—and plant construction—to be spent in LDC-B and denominated in its currency. Initial studies by MNC-A that the project would cost $20 million and the expected return would be $3.6 per year—18%, which is below the acceptable rate. This rate of return with a DES and a discount rate of 40% would be increased to 22.5%, making it an acceptable project under MNC-A's criteria. Table 8.3 compares the two alternatives.

Table 8.3
Comparing No Swaps and DES Alternatives

(In Thousands)	Alternative A: No Swaps	Alternative B: With DES
Hard currency capital needed	$10,000	$10,000
Local currency ($1 = 10AR)	100,000 ARs	100,000 ARs
Dollar cost of local currency	10,000	6,000[1]
Total dollar cost	20,000	16,000
Expected annual return	3,600	3,600
Rate of return	18%	22.5%

[1]Swapped at 40% discount.

THE MEXICAN EXPERIENCE

The Mexican debt capitalization program began with the enactment of clause 5.11 of New Money Agreements by the Mexican government. The twofold advantages of the program were listed as the reduction of Mexico's foreign debt and attraction of new foreign investment to Mexico. (The Mexican government's promotion of its DES has primarily been based on the latter.)

According to the *Operating Manual for Debt Capitalization* published by the Ministry of Finance, a foreign bank that holds Mexico's public sector debt, and more recently government guaranteed private sector debt, can exchange the debt at discounted rates with the government for *approved* investment purposes.

The government's approval process is based on a nine-category classification of investment projects. The highest category (0) is for the purchase of state-owned companies and the government will redeem the debt at its full value in pesos. The lowest category (8) is for the least desired, yet approvable, category of investment. Under category 8, the debt will be discounted by 25%—redeemed at 75% of its face value. (The figures given here refer to the peso discounting of the debt and not what the bank will receive in dollars, which will be lower, around 50–60%.)

An investment proposal submitted for debt capitalization will also be evaluated by the National Foreign Investment Commission of Mexico, which uses the following criteria for prioritizing and approving proposals:

1. Generation of foreign currency through exports.
2. Domestic production of new products, which are currently imported.
3. Transfer of high technology into Mexico.
4. High degree of integration with the domestic economy, usually measured in terms of domestic content.
5. Wholly foreign owned.
6. Smaller companies.

Other restrictions include:

1. DES cannot be used to gain ownership in industries that, under the Foreign Investment Law of 1973, are to be exclusively state-owned. These industries in-

clude: petroleum and certain other mining industries; nuclear power plants; electrical generation; railroads; telecommunications.

2. DES cannot be used to gain ownership in industries that, under different laws, are to remain 100% indigenous Mexican. These industries include: radio and television; air and bus transportation; forestry; natural gas distribution.

3. Foreign ownership in certain industries is limited to minority ownership. In these cases DES can be used only to acquire ownership below the specified minority levels. These industries are: processing of minerals; automotive parts and components; secondary petrochemical products. (Production sharing, or *maquiladora*, plants are exempt from ownership limitations, and therefore DES can be used to gain full ownership in such operations.)

Inflationary Impact

In response to the criticism that a sudden large infusion of pesos into the Mexican economy will be inflationary, the government set two limits for approval of DES applications: the monthly tentative limit of $110 million and the more definitive annual limit of $1.5 billion, both measured in the disbursement of pesos. (Depending on the distribution of the cancelled debt in different priority categories, this would mean a total debt cancellation of $1.5–2.0 billion.)

In its first year of operation (April 1986–March 1987), the Mexican government stayed within its self-established limits and approved 178 proposals resulting in the cancellation $1,513 million in public sector debt. (Only sixteen proposals were rejected outright.) Of this, the largest single conversion involved Volkswagon and the Deutsche Bank. Under this swap $141 million of Mexico's public sector debt was exchanged for $125 million in pesos. The dollar cost of this transaction in the secondary market at the time—December 5, 1985—was about $85 million. Three other car manufacturers— Chrysler, Ford, and Nissan—were also involved in debt capitalization schemes in Mexico during the same period. Their combined capitalization resulted in a total debt cancellation of $220 million. In Chrysler's case the company bought about $110 million in Mexican government debt from different banks in the secondary market for less than $60 million and exchanged them for approximately $100 million in pesos. The company also incurred a total cost including intermediary and financial advising services provided by its intermediary, Manufacturers Hanover Trust, of over $5 million. In total Chrysler received $100 million in pesos for $65 million.

During 1987 Mexico's adherence to its own limits was not as rigid. It is estimated that close to $2 billion of Mexican debt was swapped resulting in an injection of the equivalent of $1.5 billion in pesos into the Mexican economy. It is arguable how much this contributed to the country's inflation rate of 165%. After inflation reached an annual rate of 177% in January 1988, the government announced its Economic Solidarity Plan (ESP). The plan includes a variety of inflation control measures such as maintaining the peso's parity at around 2,300 per dollar, and wage and price controls. Injection of DES-generated pesos was maintained at the maximum allowable rate of the equivalent of $110 million per month. Any effect this may have had on Mexican inflation was more than offset by the success of the ESP, as Mexico's monthly inflation by the summer of 1988 had been cut to single digits and for the first half of the year was about one-half of its 1987 rate.

The most important revision of clause 5.11 came in March 1987 when the exclusivity of DES for foreign nationals was removed. Once specific guidelines regulating the participation of Mexican nationals and corporations were finalized later in the year, Mexican companies became active—albeit smaller—participants in debt capitalization schemes.

New Emphasis

By mid-1988, two industries—tourism and the *maquiladora*—were by far the major users of DES in Mexico. *Maquila* plants are exempt from maximum ownership limits otherwise imposed on the operations of foreign MNCs in Mexico, and as a result have grown rapidly both in size and in their reliance on DESs. For a foreign or Mexican investor in any of the approved industries not to use DES for financing the peso portion of its investment would be bad business and plain stupid. A deterrent may be the small size of most *maquila* operations. Despite the priority that the Mexican government gives to small investors, these investors may be reluctant to apply for DES projects in part because of lack of knowledge and internal expertise and in part because they find the waiting and other restrictions not worth the potential savings of a DES. Nevertheless, as debt capitalization becomes more familiar and more organized, smaller companies are expected to increasingly utilize this technique. Also of benefit would be the development of more active secondary markets.

Mexico's tourism industry is also greatly benefiting from DES. Numerous DES proposals have recently been approved by the Mexican government. These projects are generally small—under $10 million—but have been growing in number and significance. Also unlike the manufacturing sector, DES-financed projects in tourism are dominated by non-American, particularly Japanese, investors. The Mexican government's decision to designate three regions as potential DES approvable proposals has helped generate interest and proposals from foreign companies for DES financing of tourist facilities in these three areas of Cancun, Puerto Escondido, and Bahias de Huatulco.

Privatization

Another characteristic of DESs that has been emphasized by the Mexican government is its privatization impact. Many foreign MNCs have shown interest in obtaining ownership and control of small state-owned enterprises. The 1987 revision allowing Mexican nationals to use DES has accelerated the privatization of Mexican companies. Some foreign banks, including some of Mexico's largest creditors such as Citibank, have shown a willingness to obtain a controlling interest in Mexican banks. Once U.S. government approval is obtained (most proposals call for a higher ownership than American banks can obtain without special U.S. government approval), negotiations should progress fairly rapidly as participants are limited to the Mexican government and those individual U.S. banks that have been in an ongoing state of negotiation for rescheduling, etc., for many years.

Another characteristic of Mexico's DES—albeit not on the top of the government's priority list—allows foreign investors to swap private sector loans. This is limited to loans guaranteed by the government's Ficorca (a trust fund mechanism whereby the government guarantees the eventual repayment to foreign creditors of debts contracted by private Mexican companies) and involves a more complicated process. It is also an attractive option to many investors, both foreign and Mexican. The largest example of this type of swap to date has been the transfer of ownership of almost one-half of the Alfa Group in exchange for the cancellation of its foreign debt.

CONCLUSION

Debt-equity swaps are the most promising of all the solutions developed during recent years to remedy the staggering debt problem of the developing countries. The initial success of DES agreements is a clear indication of their potential—and also of their potential problems. The promise of the DES is that it is the first successful attempt at *negotiating a compromise* between debtor nations and their creditor banks. This is a very important first step, particularly since unlike other similar attempts, it has been void of pretentious pronouncements, rhetorical threats, and destructive caveat. DES arrangements are the first indication of a mutual understanding by all parties of the existence and the severity of the problem, one that would not dissipate either through multinationalization (a la the Baker Plan) or by politicization (Peru). The realization is a good beginning, but it is only a first step, and many problems lie ahead.

Like any other new concept, debt capitalization lacks a universal approach leaving not only the details, but also some of the major points to the negotiating parties. This places the LDC governments—and to a lesser extent the banks—in a precarious situation, because they cannot be seen as having been outdone by their respective counterparts. This lack of a general approach to DES negotiations is a natural progression in the development of a general approach to a problem, but nevertheless a risky proposition. A few breached agreements and the whole concept may lose its appeal. To avoid that fate, a better understanding of the concept is needed along with more trust among the participants. Until such time, DES arrangements, as effective as they may be, are as susceptible to a quick disappearance as many other potentially "great" solutions before them.

Chapter 9

THE DEVELOPING COUNTRIES, THE NEWLY INDUSTRIALIZED COUNTRIES, AND THE SHIFTING COMPARATIVE ADVANTAGE*

James M. Lutz

INTRODUCTION

The Newly Industrializing Countries (NICs) of the world have increasingly become important actors in the international economy. They have accounted for a larger portion of world trade in manufactured products over time, and their exports to the industrialized states have created significant adjustment problems in those countries. These exports have been one factor contributing to the increases in protectionism that have appeared in the developed states from governments under pressure from domestic interest groups (Cline, 1984; Kahler, 1985; Yoffie, 1981). These increases in exports have come at the expense of exports from plants in the developed states, at least initially since the industrialized nations were the ones that formerly dominated almost all of the trade in manufactures.

The emergence of the NICs as important participants in the export of manufactures can be seen, at least in part, as a natural outcome of a process of ongoing shifts in comparative advantage in the world economy. The NICs have been those developing states that were in the best position to move into manufacturing lines where the industrialized states no longer had a comparative advantage, even if they still retained an absolute advantage. The product life-cycle concept, for countries instead of the individual firm, also suggests that production facilities for standardized, manufactured products shift to developing countries such as the NICs in the last stage of the cycle. Such relocation occurs to take advantage of lower wages since the standardized production

*Reprinted from *The International Trade Journal,* Vol. I, no. 4, summer 1987.

techniques require less skilled, though not necessarily unskilled, labor (Gruber, et al., 1967, p. 30; Lowinger, 1975, p. 225). These new plants in developing states will produce for both their domestic markets and for other world markets to the detriment of exports from factories located in the industrialized nations. Eventually, of course, these facilities will export to the domestic markets of the industrialized states, displacing not only production for foreign markets but for domestic markets as well.

There have been some indications that shifts in comparative advantage have been present in the export mix of manufacturers for a number of developed countries (Franko and Stephenson, 1981, p. 185; Lutz and Green, 1983; Mullor-Sebastian, 1983). In addition, the product areas in which the NICs initially began to gain shares of world exports were exactly those standardized product lines in which comparative advantage was most likely to have shifted (Cline, 1984, pp. 11–13; Kihl and Lutz, 1985, pp. 86–87). There has been evidence that Japan in particular has shifted production to the NICs while expanding exports in other product areas (Hadley, 1981, pp. 309–312; Kellman and Landau, 1984; Kihl and Lutz, 1985, pp. 80–82). Some of the NICs have also displayed changing patterns of production and exports that have corresponded to the expected shifts in comparative advantage (Roe and Shane, 1979).

The final shift in comparative advantage that has been hypothesized, and the one considered in the analysis below, is the idea that production will move from the NICs to other developing states for the most standardized, labor-intensive manufactures. As a consequence of rising wage levels in the NICs and the movement to the production of more advanced items that are exported by the NICs rather than the industrialized states, the other developing countries will be able to produce and export these labor-intensive products to the world market (Krueger, 1980, pp. 241–243; Ting, 1985). The presence of this type of shift in comparative advantage in world trade is uncertain. Ting (1985) has argued that such shifts have already begun to occur, whereas others (Balassa, 1981, pp. 22–23, 217; Hansen, 1979, p. 255) have suggested that such a change was in the process of occurring. Cline (1984), however, found no evidence for such shifts of exports from the NICs to the other developing countries.

The present study attempted to determine whether there actually were shifts in comparative advantage from the NICs to other developing states for selected manufactures between 1968 and 1982. If such shifts have indeed been taking place, it would suggest that international trade has a major role to play in the industrialization process in the developing countries and that additional states will be able to diversify their exports and expand their economic base. If such shifts cannot be detected, then it would be possible that whereas changes in comparative advantage may occur in the future, for the moment they have primarily worked to the advantage of the NICs rather than providing wider opportunities for other developing countries.

METHODOLOGY

The manufactures included in the present analysis were selected from the three-digit categories of the Standard Industrial Trade Classification (SITC) system used by the

United Nations (1974, 1978, 1980, 1983). Export data were collected for all three-digit categories of SITC 8 (miscellaneous manufactures) and SITC 65 (textiles). The manufactures in the SITC 7 categories were not included since these products were not ones in which the NICs would be likely to be diverting production to other states given the nature of the manufactures (electrical equipment, nonelectrical equipment, and transportation equipment). The other portions of SITC 6 (manufactures classified by basic material component) were excluded because these other products are heavily dependent on particular natural resources (that is, wood, rubber, and various minerals). Natural resources, of course, are one of the factors of production that confer comparative advantage, and whereas exports of these products are very important to some NICs, as well as some other developing countries, the prevalence and pattern of such exports would be as much related to the availability of the resources in question as to any shifts in comparative advantage that might have occurred. Textile products, however, are exactly the type of manufactures in which other developing countries are very likely to become new exporters given the technology involved in production. Japan in the 1950s and the Asian NICs in the 1960s relied on textile exports, among other items, in the first phases of their industrialization for export processes. Some of the NICs have actually shifted portions of their textile production to other developing countries as a result of increased protectionism in the developed nations. The quotas for textile exports that have been established for the NICs have been easily met by production in the NICs, but some other developing states have underutilized their quotas. Firms in the NICs have subsequently set up new facilities in these other states to take advantage of these export opportunities that have been lost to the NICs directly (Kumar and Kim, 1984, p. 52).

Changes in export shares for the selected three-digit SITC categories were found for a group of countries for two time periods of 1968 to 1976 and 1976 to 1982. The United Nations modified the products included in the various SITC groups in the late 1970s. The number of three-digit categories was expanded, reflecting divisions of previous categories and the reassignment of products within others. Thus the data at this level for 1968 and 1982 were not directly comparable. Since 1976 was the earliest period for which there were complete data for the new categories, it was chosen as the year separating the two time periods. Detailed data on exports at the three-digit level were first available for 1968, and 1982 was the last year with complete data; therefore, these years provided the beginning and ending points. Exports for the 1968 to 1976 period were based on the earlier UN SITC categories, of which there were a total of twenty-five. For the 1976 to 1982 period, the data utilized the new categories, which totalled thirty-seven. The division into two time periods, although necessary given the nature of the data categories and modifications in them, was also useful since the first period was one in which international trade was generally expanding, whereas the second was a period in which there were a variety of international economic problems. It is quite conceivable that any shifts in comparative advantage that were present would have been different in such dissimilar contexts.

There were sixteen individual countries and two residual groups of countries for which the export data were collected and included in the analysis. The total exports by product category were first collected to provide a base figure for the years utilized. Five NICs were included—Hong Kong, Korea, Singapore, Brazil, and Mexico. These five states, as well as Taiwan, are invariably included in any list of NICs. The inclusion of Taiwan would have been very useful for the present study, but the United Nations stopped reporting separate trade data for Taiwan with the admission of the People's Republic of China to the organization. Eleven other individual developing countries were included—Malaysia, Thailand, Indonesia, India, Pakistan, Turkey, Egypt, Argentina, Colombia, Uruguay, and El Salvador. These countries have been either large exporters (for developing states) of some manufacturers, or they are states that potentially might become the NICs of the future. In either case, they are the countries likely to have gained from any shifts in comparative advantage that may have occurred. This group also included countries in a number of different geographical areas. Two residual groups of countries were included in the analysis. The first consisted of the developed countries in the world to provide an indication of their export levels in the selected manufacturers. The second was a group consisting of all the other developing countries to take into account their possible trade gains from changes in the international economy. This group included states that only appeared among the top exporters for a few products. Their impact was aggregated since the UN reporting procedure included only export data for the top exporters in each SITC category. Collectively, however, these states did have some impact on exports for virtually all the three-digit product categories.

The changes in total exports in the selected SITC categories are shown in Table 9.1 for 1968, 1976, and 1982. The effects of the changes in the SITC categories can be seen in the two sets of figures for 1976. The differences are not generally major, but are present. The share of the developed countries in the selected manufactures declined in both periods in the aggregate, indicating that some changes had been occurring. The greatest changes for this group of states was from 1968 to 1976 when international trade was expanding. Both the NICs and some of the other developing states gained overall shares of the total exports in both time periods. The fact that the NICs gained in terms of overall export shares was important for the present analysis since it meant that shifts in comparative advantage were at least possible and could be detected. The gains of the five NICs, in fact, were sometimes considerable ones. Of the eleven individual developing countries, India, Pakistan, and Egypt had declining shares of the total exports of the selected manufactures from 1968 to 1982. The other states either gained shares of the overall market or held their own for the fourteen-year period. Thailand, Turkey, and Malaysia had the largest gains overall. More of the states in this group gained from 1968 to 1976 than in the later period, but there were increases for at least some in both time periods. The other developing countries group gained from 1968 to 1976 but lost significant ground from 1976 to 1982. There was obviously no shift that worked to the advantage of this collective group of countries during the second time period.

In order to test for shifts in comparative advantage among the countries included in the study, the changes in export shares for the individual product categories at the three-digit level for the countries and the two residual groups of states were correlated with each other. In the case of the developed countries group, it was expected that there

Table 9.1

Shares of World Exports of Selected Manufactures

Country	1968		1976[1]		1976[2]		1982	
	Volume (mil.)	Percent	Volume (mil.)	Percent	Volume (mil.)	Percent	Volume (mil.)	Percent
Total	$25,336	100.0	$93,219	100.0	$96,589	100.0	$180,380	100.0
Developed Countries	22,287	88.0	76,229	81.8	77,196	79.9	142,084	78.8
Hong Kong	1,214	4.8	5,721	6.1	5,730	5.9	12,767	7.1
Singapore	103	0.4	679	0.7	664	0.7	1,672	0.9
Korea	232	0.9	2,329	2.5	3,886	4.0	8,790	4.9
Malaysia[3]	17	0.1	268	0.3	296	0.3	474	0.3
Thailand	12	0.0	283	0.3	280	0.3	973	0.5
Indonesia	1	0.0	21	0.0	39	0.0	167	0.1
India	506	2.0	1,238	1.3	1,230	1.3	1,795	1.0
Pakistan	286	1.1	533	0.6	440	0.5	1,164	0.6
Turkey	8	0.0	324	0.3	319	0.3	1,239	0.7
Egypt	132	0.5	298	0.3	284	0.3	158	0.1
Brazil	19	0.1	665	0.7	690	0.7	1,478	0.8
Mexico	60	0.2	250	0.3	278	0.4	1,150	0.6
Argentina	24	0.1	126	0.1	95	0.1	142	0.1
Colombia	14	0.1	168	0.2	160	0.2	341	0.2
Uruguay	28	0.1	95	0.1	143	0.1	144	0.1
El Salvador	35	0.1	70	0.1	72	0.1	193	0.1
Other Developing Countries	358	1.4	3,920	4.2	4,785	4.9	5,640	3.1

[1] 1978 SITC categories
[2] 1979 SITC categories
[3] West Malaysia, Sabah, and Sarawak in 1968
Compiled from United Nations, *Yearbook of International Trade Statistics*, various years.

would be strong negative associations, particularly with the NICs. The negative associations between a group of countries with declining shares and states that had been expanding their exports would indicate that the NICs had indeed gained markets from the industrialized nations. As for shifts from the NICs to other developing countries, if such changes were occurring, they would also be indicated by negative associations when both the NIC and the other developing country had gained in terms of overall markets. If both states had been gaining, the negative association between them would indicate that their negative gains occurred in different product areas. Such differential gains would provide evidence that there were indeed shifts from the NICs to other developing states since it would be unlikely that the other states would have been gaining in more technology intensive products or those requiring higher skill levels.

In addition to deriving coefficients between pairs of countries based on the simple percentage changes in exports in the selected SITC categories, the coefficients were also weighted by the total volume of exports at the end of each period in each three-digit category. Thus the products in which there were larger volumes of trade were given increased importance rather than treating all the three-digit categories equally. Products with larger volumes of exports are ones in which shifts in comparative advantage may be more likely to occur (Lutz and Green, 1983); consequently, the weighting procedure may reveal patterns that the simple correlations would not have provided.

RESULTS

All the significant correlations between pairs of countries for the 1968 to 1976 period are shown in Table 9.2. Increase, decrease, and stable refer to the changes in export percentages, or lack thereof, that are found in Table 9.1. Whereas the present study is primarily concerned with the interactions between the NICs and developing countries, the presentation of all the association aids in providing a general context and might also identify countries that deviate from a number of broader patterns. The negative associations between four of the NICs and the developed countries group indicates that there were market shifts to the NICs at the expense of the industrialized states in this period as might be expected. There were also some indications of shifts to a few of the other developing countries, but the associations were generally not as strong as the case of the NICs. El Salvador's positive association with the industrialized countries tends to indicate that its level of exports for the selected manufactures was tied to activity in the developed states rather than being a recipient of shifts in comparative advantage from them. Pairs of NICs generally had positive associations with each other, indicating that their gains were often in the same product categories. The negative link between Hong Kong and Mexico, however, could indicate that these two countries may have been competing in some markets or perhaps that an export advantage in some products may have shifted from Hong Kong to Mexico, the much smaller overall exporter.

The association of the NICs with the other developing states was generally positive.

Thus both countries in each pair were gaining in the same product categories rather then different ones when both states increased their relative share of the export market. As a result, these positive associations provide no evidence that shifts in comparative advantage had been occurring but rather that there was complementary export expansion for country pairs. Mexico is a partial exception to this pattern of positive associations, indicating that it may have been following a different pattern from the other NICs. The relatively small negative association between Brazil and Pakistan indicates that some of Brazil's gains in markets in this period were probably at the expense of the latter state, which lost some of its markets.

Many of the associations among the non-NIC developing countries were also ones that were complementary in nature, as evidenced by positive correlations beween many pairs of countries. India, Pakistan, and Egypt, however, the countries that had relative declines in this period, had negative links with a number of other states that gained markets. Thus these developing countries that gained apparently captured some markets from these three states rather than gaining them as a result of shifts in comparative advantage from the NICs. El Salvador again had a different pattern from the other developing countries, providing additional evidence that its export activities were different from most of the other states included in the analysis.

From 1976 to 1982 the pattern of the associations differed from the earlier period. In part, the differences reflect the fact that fewer developing countries actually increased their share of the exports of the selected manufactures. Mexico and Hong Kong gained exports from the developed states, but Brazil's gains were now in areas where the industrialized countries maintained their markets (see Table 9.3). There was also very little indication that gains by the various NICs were in the same product categories given the lack of positive associations among them. The relationships between particular NICs and another developing country were also no longer generally complementary ones. Thailand and Malaysia still had positive associations with some of the NICs, but in other cases the gains in exports by the NICs were apparently in part at the expense

Table 9.2

Significant Correlations of Changes in Exports for Country Pairs, 1968–1976

	Measure	
Country Pairs[1]	Change in Export Share	Weighted Change in Export Share
Developed Countries and Other Countries		
Developed Countries (D)—Hong Kong (I)	−.73***	−.70***
Developed Countries (D)—Singapore (I)	—	−.39*
Developed Countries (D)—Korea (I)	−.71***	−.81***
Developed Countries (D)—Brazil (I)	−.35*	—
Developed Countries (D)—Other Developing Countries (I)	—	−.36*
Developed Countries (D)—Argentina (S)	−.42*	—
Developed Countries (D)—Uruguay (S)	−.45*	—
Developed Countries (D)—El Salvador (S)	—	.38*
Developed Countries (D)—India (D)	−.36*	−.54**

Table 9.2 *continued*

Country Pairs[1]	Change in Export Share	Weighted Change in Export Share
NICs and NICs		
Hong Kong (I)—Singapore (I)	—	.53**
Hong Kong (I)—Korea (I)	—	.36*
Korea (I)—Brazil (I)	.36*	.38*
Hong Kong (I)—Mexico (I)	−.36*	−.37*
NICs and Developing Countries		
Singapore (I)—Malaysia (I)	.45*	.39*
Korea (I)—Colombia (I)	.41*	—
Korea (I)—Other Developing Countries (I)	.42*	.50**
Mexico (I)—Thailand (I)	.36*	.37*
Brazil (I)—Turkey (I)	.43*	—
Hong Kong (I)—Argentina (S)	.37*	—
Hong Kong (I)—Uruguay (S)	.40*	—
Brazil (I)—Argentina (S)	.43*	—
Brazil (I)—Uruguay (S)	.43*	—
Mexico (I)—Indonesia (S)	−.50**	−.40*
Mexico (I)—El Salvador (S)	−.36*	—
Brazil (I)—Pakistan (D)	−.34*	—
Developing Countries and Developing Countries		
Thailand (I)—Colombia (I)	.39*	.57**
Colombia (I)—Other Developing Countries (I)	.40*	—
Turkey (I)—Other Developing Countries (I)	−.41*	—
Turkey (I)—Uruguay (S)	.62***	—
Turkey (I)—Argentina (S)	.78***	.45*
Thailand (I)—El Salvador (S)	−.69***	−.61***
Colombia (I)—El Salvador (S)	−.34*	−.61***
Turkey (I)—Egypt (D)	.47**	.79***
Other Developing Countries (I)—Egypt (D)	—	−.40*
Other Developing Countries (I)—Pakistan (D)	−.76***	−.58***
Other Developing Countries (I)—India (D)	−.52**	—
Argentina (S)—Uruguay (S)	.94***	.49**
El Salvador (S)—India (D)	—	−.52**
Uruguay (S)—Egypt (D)	—	−.52**
Pakistan (D)—India (D)	.85***	.84***

[1](I)—increase in share of total world exports of selected manufactures; (D)—decrease in share of total world exports of selected manufactures; (S)—no change in share of total world exports of selected manufactures.
* = .01   ** = .05   *** = .001   —association not significant   n = 25

of a number of other developing countries. The other developing countries group in particular suffered market losses that were negatively associated with gains by a number of the NICs. Rather than there having been a shift in comparative advantage from the NICs to other developing states, the NICs instead seemed to have captured markets from them.

The associations between the various developing countries displayed a mixed pattern.

Sometimes export positions were positively associated and at other times negatively linked. Positive correlations among Thailand, Malaysia, Indonesia, and Colombia indicate that these four countries were performing similarly in many of the same product categories. As was the case for the first period, losses in export shares by Egypt and India were matched by gains by a number of other countries, providing support for the idea that there was competition for the same markets among a number of developing states.

CONCLUSIONS

Overall, the preceding analysis provided very little evidence that there actually had been shifts in comparative advantage from the NICs to the other developing countries as had been suggested, although there was evidence that such shifts were occurring between the developed states and the NICs. One possible exception to this pattern might have been Mexico. Although Mexico was treated as an NIC, its levels of exports in 1968

Table 9.3
Significant Correlations of Changes in Exports for Country Pairs, 1976–1982

Country Pairs[1]	Measure	
	Change in Export Share	Weighted Change in Export Share
Developed Countries and Other Countries		
Developed Countries (D)—Hong Kong (I)	−.48***	−.42**
Developed Countries (D)—Mexico (I)	−.32*	−.28*
Developed Countries (D)—Brazil (I)	.35*	.40**
Developed Countries (D)—Turkey (I)	−.34*	−.29*
Developed Countries (D)—Malaysia (S)	—	−.28*
Developed Countries (D)—India (D)	−.31*	−.33*
Developed Countries (D)—Other Developing Countries	−.40**	−.36*
NICs and NICs		
Korea (I)—Brazil (I)	—	.31*
NICs and Developing Countries		
Singapore (I)—Thailand (I)	.30*	.33*
Korea (I)—Thailand (I)	.28*	.44**
Korea (I)—Malaysia (S)	.32*	.37*
Korea (I)—Argentina (S)	−.28*	—
Korea (I)—El Salvador (S)	−.35*	−.50***
Korea (I)—Uruguay (S)	−.55***	−.46**
Hong Kong (I)—Other Developing Countries (D)	−.48***	−.42**
Korea (I)—Other Developing Countries (D)	−.50***	−.50***
Brazil (I)—Other Developing Countries (D)	−.64***	−.72***
Singapore (I)—Other Developing Countries (D)	—	−.33*
Mexico (I)—India (D)	−.27*	—

Table 9.3 *continued*

Country Pairs[1]	Change in Export Share	Weighted Change in Export Share
	Measure	
Developing Countries and Developing Countries		
Thailand (I)—Indonesia (I)	.59***	.57***
Thailand (I)—Malaysia (S)	.28*	.32*
Indonesia (I)—Malaysia (S)	—	.43**
Thailand (I)—Colombia (S)	.46**	.34*
Indonesia (I)—Colombia (S)	.51**	.34*
Thailand (I)—El Salvador (S)	—	−.32*
Pakistan (I)—El Salvador (S)	−.37*	−.29*
Pakistan (I)—India (D)	−.61***	−.69***
Thailand (I)—Egypt (D)	−.44**	−.28*
Indonesia (I)—Egypt (D)	−.28*	—
Argentina (S)—Uruguay (S)	.65***	.71***
Argentina (S)—Malaysia (S)	−.34*	—
Uruguay (S)—Malaysia (S)	−.45**	—
Argentina (S)—Colombia (S)	—	−.50***
Uruguay (S)—Colombia (S)	−.33*	—
Colombia (S)—Egypt (D)	−.46**	—
Argentina (S)—Egypt (D)	—	−.29*
Uruguay (S)—Egypt (D)	.30*	—
Uruguay (S)—Other Developing Countries (D)	.28*	.31*
El Salvador (S)—Other Developing Countries (D)	.33*	.37*

[1](I)—increase in share of total world exports of selected manufactures; (D)—decrease in share of total world exports of selected manufactures; (S)—no change in share of total world exports of selected manufactures.

* = .01   ** = .05   *** = .001   —association not significant $n = 37$

for the selected manufactures was relatively low, and its pattern of associations was different from that of the other NICs. During the 1968 to 1976 period, Mexico may have been in the process of moving to the status of an NIC and may have profited from shifts in comparative advantage, perhaps from Hong Kong. Although this one case is hardly conclusive, it might indicate that states that have achieved an appropriate level of industrialization and that are what might be termed near-NICs are the developing countries most likely to be able to gain from the hypothesized shifts in comparative advantage from existing NICs.

The lack of evidence for shifts in comparative advantage from 1976 to 1982 and the presence of evidence of NIC gains from other developing states, as well as the evidence of competition among the non-NIC developing countries, could all reflect at least in part the downturn in the international economy that took place in this period and the economic problems that most countries in the world were facing. The increase protectionism in the industrialized states could also have played a role, particularly in the area of textiles, with the negotiation and implementation of the Multi-Fibre Textile Agreements. Clothing and footwear were also areas subject to increased protection, and these are product areas in which many developing countries have export potential (Pelzman, 1984). The presence of these protectionist practices would have limited the opportunity for shifts in comparative advantage to occur. Protectionism in EC countries would have had an impact in particular since it would maintain higher levels of intra-EC exports and thus keep the share of the developed countries in the overall world market higher. This limit on shifts away from the EC countries could perhaps have made it less likely for NICs to shift production facilities into new product lines and at the same time made it more likely that they would maintain older export production, limiting the opportunity of other developing countries to move into new export areas. Turkey's gains in exports in this period, contrary to the prevailing trend, provides some support for this possibility since Turkey was less affected by EC limitations on imports given its economic agreements with the EC.

The 1968 to 1976 period was not a time of difficulties in the international economy, but even with an expansion of world trade, there was still little evidence of shifts in comparative advantage from the NICs to other developing states. In those cases of significant associations between NICs and developing countries where both increased their export shares, the evidence was primarily for the presence of complementary gains rather than for shifts. One possible reason for complementary export gains may have been increasing intraindustry specialization involving developing countries. Such specialization would mean increases of exports for all the countries involved in such an industrial sector. The presence of this type of specialization has been noted for Japan, the Asian NICs, and other Asian developing states in a number of manufacturing areas (Masahide, 1984, p. 145; Toyne et al., 1984, pp. 152, 157). The positive associations in Table 8.3 among the ASEAN states of Thailand, Indonesia, Malaysia, and Singapore provide some additional support for the idea that such specialization and economic cooperation can have a positive effect on the ability of countries to simultaneously gain markets for exports in some of the same product categories.

The indications of competition among the non-NIC developing countries for export markets that was present both time periods used suggests that export expansion by one developing country often does not result from shifts in comparative advantage from the industrialized states or the NICs. Rather, the gains by some of the developing countries that have occurred have apparently been at the expense of existing exporters. India and Egypt were cases in point in the above analysis and Pakistan to a lesser extent. Thus one country's progress in terms of exporting manufactures to the world market may result from a variety of factors. If the gains by one developing country essentially come at the expense of another, the possibility of net future gains for non-NIC developing countries is obviously limited.

Overall, the above results provided little evidence for the presence of a process of the progressive shifting in comparative advantage from the industrialized states to the NICs and from the NICs to other developing states. In times of expanding world trade such shifts were not evident, and in times of international recession the developing states lost markets to the NICs, the most industrialized developing countries. Thus in times of worldwide economic recession and increasing protectionism, these other developing states will be the ones that face the greatest hardships. Whereas shifts in comparative advantage that benefit non-NIC developing countries may yet appear in the future, there is not much evidence that the process has been operative to date. The other developing nations may ultimately have to achieve a level of development that permits intraindustry specialization or hope for a decline of protectionism in the developed countries.

References

Balassa, Bela. 1981. *The Newly Industrializing Countries in the World Economy*. New York: Pergamon.

Cline, William R. 1984. *Exports of Manufactures from Developing Countries: Performance and Prospects for Market Access*. Washington, D.C.: Brookings Institution.

Franko, Lawrence G., and Sherry Stephenson. 1981. French Export Behavior in Third World Markets, in Center for Strategic and International Studies (ed.): *World Trade Competition and Third World Markets*. New York: Praeger, pp. 171–251.

Gruber, William H., Dileep Mehta, and Raymond Vernon. 1968. The R&D Factor in International Trade and International Investment of United States Industries. *Journal of Political Economy* 75 (1): 20–37.

Hadley, Eleanor G. 1981. Japan's Export Competitiveness in Third World Markets, in Center for Strategic and International Studies (ed.): *World Trade Competition and Third World Markets*. New York: Praeger, pp. 252–330.

Hansen, Roger D. 1979. Trade, the Developing Countries, and North-South Relations, in Institute for Contemporary Studies (ed.): *Tariffs, Quotas & Trade: The Politics of Protectionism*. San Francisco: Institute for Contemporary Studies, pp. 247–268.

Kahler, Miles. 1985. European Protectionism in Theory and Practice. *World Politics* 37 (4): 475–502.

Kellman, Mitchell, and Daniel Landau. 1984. The Nature of Japan's Comparative Advantage, 1965–80. *World Development* 12 (4): 433–438.

Kihl, Young Whan, and James M. Lutz. 1985. *World Trade Issues: Regime, Structure, and Policy*. New York: Praeger.

Krueger, Anne O. 1980. LDC Manufacturing Production and Implications for OECD Comparative Advantage, in Irving Leveson and Jimmy Wheeler (eds.): *Western Economies in Transition: Structural Change and Adjustment Policies in Industrial Countries*. Boulder, Co.: Westview, pp. 219–250.

Kumar, Krishna, and Kee Young Kim. 1984. The Koran Manufacturing Multinationals. *Journal of International Business Studies* 15 (1): 45–61.

Lowinger, Thomas C. 1975. The Technology Factor and the Export Performance of U.S. Manufacturing Industries. *Economic Enquiry* 13 (2): 221–236.

Lutz, James M., and Robert T. Green. 1983. The Product Life Cycle and the Export Position of the United States. *Journal of International Business Studies* 14 (3): 77–93.

Masahide, Shibusawa. 1984. *Japan and the Asian Pacific Region*. New York: St. Martin's.

Mullor-Sebastian, Alicia. 1983. The Product Life Cycle Theory: Empirical Evidence. *Journal of International Business Studies* 14 (3): 95–105.

Pelzman, Joseph. 1984. The Multifiber Arrangement and Its Effects on the Profit Performance of the U.S. Textile Industry, in Robert E. Baldwin and Anne O. Krueger (eds.): *The Structure and Evolution of Recent U.S. Trade Policy*. Chicago: University of Chicago Press, pp. 111–141.

Roe, Terry, and Mathew Shane. 1979. Export Performance Marketing Services, and the Technological Characteristics of the Malaysian Industrial Section. *Journal of Developing Areas* 13 (2): 175–189.

Ting, Wenlee. 1985. *Business and Technological Dynamics in Newly Industrializing Asia*. London: Quorum Books.

Toyne, Brian, et al. 1984. The International Competitiveness of the U.S. Textile Mill Products Industry: Corporate Strategies for the Future. *Journal of International Business Studies* 15 (3): 145–165.

United Nations. *Yearbook of International Trade Statistics*. New York: United Nations Statistical Office, various years.

Yoffie, David B. 1981. The Newly Industrializing Countries and the Political Economy of Protectionism. *International Studies Quarterly* 25 (4): 569–599.

Part Three

Special Issues

Each of the three chapters in Part Three is an examination of one of the most serious issues confronting international trade. In Chapter 10, Bernard Sarachek analyzes what could potentially become one of the most significant international economic events of the last quarter of the twentieth century. A single European market will not only create the world's largest economic unit, but as significantly, it will give Europe a political clout it has not enjoyed since World War II. In addition to an examination of the Single European Act (SEA), Sarachek discusses some probable effects of the SEA on trading and investment relations between the European Community and the rest of the world. Basic to his discussion is the proposition that the SEA will accelerate the development of already evolving relationships rather than create entirely new types of relationships.

Sarachek argues that the movement toward greater market unification will result in more protectionist policies in Europe. This will accelerate the new trend that is making the world tilt away from reliance on generalized rules of free trade toward particularized negotiated agreements. Consequently, Sarachek concludes, a unified European market will increase competitive challenges to non-EC economies, including the United States.

One of the implications of the creation of regional trading blocs is the inevitable increase in international investment. In Chapter 11, Darwin Wassink and Robert J. Carbaugh examine international joint ventures in one of the most significant and most internationalized industries—the automobile industry. They point out that the trend toward internationalization of the American automobile industry is accelerating and taking different forms. In addition to joint ventures, it ranges from U.S. automakers buying large minority shares in foreign auto markets to the marketing of foreign-produced cars under domestic automaker nameplates, and from the production of foreign cars in the United States to the increased installation of foreign-made parts in American automobiles.

Wassink and Carbaugh postulate that international joint ventures in the automobile industry can yield both welfare-increasing and welfare-decreasing effects for the domestic economy. They discuss a model to measure the welfare effects of international joint ventures and conclude by applying their model to the specific case of the New United Motor Manufacturing, Inc. (NUMMI), a 50-50 joint venture agreement between General Motors and Toyota Motor Corporation to produce Chevrolet Novas and small trucks in GM's idle Fremont plant.

The impact of foreign competition on domestic employment has long been a cause for concern among policymakers and practitioners as well as the students of international trade. In Chapter 12, Catherine Mann examines the specific impact of foreign competition on employment in certain import-sensitive U.S. industries. Her objective is to focus on the general determinants of domestic employment when an industry is faced with foreign competition in prices and quantities. To that end, Mann develops a three-factor production function. The point of her estimation equation is to determine (1) whether competition for market share, as well as in prices, is an important determinant of domestic employment, and (2) whether foreign competition in prices and quantities is *the* most important determinant of domestic employment. The conclusion of the study is that domestic economic conditions are far more important than foreign competition in determining employment levels. Therefore, Mann concludes that protectionism will be an inefficient mechanism for alleviating domestic employment problems that are caused by internal and not external sources.

Chapter 10

THE TRADE IMPLICATIONS OF THE SINGLE EUROPEAN ACT

Bernard Sarachek

INTRODUCTION

In 1985 the European Council of the Heads of State asked the EC Commission to draft proposals that would move the EC toward true economic unification by 1992. The Commission proposed almost 300 directives, which collectively constitute the Single European Act (SEA). Broadly, the goals of the SEA are: (1) to intensify a sense of "European" regional identity, (2) to accelerate economic growth by eliminating duplication and by encouraging efficient location and scale economies, and (3) to compete with Japan and the United States by accelerating the pace of research and development within the EC. The task of reconstructing and unifying the EC cannot be entirely self-contained. This mammoth undertaking must have ramifications on other regions and their trading relations with the EC. This chapter focuses on some possible external impacts of the SEA.

THE SEA AND EUROPEAN INTEGRATION

The SEA is an attempt to remove restrictions to the movement of goods, people, capital, media, and information across EC internal borders. National barriers to services would be eliminated. Banking, financial, computer, telecommunication, and many other services could become freely deliverable across national boundaries within the EC. The SEA would harmonize EC standards pertaining to health, consumer protection, and technical product, and production specifications. Accounting standards and the standards regulating the practice of professional groups would be harmonized, enabling certified professionals to practice across borders. Capital movements and trading patterns would conform closer to true market efficiencies as distorting differences in fiscal and monetary practices of nations are eliminated. The European patent system would be perfected by eliminating national differences and shifting patent regulation to the EC Community level.

Economic unification would also be fostered by non-SEA programs, including the Eurotunnel connecting Britain to the continent, the European Monetary System and various technology consortia such as the Airbus Industries, the European Space Agency, Eurika, Euratom, and the EC's four Joint Research Centers. The wave of industrial denationalization occurring during the 1980s also contributes to the economic unification of the EC.

The study headed by Paolo Cecchini, and sponsored by the EC Commission, optimistically describes the benefits the Community would derive from greater economic unification. That study estimates that the SEA will create two–five million additional jobs in the EC, while adding between 5–7% to the Community's GNP (Cecchini, 1986).

PROBABILITY OF SUCCESS

Being primarily economic rather than political, the process of unifying Europe has been particularly complex. Political unification in other historical instances has usually preceded economic unification. This, for example, was the case when the original thirteen American states formed the United States. It was also the case when the Europeans delineated each of their various colonies around the world, and when the tsars expanded Russia from Europe to Siberia. Political unification of a relatively few critical institutions is usually easier to achieve than economic unity, especially if most citizens' political awareness is underdeveloped or focused on local rather than national matters. Economic unification, by contrast, invariably boils down to sculpting and interweaving a great many institutions in which innumerable individuals and groups have vested interests to defend.

Initial attempts at political unification would have been impossible in an economically advanced region such as Europe, with its strong nationalistic jealousies and well-defined cultural heritages. Countries such as Belgium, Yugoslavia, Spain, and the United Kingdom cannot fully resolve their internal cultural differences. How could the twelve members of the EC hope to achieve political unification? Since immediate political unification was too herculean an effort, Europeans have had to be content with the tedious microsurgery of forging economic unification bit by bit.

Viewed in this light, there is little reason for skepticism or pessimism regarding the SEA's chances of success. Success must be measured in degrees. It is not a "go, no-go" proposition. Already, the EC has come a long way toward greater market unification since its official beginnings in 1957. This process can be expected to continue, albeit in fits and starts.

The current merger movement and the wave of cooperative arrangements set off in business, finance, and banking by the awareness of 1992's competitive threats and opportunities have undoubtedly moved the EC a giant step toward greater unification. Even companies in non-EC countries have been induced to seek mergers to assure themselves of market niches within a potentially unified EC, or to form stronger economic entities within their own home markets that could fend off more vigorous competition from newly merged EC firms. Recent denationalization and deregulations of various industries within the EC have also fueled the drive to merge, ally, and internationalize. Even if 1992 falls short of expectations, momentum toward unification is real.

Still, it must be acknowledged that Europe is far from united in its acceptance of the SEA. The peripheral poor of the EC (that is, Ireland, Greece, Portugal) welcome the added employment the SEA might bring. At the same time, however, they fear that economic unification will flood their domestic markets with other EC countries' goods, and their native businesses and resources will be acquired by firms from other EC nations. Proposed regional harmonizations of taxation and banking laws mean that Luxembourg risks its privileged position as a tax haven, offshore banking center, and shopping haven. London risks a diminished role as the financial capital of Europe if an EC central bank is created and headquartered elsewhere, or if monetary unification leads to regulation of the Euro-money markets. Business within the prosperous Munich-Lyon-Milan triangle will disproportionally benefit from the SEA, whereas the depressed coal- and steel-producing areas of Britain, Lorraine, and the Ruhr could suffer diminished economic roles. Nationally based labor unions will find it necessary to negotiate with larger enterprises dispersed throughout the EC. More heavily unionized countries such as Britain and West Germany fear that the SEA will induce job migrations to lower labor cost countries, and will result in a general reduction in the working standards of their workers. The EC Commission's desire to eliminate company practices such as the issuance of bearer securities, the use of "silent reserves," and corporate charter restrictions on the voting rights of alien stockholders could expose companies to greater risks of unfriendly takeovers.

The SEA's goal of forging a European identity involves adjustments in the existing EC political institutions. The review and decision-making powers of the European Assembly will be strengthened. Decisions of the Council of Ministers are currently based on majority vote rather than unanimous agreement, as in the past. A Court of First Instance has been established below the Court of Justice. There is even talk of changing the selection process for the EC president to one of popular election. Changes such as these may augment the sovereignty of the EC's political machinery, but they can only come at the cost of a more restricted sovereignty for member nations. Indeed, many fear that the SEA could result in a politically more centralized Europe that will impose too many social programs and too much Eurocratic bureaucracy rather than establish a more open competitive environment. Fears of restrictive welfare programs and inefficiently centralized bureaucracy are particularly strong in the U.K. and Germany.

The simple fact is that there will be winners and losers within the EC. For a few, the SEA could represent the possibility of absolute losses. Even if some areas or groups gain absolutely but lose relatively to others, adverse consequences can follow in the form of diminished political influences for those relative losers within the European Community.

Economic protectionism may be the price the EC must pay to gain support for the SEA from all of its constituencies. Concern over possible EC protectionism is not limited to EFTA nations, North America, and Japan. Communist countries of Eastern Europe and the Muslim countries of Africa and the Middle East have felt this concern. It is partly reflected in Morocco's unsuccessful attempt to join the EC, and Turkey's current interest in joining.

Austria will probably apply for membership in the EC sometime during 1989, though the EC Commission has repeatedly stated that no new members would be accepted until the SEA has successfully created a unified market. Norway is another EFTA country that is seriously considering the possibility of joining the EC. Still other EFTA nations could follow in order to take advantage of the opportunities that EC membership offers and to avoid protective exclusion from EC markets. This could result in the effective demise of EFTA. Even if it survives, it will be effectively reduced to little more than the EC's "shadow."

THE SEA IN WORLD CONTEXT

The effects of the SEA on non-EC nations will probably not be unique. The SEA will contribute to evolving tendencies that already exist in the world trading system. For example, the world has been experiencing a trend toward greater monetary and industrial globalization. This was dramatically demonstrated in October of 1986 when the British financial community experienced its "Big Bang" of deregulation. Nations have discovered that their policies are becoming increasingly interdependent. Changes in fiscal budgetary and monetary policies have much more immediate impacts on exchange rates and capital flows between nations than in earlier decades. Unintended consequences frequently follow, both for the nation that initiates a policy change and for other nations.

As national discretion in matters relating to fiscal and monetary policies diminishes, fewer tools remain available to governments attempting to preserve jobs and domestic economic growth. Trade protection and export stimulation become increasingly attractive policies. This trend exists even without the SEA, but to the extent that the goal of European economic unification diminishes the discretionary fiscal and monetary policies of member nations, it increases the value of trade protection to the Community.

Protectionist sentiments today are still rather moderate among the industrialized nations. The experiences of the 1930s have left a deep impression concerning the futility of extreme autarky. Neither an abiding faith in free trade nor a commitment to protectionism can be expected to mark the future of world trade. The consequence may well be an intermediate trade pattern that mixes elements of protection and free trade, but is predominantly characterized by bilateral and multilateral regulation of trade in particularly strategic or trade-sensitive industries. More frequently than in the recent past decades, trade agreements will give differing privileges and duties to each nation, rather than establishing a few globally recognized rules applicable to all nations.

The current and previous EC commissioners for external relations have each indicated that the EC would seek something other than "rigid maximalist positions" toward free trade, and that negotiation is the key to enhanced trade (Andriessen, 1989; cf. Choate and Linger, 1988; Rowley, 1988). The SEA will reenforce the Commission's role as the bargainer for the EC. By further unifying the European bloc of nations, the SEA will set the stage for increased particularized bilateral and multilateral bloc negotiations. The goal of achieving generally applicable world trading rules based on traditional free trade principles will recede, and the focus will shift toward negotiating more particularized trading relationships.

A BUSINESS IDENTITY FOR THE COMMUNITY

The EC will not unify its markets merely to open them to penetration by non-Europeans. Europe must be convinced that local affiliates are "European" rather than mere extensions of their foreign parent firms. IBM-Europe exemplifies a subsidiary that has gone far toward achieving a European identity. A 1978 study commissioned by the French president identified IBM as a foreign enterprise whose dominance in the computer industry threatened France's security, its citizens' civil liberties, and its government's integrity (Nora and Minc, 1981). During the early 1980s, IBM was also the object of the largest antimonopoly investigation ever conducted by the EC Commission.

IBM substantially revised its image, expanding its R&D operations in Europe. The company bid successfully for research funds granted by the EC. IBM-Europe's management meets regularly with representatives of the EC Commission to reduce the possibility of running afoul of the EC's antimonopoly regulation. IBM-Europe was decentralized in 1986, shifting many decision-making powers from the Paris headquarters to its various national subsidiaries in Europe. At the same time, however, IBM continues to follow a regional policy of producing different products in each of its fifteen European plants, so that each plant supplies all of Europe. IBM has also negotiated the possibility of selling parts and personal computers under European competitors' labels.

Like IBM, after 1992 other U.S. multinationals will have to share their technology more readily with Europe. Local subsidiaries will have to assume distinctly European identities well differentiated from those of their U.S. parent companies.

To assume the full character of a European company, local subsidiaries of foreign firms will find it necessary to rely on local sourcing. Already subsidiaries of companies like DuPont and 3M source almost entirely from within Europe. Thus far the Europeans have been relatively moderate in their demands that U.S. firms source locally. Having seen the advance of the Japanese in the U.S. market, and currently watching increased Japanese incursions into their own markets, EC nations are much more sensitive to the threat of Japanese encroachments. Products produced in the United States by Japanese firms have been treated as Japanese products for purposes of EC import restrictions. For example, the EC has counted U.S. manufactured exports of Honda automobiles as Japanese imports. At least 60% of a product must be sourced from within Europe to be considered as European-produced. The EC is currently considering raising the local content requirement for foreign subsidiaries of Japanese firms to an even higher percentage (Lubin, 1989; Nelson and O'Boyle, 1988).

The development of European identities will not be limited to affiliates of non-EC firms. For firms that are rapidly expanding regionally, such as Philips, Siemens, Olivetti, Amrobank, and Volkswagen, their "home country" is starting to appear as the EC rather than their original state of origin. As part of the drive toward market unification, EC member nations have been encouraged to cease the practices of favoring "national champions" in matters relating to government contracting, subsidies, and legislation. It remains to be seen whether a new brand of EC regionwide "national champions" will arise to receive any special favors that the political machinery of the EC could dispense.

U.S. "INDUSTRIAL POLICIES"

By contributing to the EC's economic development and by stimulating the growth of larger European multinational corporations, the SEA should have the effect of intensifying competition in global markets. This will add to the inducements that already exist for the U.S. government to alter its own approaches to business. Some specific areas are discussed below.

1. Globalization of finance and banking has intensified the need to revise the Glass-Steagle Act. Europe's current merger movement in banking and finance in anticipation of 1992 merely adds to this need. The separation of commercial and investment banking mandated by the Glass-Steagle Act places domestic U.S. banking institutions at competitive disadvantages. Domestic U.S. investment banks are denied the benefit of the capital support that commercial banks can obtain from customers' deposits, whereas commercial banks are denied access to the profit opportunities to be found in investment banking. By comparison, the international European banks have the competitive advantage of being able to practice "universal banking," uniting all phases of commercial and investment banking both domestically and internationally.

The Glass-Steagle Act could also fall victim to the EC's demands for reciprocity. If U.S. banks are allowed to enter or remain in Europe and practice universal banking, EC banks should be permitted to compete as universal bankers within the United States. The United States will be hard put to resist EC demands for reciprocity, especially since many of the largest U.S. banks already favor the repeal of Glass-Steagle.

2. Despite Americans' customary suspicions of government-business alliances, the U.S. government does not assume a "hands-off" stance toward business. Traditionally, U.S. industrial policy has been one of propping up declining industries and neglecting industries (excepting agriculture and defense) where U.S. competitive advantages are strong. Unlike Japan and Europe, the United States prefers to protect declining industries such as shoes, textiles, and steel, rather than push forefront industries in which it has its strongest comparative advantages.

The numerous government-sponsored technology consortia created within the EC follow Japan's practice of supporting sunrise industries. The EC views the closing of its high technology gap with the United States and Japan as vital to its future welfare (cf. Pierre, 1987). If the SEA intensifies competition in forefront industries, present U.S. government industrial policy will appear all the more unrealistic. Hopefully, competition may eventually convince the U.S. government to support positions of business strength rather than protect positions of weakness.

3. A new pattern of inter-firm competition has emerged around the industrial world. The classical Ricardian-Marshallian model identified competition as a market condition in which individual firms operate autonomously. Cooperative arrangements among firms traditionally were identified as collusion, the very antithesis of competition. However, as Harrigan (1986) has indicated, it is increasingly the case that modern competitors within the same industry will form partial alliances in selected stages of research, production, or marketing. The purposes of these partial alliances are *inter alia,* to increase productive efficiencies, reach otherwise inaccessible markets, create new innovations, and in general gain the competitive strength.

Competition-cooperation arrangements may take a wide variety of forms such as joint ventures, countertrade piggyback marketing arrangements, and joint research and development of new products. Competition-cooperation is apparent in highly competitive mature industries such as steel, beverages, and automobiles as well as in competitive high technology industries such as computers, telecommunications, and biotechnology. It characterizes almost any highly competitive global industry.

The SEA will intensify the need to resort to competition-cooperation arrangements by increasing global competitive pressures. Certainly the EC and its various member nations have favored, and even subsidized, consortiums of firms in industries in which Europeans are competitively behind the United States or Japan.

Within the United States this competition-cooperation pattern most frequently combines U.S. firms with foreign firms. This seems reasonable since alliances frequently seek some benefits that could only come by combining partners foreign to one another. One partner, for example, might seek foreign technological know-how, whereas the other might seek access to a market that would be otherwise blocked by some government action. However, to some degree a number of alliances between U.S. firms and foreign firms must be credited to the fact that the U.S. courts would tolerate alliances with foreigners that they would not tolerate between domestic American firms. If GM and Toyota form a joint venture, our antitrust authorities raise no objection. If United Air Lines and British Airways pool ground facilities and various customer services at U.S. airports connecting domestic and international routes, the government says nothing. Such arrangements would be unthinkable between GM and Chrysler, or Pan American and United.

American courts may finally recognize that U.S. industries cannot be evaluated exclusively in terms of the domestic U.S. market. If this pattern of competition-cooperation strengthens European competitors, and if Europe does become more protectionist, the need for U.S. firms to cooperatively muster their competitive efficiencies will rise proportionately.

The competitive pressures of foreign trade have already forced the United States to take some steps down the road toward greater relaxation of our antitrust laws. For example, the Export Trading Company Act of 1982 enables competitors to share information and export through the same trading company while remaining exempt from criminal prosecution under the antitrust laws. Moreover, the National Cooperative Research Act of 1984 increases the freedom of firms to form joint research and development ventures. (Joint research and development ventures could still be held in violation of the antitrust laws, but they cannot be deemed illegal per se.)

4. No county has extended its legal jurisdiction extraterritorially to the extent and frequency of the United States. This has caused resentment among most European nations. Several European nations have created laws preventing their citizens from providing information to foreign courts.

Both the EC Court and Commission have shown much greater willingness than individual member nations to extend European law extraterritorially. To the extent that the governmental machinery of the EC will grow in importance relative to that of member nations, the United States could find it much easier to negotiate mutual accommodations regarding appropriate extraterritorial legal uses. This has importance for antitrust enforcement, securities regulation, banking regulation, environmental controls, and consumer protection, to mention a few areas.

EASTERN AND WESTERN EUROPE

Despite Eastern Europe's concern that the EC might become overly protectionist, economic reunification of Eastern and Western Europe now seems imminent. The temporal coincidence of *perestroika* and the SEA can benefit both Western and Eastern Europe. These two agendas share the fact that they seem to be irreversible, even if they do not turn out to be as successful as their advocates would wish. Strong historic, cultural, and economic ties persist between parliamentary and Communist Europe. These ties are particularly strong between West Germany and France, on the one hand, and Eastern Europe, on the other. Austria and Switzerland are important economic and political bridges between Eastern and Western Europe. Should they enter the EC, they will bring with them an extensive infrastructure of business contacts with Eastern Europe.

Militarily, economic interdependence is the best defense Western Europe could establish against any remaining Eastern European threat. From a Soviet perspective, if *perestroika* is an admission of military defeat, it is better to "surrender" to Western Europe. The United States and Japan are the world's two economic superpowers. Closer ties to them would reduce the Soviet's bargaining power and increase its economic dependency. The Soviets will have greater policy space for maneuver by building their strongest ties to a confederation of Western European nations. Conversely, the reconstruction of East-West ties within Europe would weaken the political and military threat against the USSR posed by the Atlantic Alliance. Certainly, this was a major concern expressed by the U.S. government, for example, in 1980–1981 when the agreement was reached to build a pipeline between the USSR and several Western European countries to supply Western Europe with Siberian natural gas.

In June 1988 the Council for Mutual Economic Assistance (COMECON) formally recognized the EC for the first time. Officials from the two regional associations met to discuss the improvement of economic ties between them. Each COMECON country has established, or is planning to establish, formal diplomatic links directly with the EC. One COMECON country, Hungary, has even been reported to be flirting with the possibility of eventually becoming a member of the EC ("Hungary," 1988).

Since the pact between COMECON and the EC was concluded, a significant increase in economic contacts has taken place between EC countries and the USSR. Private Western European bankers in 1988 and 1989 extended approximately $6 billion of new loans to the USSR European companies have entered into numerous deals to help modernize Soviet industry. Some European diplomats have expressed interest in having their governments extend foreign aid to the USSR.

Such pan-European ties constitute a threat to COCOM, the watchdog arrangement established to ensure that strategic products and technology are not exported to Marxist-Leninist countries. Increasingly, the United States' European allies are chafing under the restrictions that COCOM imposes on their trade contacts with COMECON countries. Furthermore, COCOM is inconsistent with the goal of European market unification since it necessitates the issuance of reexport licenses restricting the free movement of goods between EC member nations, whether those goods originated within or outside the EC. It is, of course, possible that EC communitywide enforcement of COCOM could result. How that might work is still unclear. In any event, should the responsibility for the enforcement of COCOM be shifted more fully from individual member states to the EC, tensions concerning the proper locus of sovereignty might well be aggravated.

Any European reconciliation will also make it easier to draw the nations of EFTA further into the EC's sphere of economic influence. For example, East-West reconciliation would eliminate any external political block to Finland's membership in the EC.

THE FUTURE OF EC

At least one additional question remains to be discussed when considering the ramifications of the SEA. Will the EC continue to expand geographically, and if so, to what extent will it be able to expand?

Any EFTA nation could be introduced into EC membership without engendering particularly great stress on the EC's internal unity. Some EFTA nations such as Switzerland and Finland might themselves experience significant internal political strains. However, the industries, monetary systems, and general economic life of EFTA have become so harmonized and interdependent with the EC that membership would do relatively little to change their economic relations to the current members of the Community.

Countries such as Turkey and Morocco constitute real dilemmas. Middle Eastern and North African nations have very different ethnic and religious backgrounds from the EC nations. Their economies frequently compete with the southern members of the EC, particularly in agriculture and with regard to labor skills. In the case of Turkey, for example, some EC nations are content to see Greek-Turkish tensions perpetuate, and experience discomfort when those tensions ease. Middle Eastern and North African countries either have fragile parliamentary democratic political systems, or have political systems that would not be considered as parliamentary democracies by the EC.

The EC faces some major contradictions. The more members it includes, the more difficult it is to achieve a consensus regarding the role and future of the association. Furthermore, the more members included, the greater the possibility that member nations may have economies that compete rather than complement one another. Workers in wealthier members fear the competition of lower cost workers in poorer members. Wine growers in France may resent the competition of wine growers in Italy, Spain, or Portugal. And so it goes.

A fashioning of greater economic and political unity within the EC, as the SEA attempts, will eventually moderate these internal stresses as the populace of the EC moves closer to accepting a common identity. Unification, however, reduces the association's ability and willingness to absorb additional nations as new members.

At the same time that enlarging the number of member nations generates increased internal stresses and increases the difficulty of accepting still more members, the impulse for the EC to continue to expand remains. It is politically dangerous—and therefore economically dangerous—for the EC not to continue its expansion. The admission of Greece, Spain, and Portugal into the EC reenforced their fledgling democracies and added insurance against the possibility that fascism or communism would reappear on the southern flank of the EC. Just so, the EC may feel the compulsion to consider Turkey and other nations for potential membership. A democratic Turkey, reenforced by membership in the EC, could exert an influence on its own Muslim neighbors, encouraging them to reject radicalism either of a religious fundamentalist caste or of a Marxist-Leninist one. Furthermore, if the SEA will be a step toward solidifying a European trading bloc in competition with the Pacific Rim region, it follows that the competitive capabilities of the EC will be enhanced by continuing its expansion in order to integrate more national economies and gain greater access to more markets and resources.

Somewhat similar dilemmas for the EC might be in store if reconciliation does take place between Eastern and Western Europe. An Eastern European country—Hungary or Poland, for example—may actually request membership some day. Would there be a temptation for the EC to reject these applicants due to the fact that their modern political institutions are unlike those of the EC, and due to differences in their economic levels of attainment and the manners by which their economies are organized? At the same time, would the EC feel the compulsion to consider such applicants in order to open wider the economic doors to its neighbors and in order to foster more democratic political traditions in nations neighboring the EC?

One way that the EC may fend off this dilemma is to support the existence of other blocs of countries by sharing with them some of the benefits to be derived from EC economic unification. If the envisioned European Economic Space would provide sufficient access of EFTA nations to the EC, EFTA nations would have less motivation to formally join the EC. Perhaps a similar arrangement may someday be worked out between the EC and COMECON, so that the benefits to an individual Eastern European country of closer involvement in the EC's market would come through that country's COMECON membership rather than at the expense of that nation's allegiance and support for COMECON.

CONCLUSIONS

Since World War II, the world's economic center of gravity has been shifting from the Atlantic to the Pacific. The Single European Act was born in large measure out of the realization that Europe must become more unified if it is to regain its competitiveness with the Pacific Rim. If Europe were to achieve the type of growth and development that would place it fully on par with the Pacific Rim, one could predict a world in which relatively equivalent interdependence would occur between Europe, the United States, Japan, and the rapidly expanding economies of East and Southeast Asia. This, however, will probably not be the case. A low-growth aging population, problems of national and ethnic diversities, natural resource limitations, and the prior existence of well-defined national economies with differing national institutions are among the constraints that limit Europe's drive to achieve a competitive par with the Pacific Rim.

This does not negate the fact that important strides toward growth, technological advancement, and economic unification will be made as a consequence of the SEA. However, it is doubtful that Europe will experience the dramatic sort of economic expansion that has been witnessed in East and Southeast Asia. It is for this reason that we may expect to see a world dominated by two major trading areas—a reunified Europe and the Pacific Rim. European unification is, after all, a defensive strategy. To unify in order to diminish its internal diversities and to reformulate its industry and technology in a more competitive fashion, Europe will probably tend to become more inward looking.

As an essentially defensive strategy, it is reasonable to suppose that the SEA will reenforce world trading patterns already in the making rather than generate newer ones. This is true whether the patterns are the definition of two predominant trading areas, the reenforcement of competition-cooperation market patterns in world industries, the shift from generalized rules of world trade to more particularized negotiated agreements, the decline of EFTA, or the growth of governments' support for national sunrise industries.

References

Andriessen, Frans. 1989. Close U.S. EC Cooperation Vital for World Trade. *Europe* No. 284, pp. 14–15.

Cecchini, Paulo, *et al.* 1988. *The European Challenge: 1992*. Gower: Aldershot.

Choate, Pat, and Juyne Linger. 1988. Tailored Trade. *Harvard Business Review* 66 (1): 86–93.

Harrigan, Kathryn R. 1986. *Managing for Joint Venture Success*. Lexington, MA: Lexington Books.

Hungary Looks West. 1988. *Wall Street Journal*. November 14, p. B28.

Lubin, Joann S. 1989. Japanese Auto Makers Jostling Past EC's Import Curbs. *Wall Street Journal,* March 17, p. A8.

Nelson, Mark M., and Thomas F. O'Boyle. 1988. EC's Auto Plan Would Keep Japan at Bay. *Wall Street Journal,* October 27, p. A10.

Nora, Simon, and Alain Minc. 1981. *The Computerization of Society*. Cambridge: MIT Press.

Pierre, Andrew J. (ed.). 1987. *A High Technology Gap?* New York: Council on Foreign Relations.

Rowley, Anthony. 1988. Twelvefold Reciprocity. *Far Eastern Economic Review* 141 (29): 65.

United Nations. 1987. *United Nations Demographic Yearbook, Population and Vital Statistics*. New York: United Nations.

Chapter 11

WELFARE EFFECTS OF INTERNATIONAL JOINT VENTURES IN THE WORLD AUTO INDUSTRY

Darwin Wassink and Robert J. Carbaugh

The American auto industry is undergoing an evolution in which the "all-American car" is rapidly becoming a thing of the past. Although American automakers will continue to develop and build their own midsize and large autos in the United States, they are turning over increasing amounts of small car production to foreign competitors, mainly the Japanese. This process intensifies the demands for protectionism among American auto workers. Reflecting this trend, in 1984 General Motors, Inc. and Toyota, Inc. of Japan formed a joint venture that assembles subcompact autos for sale in the United States. This chapter examines possible welfare effects of international joint ventures among competing auto producers.

INTERNATIONAL JOINT VENTURES

The trend toward the internationalization of the American auto industry is documented by an increasing variety of commercial interrelationships between American and foreign automakers. For example, General Motors owns 34% of Isuzu and 5% of Suzuki; Ford owns 25% of Mazda; and Chrysler owns 15% of Mitsubishi. Internationalization also includes the production of foreign cars in the United States—such as Accords being produced in the Honda plant in Marysville, Ohio—just as it does the production of American-brand cars overseas, such as the Ford Escort being manufactured in Western European plants. It involves the marketing of foreign-produced autos under domestic nameplates, such as the Chrysler Colt produced in Japan by Mitsubishi and shipped to the United States. The installation of foreign-produced components in U.S. automobiles also reflects the internationalization trend. Finally, the General Motors-Toyota and Chrysler-Mitsubishi joint ventures, to assemble subcompact cars in the United States, indicates a fundamental shift in thinking about the way to produce and market automobiles. Table 11.1 summarizes the Japanese-managed auto assembly plants in the United States as of 1989.

If a company is to participate in international business, it must enjoy some advantage over foreign firms. A cost advantage is necessary if the company is to export. Licensing is profitable only if the company owns a production process or patent that can be transferred overseas for a fee. Establishing foreign subsidiaries requires the company to have an advantage over local firms in the country where the subsidiary is established.

In a trend that accelerated during the 1980s, companies have linked up with their former rivals in a vast array of joint ventures. A *joint venture* is a business organization established by two or more companies that combine their skills and assets. It may have a limited objective (e.g., research or production) and be short-lived. Joint ventures may be multinational in character, involving cooperation among domestic and foreign companies. Joint ventures differ from mergers in that they involve the creation of a new business firm, rather than the union of two existing companies. Table 11.2 provides examples of recent joint ventures between Japanese and Western motor vehicle assemblers.

There are several types of international joint ventures. First is a joint venture formed by two firms that conducts a business in a third country. For example, an American and a British oil firm may form a joint venture for oil exploration in the Middle East. Next is the formation of a joint venture with local private interests. Honeywell Information Systems, Inc. of Japan was formed by Honeywell, Inc. of the United States and Mitsubishi Office Machinery Co. of Japan to sell information systems equipment to the Japanese. Last is a joint venture that includes local government participation. Bechtel Co. of the United States, Messerschmitt-Boelkow-Blom of West Germany, and National Iranian Oil Co. (representing the government of Iran) formed Iran Oil Investment Co. for oil extraction in Iran.

The joint ventures between U.S. and Japanese auto manufacturers have been formed to provide benefits to both the U.S. and Japanese firms. U.S. auto manufacturers see the joint venture as a method of learning more about the efficiencies of Japanese production techniques. This, they believe, will allow them to reduce production costs and improve efficiency over those levels that would occur if they undertook production on

Table 11.1

Japanese-Managed Assembly Operation in the United States, 1989

Company	Product	Capacity	Start Date
Honda	Accord, Civic	360,000	1982
Nissan	Sentra/pickup	240,000	1983
NUMMI	Nova/Corolla FX16	250,000	1984
Mazda	MX-6/Probe	300,000	1987
Diamond-Star	Mirage/Colt	240,000	1988
Toyota	Camry	200,000	1988
Suburu/Isuzu	Small car/small truck	120,000	1989
		1,710,000	

Source: Wall Street Journal, various issues.

Table 11.2
Ventures between Japanese and Western Motor Vehicle Assemblers

Joint Ventures

Name of Venture	Partners	Initiated	Location	Activity
Alfa Romeo Nissan Automobiles (ARNA)	Nissan/ Alfa Romeo	1980	Naples, Italy	Assembly of cars and light trucks, some joint design of the body
New United Motor Manufacturing (NUMMI)	General Motors/ Toyota	1984	Fremont, California	Assembly of a preexisting Toyota design
Diamond-Star Motors	Chrysler/ Mitsubishi Motors	1985	Bloomington, Illinois	Assembly of a small car, some joint design of the body
	General Motors/ Suzuki	1986	Ingersoll, Ontario	Assembly of preexisting Suzuki design

Collaborations[1]

Partners	Activity	Date Initiated
Honda/BL	Joint design and shared production of XX and YY models	1973
Daimler-Benz/ Mitsubishi Motors	Joint design and production of a light commercial vehicle in Spain	1984
Ford/Mazda	Production in a Mexican Ford facility of a Mazda-designed product using Mazda's process technology and process engineering/management assistance	1984

[1]"Collaboration" suggests the joint design or manufacture of products without the creation of a shared-equity, legal entity.
Source: Adapted from James Womack, Multinational Joint Ventures in Motor Vehicles, in David Mowery (ed.): *International Collaborative Ventures in U.S. Manufacturing* (Cambridge, MA: Ballinger, 1988), p. 314.

their own. Japanese producers see these joint ventures as an additional method of penetrating the American market as well as, and probably more importantly as, a way to reduce their vulnerability to potential protectionist actions by the United States.

International joint ventures can yield both welfare-increasing effects and welfare-decreasing effects for the domestic economy. Joint ventures lead to *welfare gains* when: (1) the newly established joint venture adds to preexisting productive capacity and fosters additional competition, (2) the newly established joint venture is able to enter new markets that neither parent could have entered individually, (3) the joint venture yields cost reductions (e.g., economies of scale) that would have been unavailable if each parent performed the same function separately. However, the formation of a joint venture may give rise to increased *market power,* suggesting greater ability to influence market output and price. This could especially occur when the joint venture is formed in markets in which the parents conduct business. Under such circumstances, the parents, through their representatives in the joint venture, agree on prices and output in the very market that they themselves operate. Such coordination of activities limits competition, reinforces upward pressure on prices, and lowers the level of domestic welfare.

The example below contrasts two situations: (1) where two competing firms sell autos in the domestic market, and (2) where the two competitors form a joint venture that operates as a single seller (i.e., monopoly) in the domestic market. We would expect to see a higher price and smaller quantity in the case where the joint venture behaves as a monopoly. This will always occur as long as the marginal cost curve for the joint venture is identical to the horizontal sum of the marginal cost curves of the individual competitors. The result of this *market-power effect* is a deadweight welfare loss for the domestic economy—a reduction in consumer surplus that is not offset by a corresponding gain to producers. If, however, the formation of the joint venture entails *productivity gains* that neither parent firm could realize prior to its formation, domestic welfare would be increased. This is because a smaller amount of the domestic economy's resources is now required to produce any given output. Whether domestic welfare rises or falls because of the joint venture depends on the magnitudes of these two opposing forces.

Figure 11.1 illustrates the welfare effects of two parent firms that form a joint venture in the market in which they operate. Assume that Sony Auto Co. of Japan and American Auto Co. of the United States are the only two firms producing autos for sale in the U.S. market. Suppose each firm realizes constant long-run costs, suggesting that average total cost equals marginal cost at each level of output. Let the cost schedules of each firm prior to the formation of the joint venture equal $MC_0 = ATC_0$, which equal $10,000. $MC_0 = ATC_0$ thus becomes the long-run market supply schedule of autos.

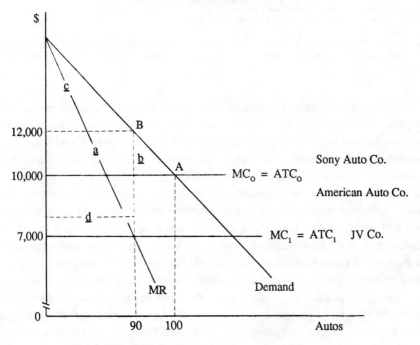

Figure 11.1. Welfare effects of an international joint venture.

Assume that Sony Auto Co. and American Auto Co. initially operate as competitors, charging a price equal to marginal cost. In Figure 1, market equilibrium exists at point *A* where 100 autos are sold at a price of $10,000 per unit. Consumer surplus totals area *a* + *b* + *c*. Producer surplus does not exist given the horizontal supply curve of autos. Now suppose the two firms announce the formation of a joint venture known as JV Co., which manufactures autos for sale in the United States. Assume the autos sold by JV Co. replace the autos sold by the two parents in the United States.

Suppose the formation of JV Co. entails new production efficiencies, which result in cost reductions. Let JV Co.'s cost schedule, $MC_1 = ATC_1$ be located at $7,000. As a monopoly, JV Co. maximizes profit by equating marginal revenue with marginal cost. Market equilibrium exists at point *B*, where 90 autos are sold at a price of $12,000 per unit. The price increase leads to a reduction in consumer surplus equal to area *a* + *b*. Of this amount, area *a* is transferred to JV Co. as producer surplus. Area *b* represents the loss of consumer surplus not transferred to JV Co., and becomes a deadweight welfare loss for the U.S. economy (i.e., consumption effect).

Against this deadweight welfare loss lies the efficiency effect of JV Co., which entails unit costs falling from $10,000 to $7,000 per auto. JV Co. can produce its profit-maximizing output, 90 autos, at a cost reduction equal to area *d* as compared to the costs that would exist if the parent firms produced the same output. Area *d* thus represents additional producer surplus, which is a welfare gain for the U.S. economy. The analysis concludes that for the United States, the formation of JV Co. is desirable if area *d* exceeds area *b*.

It has been assumed that JV Co. entails cost reductions that are the basis for output and price determination (MC_1), which are unavailable to either parent as a stand-alone company. Whether the cost reductions benefit the overall U.S. economy depends on many factors. If the cost reductions result from *productivity improvements* (e.g., new work rules leading to higher output per worker), a welfare gain exists for the economy since fewer resources are required to produce a given number of autos and can be shifted to other industries. However, cost reductions stemming from JV Co.'s formation can be *monetary* in nature. To the extent that JV Co., being a newly formed company, is able to negotiate wage concessions from domestic workers, that could not be achieved by American Auto Co., the cost reductions would represent a transfer of dollars from domestic workers to the economy (consumers in terms of lower prices and JV Co. profits). This share of the lower costs (area below the dashed line within *d*) is not a welfare gain for the U.S. economy. The analysis of the desirability of this joint venture depends on the area above the dashed line in *d* being greater than the area *b*.

Another factor is the effect of the joint venture on Sony Auto Co.'s profits. Before the establishment of the American joint venture, Sony Auto Co. earned profits on its auto production in Japan. After shifting production to the joint venture, Sony profits are earned in the United States and repatriated to Japan. However, in this case they are subject to the U.S. corporate income tax. To the extent that these tax revenues are an addition to the U.S. economy, that would not have resulted from the separate companies; this would lower the dashed line in area *c* and increase the welfare benefits to the U.S. economy.

NEW UNITED MOTOR MANUFACTURING, INC.

A widely publicized international joint venture was announced in 1983 by General Motors and Toyota Motor Corporation, the first and third largest auto companies in the world. With the approval of the Federal Trade Commission, the two competitors agreed to form a new separate corporation for a twelve-year period, called New United Motor Manufacturing, Inc. (NUMMI). General Motors and Toyota each own half of NUMMI.

Located at an idle GM plant in Fremont, California, NUMMI produces Chevrolet Novas, a compact car based on the design of the Toyota Corolla, as well as small trucks. The Nova does not represent a new car developed for the American market. Toyota designed the manufacturing layout, coordinated acquisition and installation of equipment, and implemented its production system. NUMMI has a production capacity of 200,000 Novas per year. The Novas are sold to General Motors for distribution through its dealers. General Motors has the sole responsibility for pricing the vehicle. Toyota and other Japanese manufacturers supply approximately 50% of the value of the vehicle. Major components supplied by the Japanese include engine and transmission, whereas the Fremont plant conducts stamping and assembly. American companies supply to NUMMI such items as batteries, glass, headliners, paint and sealants, and air-conditioner components.

General Motors' announced goal was to learn the Japanese art of management and small car manufacturing by getting a first-hand look at how Toyota organizes its operations, motivates its workers, and locates machines and materials. General Motors maintained that if it learned how to build lower cost cars, it would transfer those cost-saving methods to its other plants. It was estimated that General Motors would save as much as $1,000 per car because it did not have to design a new auto from the ground up. Using Japanese-made components was estimated to save an additional $700 per car ("The All-American Small Car," 1984).

NUMMI's production system is based on that of the Toyota Motor Corporation. Two of the more important production techniques used by NUMMI are the "just in time" and "Jidoka" quality principles. The "just in time" system of parts logistics results in NUMMI carrying only three to four days of parts inventory with little or no warehousing in between. This system of tightly controlled parts inventories and close coordination with suppliers is intended to avoid production bottlenecks and yield operating efficiencies. The "Jidoka" technique results in machines or the production process itself stopping automatically in abnormal situations, such as a machinery breakdown, permitting speedy correction of the situation. Stopping the production line in case of some abnormality also applies to workers, who have a stop button at each job site and the authority to stop the production process at their discretion.

Another potential area of cost savings comes from NUMMI's efforts to eliminate the job demarcation problems that plague most American auto plants. NUMMI utilizes simpler and more flexible job classifications, work rules, and procedures, which are intended to increase labor productivity. In the manufacturing area, there are two groups of employees—production workers and skilled trade workers. The latter group consists of three classifications—tool and die, power house skilled tradespeople, and general maintenance skilled tradespeople. In contrast, some GM plants have more than 100 job classifications. On NUMMI assembly lines, employees work in teams of five to ten members, each person performing up to fifteen separate jobs. Every production worker learns the job of everyone else on the team in case of absence. Workers regularly rotate jobs for fairness and to relieve boredom. Each team has complete jurisdiction over its own operation, including quality and any improvements in the production process. NUMMI management thus has greater flexibility in assigning jobs, which permits fewer assemblers and quality inspectors to be hired. In return for these concessions from the UAW union, NUMMI pays its workers prevailing wage and benefit rates for new hires in the industry. NUMMI has pledged that its workers would not lose jobs because of automation.

For Toyota, NUMMI represents a relatively low-cost opportunity to test the transferability of its production techniques overseas. It provides Toyota a quick way to learn how to operate in the United States with a partner who knows the ins and outs of the American auto market. Toyota also views a manufacturing foothold in the United States as insurance against rising U.S. protectionism.

The above advantages were confirmed by Toyota's December 1985 announcement to locate its first U.S. car assembly plant in Georgetown, Kentucky. Toyota plans to build as many as 200,000 midsize Camry models a year for the U.S. market by 1990. Toyota indicated that UAW representation at the Georgetown plant will probably come as a matter of course. By choosing Georgetown, Toyota is locating itself amid automotive supply companies, many of which are Japanese. This will help enable Toyota to maintain a tightly controlled parts inventory system with suppliers. It was also indicated that the mid-South provided an atmosphere where Toyota knows the Japanese have succeeded in the past (e.g., Honda's plant in Ohio, Nissan's plant in Tennessee). What's more, workers in the mid-South have not demanded the same restrictive work rules that are found in most Big Three plants, which are viewed as a major source of Japanese automakers' cost advantage ("Toyota," 1985).

When the Federal Trade Commission accepted a consent agreement with General Motors and Toyota, the Commission majority cited three major procompetitive benefits for the automobile industry from the joint venture: (1) it would likely increase the total number of small cars available in America, allowing consumers greater choice at lower prices, (2) the joint-venture car would cost less to produce than if General Motors was forced to rely on other alternatives, and (3) the venture permitted a valuable opportunity for General Motors to complete its learning of the more efficient Japanese manufacturing techniques.

Dissenting commissioners argued that since the joint venture was the offspring of the first and third largest auto manufacturers in the world, competition would be lessened and new car prices would increase. Also, General Motors and Toyota would be able to exchange anticompetitive information, thus blunting competition. Any efficiencies that General Motors might learn from Toyota would be limited mainly to assembly and stamping processes, since Toyota designed the new car and produced the sophisticated components in Japan. Furthermore, it was argued that General Motors had already implemented many Japanese techniques without Toyota's help, and that process would continue unabated. It was maintained that General Motors could learn about efficiencies from its two other Japanese partners and did not need Toyota ("The GM-Toyota Linkup," 1984).

Critics of NUMMI also maintained that it would result in job losses for Americans. At the NUMMI plant, up to 3,000 new jobs would be generated. However, only 50% of the Nova is sourced in the United States, the remainder representing Japanese production. Because the Nova was to replace GM's Chevette, with almost 100% American content, the result would be an overall job loss for U.S. workers. Moreover, most sophisticated systems and components for the Nova would be produced in Japan, providing high-skilled jobs for the Japanese. Back in America, workers put the final pieces together, resulting in low-skilled jobs that would become increasingly automated in the years ahead (General Motors Corp., 1983).

In terms of the model in Figure 11.1, it appears that the cost reductions that accrue to NUMMI, compared to the costs achieved by General Motors when it produces compact autos independently, can be attributed to two sources. First, there will be significant cost reductions from the imported components produced by Toyota. This estimated cost reduction of $700, as reported in *Business Week,* is not a saving to the U.S. economy. It reflects a reduction based on the lower production costs in Japan. But this benefit would equally accrue to the U.S. consumer if Japanese autos were instead imported. The same would be true of the cost savings from design and research done in Japan rather than in the United States.

The important cost savings for the U.S. economy are the productive efficiencies that result from the adoption of Toyota labor practices and assembly line organization of the NUMMI plant. The amount of these savings has not been made public by NUMMI and is difficult to evaluate from the outside. However, critics of the FTC decision to consent to the joint venture estimated NUMMI's efficiency gains to be only $200 per vehicle, resulting in $40 million in total efficiency gains (NUMMI's production capacity equals 200,000 Novas per year) ("Future," 1984). It is likely that General Motors would contend that these figures underestimate NUMMI's efficiency gains. But it appears that the immediate benefits of NUMMI will be modest.

At the assembly plant level, the NUMMI venture has been quite successful in achieving efficiency gains. Table 11.3 provides comparisons of NUMMI's labor productivity (worker hours per vehicle) compared to its sister Toyota plant in Japan, which produces an identical vehicle, and with typical "low-tech" and "high-tech" GM plants located in the United States. A high-tech plant is one that has been recently retooled and utilizes state-of-the-art technology and automation. It should be noted that the equipment at the NUMMI plant is rather conventional by standards of the world auto industry and the degree of automation in the NUMMI plant is below that of GM's high-tech plants.

As Table 11.3 illustrates, NUMMI has eliminated more than 40% of the worker hours involved in manufacturing an auto, as compared to the older, low-tech GM plants. Moreover, NUMMI utilizes 30% less labor than GM's most recent and highly automated manufacturing plants. What's more, the quality level of vehicles has consistently exceeded the quality level of vehicles produced at other GM plants. The reasons underlying NUMMI's productivity success have been previously discussed—multiskilled

Table 11.3

Comparisons of Labor Productivity (worker hours per vehicle): NUMMI, Toyota of Japan, General Motors of the United States

| | General Motors | | NUMMI | Toyota of Japan |
	Low-Tech Plant	High-Tech Plant		
Worker Hours Per Vehicle	33.4	27.0	19.0	15.7
Percentage Difference from NUMMI	+76%	+42%	—	−17%

Source: James Womack, Multinational Joint Ventures in Motor Vehicles, in David Mowery (ed.): *International Collaborative Ventures in U.S. Manufacturing* (Cambridge, MA: Ballinger), p. 322.

workers in teams, relations with input suppliers, efforts to eliminate inventories, and the philosophy of continuous improvement in productivity.

The strongest support for the joint venture might be based on the potential learning-by-doing that could be transferred later to the organization of production in other auto manufacturing facilities of General Motors. This possibility goes beyond our model and will continue to be a hypothetical benefit for years to come. It will not only be difficult to measure these gains, but nearly impossible to construct a counterfactural of how organization change would have occurred without this joint venture experience. As a result, it seems inappropriate to attribute large efficiency benefits to NUMMI.

Critics of the joint venture have expressed concern that the cooperation of Toyota and General Motors will lead to a joint exercise of market power. In 1984 Toyota and General Motors sold 1,559,980 vehicles rated as subcompacts or compacts out of an industry total of 5,300,000 small cars sold. As the dominant firms in the industry, Toyota and General Motors might use their market power to raise auto prices. If other companies followed the price increase of General Motors and Toyota, the losses to the American consumer could easily exceed the efficiency gains on the small number of cars produced by NUMMI.

If the projected efficiency gains of $200 per vehicle for annual output of 200,000 vehicles are achieved by NUMMI, this $40 million gain would be offset by a price increase of only $7.50 per vehicle for the 5,300,000 small cars sold in 1984. If only General Motors and Toyota raise prices on their models to reduce competition for the Nova, and other small car producers do not follow the price increase, a price increase of $25.65 on their models would offset the efficiency gains of NUMMI. If price increases in small cars spill over into price increases for large cars, as would be expected, it would require smaller price increases to offset projected efficiency gains of NUMMI.

Pricing behavior of General Motors and Toyota in the 1986 model year and after has been difficult to evaluate. Toyota prices are likely to be influenced by changing exchange rates, as well as changing market conditions in the United States. In the initial price announcements of General Motors, the increases in prices for models carried over from the 1985 model year showed approximately a 5% increase for small cars comparing 1985 model initial prices and 1986 model initial prices. For large and luxury model cars, the price increase were substantially lower, whereas for midsize models the price increases by General Motors were larger. However, if the price increases on small cars were only 1% higher in 1986 than with full competition, this would amount to a $50 to $70 increase, which would more than eliminate NUMMI's efficiency benefits to American consumers.

CONCLUSIONS

The overall impact of international joint ventures in the U.S. automobile industry will depend on two factors that are difficult to quantify. Most analysts indicate that the immediate efficiency gains from joint-venture auto production are relatively small. But if these gains can be transferred to all auto production by U.S. firms in a more rapid and efficient manner as a result of this process, the gains could be significant. The potential for losses to the U.S. economy depends on the effect of the joint venture on the competitiveness of the automobile market. If joint-venture production simply replaces former domestic production, as the Nova replaces the Chevette, and the cooperating firms develop implicit arrangements to segment the market and avoid direct competition, the resulting market power could lead to higher profits at the expense of the American consumer. Any business arrangement that allows firms in an oligopolistic market to cooperate tends to raise economists' suspicions. Whether the FTC decision to consent to international joint ventures was good or bad will remain difficult to evaluate. However, it appears the NUMMI's efficiency gains have been considerable relative to other GM manufacturing plants.

References

The All-American Small Car is Fading. 1984. *Business Week,* March 12.

Future of the Automobile Industry. 1984. Hearing Before the Subcommittee on Commerce, Transportation, and Tourism, U.S. House of Representatives, February 8, p. 286.

The GM-Toyota Linkup Could Change the Industry. 1984. *Business Week,* December 24.

General Motors Corp. and Toyota Motor Corp.: Proposed Consent Agreement With Analysis to Aid Public Comment. 1983. *Federal Register* 48(250): 67246–67257.

Toyota is Said to Pick Site in Kentucky for its First Car Assembly Plant in U.S. 1985. *Wall Street Journal,* December 4.

Chapter 12

FOREIGN COMPETITION AND EMPLOYMENT IN IMPORT-SENSITIVE U.S. INDUSTRIES*

Catherine L. Mann

INTRODUCTION

The more strident call for protecting import-sensitive industries in the United States generates renewed interest in estimating the effectiveness of existing international trade policies designed to aid domestic industries. If existing programs have not prevented debilitating import competition, then it must be determined whether the cause is misjudging the characteristics of foreign competition, mistargeting policy tools, or a lack of real intent to protect. The logical progression of analysis: (1) identifies stricken industries, (2) categorizes the observed decline in industry performance, and (3) estimates what portion of the observed decline is due to foreign competition.

Previous research takes three directions. Two stress the importance of quantity of imports, the other the price of imports. However, for a number of reasons, including flexible exchange rates, foreign countries' domestic growth strategies, and heterogeneous products, the observable foreign price data may not reflect all facets of import competition. Yet quantity data alone cannot capture the causal element of import penetration. Therefore, any analysis of import competition must include both foreign prices and a measure of domestic market share penetration by quantity of imports that captures escape-clause quota protection and other nonprice determinants of demand. In addition, when estimating the effects of existing trade policy, it is crucial to keep in mind that short-run fixity of capital stock may be a quite important determinant of the structural model.

This chapter is organized as follows: the next short section puts this study in the context of the literature. Sections three and four summarize the model and formally

*Reprinted from *The International Trade Journal*, Vol. II, no. 4, summer 1988.

develop the estimation equation, which is presented in section five. Section six describes the industries and data. Section seven shows the results. Section eight concludes.

LITERATURE

Analyzing and estimating the impact of imports on domestic employment is not a new project. Historically, these analyses used either the accounting technique or the elasticity method. More recently, general equilibrium models have been employed.

The accounting technique (Frank, 1977; Krueger, 1980a) estimates what percent of employment growth is generated from growth in domestic and foreign demand, import growth, and labor productivity growth. The input-output elasticity technique (Bayard and Orr, 1979) estimates the change in job opportunities resulting from tariff changes and demand growth. The general equilibrium structure (Grossman, 1987) estimates the employment elasticity with respect to foreign price, real wages, and demand growth.

What is interesting is that all these methods conclude that import competition causes only a small fraction of employment losses for most industries. The bulk of employment change comes from changing labor productivity, real wages, general levels of demand, or changes in expenditure patterns. The fact that these results seem to hold up using a variety of methods suggests robustness, and makes it difficult to comprehend the continued vociferousness of labor and industry. Moreover, these results suggest why protection may not be effective in preventing employment losses. Are there other effects not captured in the foregoing analyses?

Martin and Evans (1981) outline several problems with these noncausal techniques. First, the fundamental issue is that the discrete time decomposition of employment growth used by Frank (1977) and Krueger (1980a) ignores the interaction term between employment and output growth, assuming it to be second-order small. However, if this assumption fails, the interaction term reappears in either productivity growth or demand growth, biasing upward the relationshp between employment growth and either demand growth or productivity growth. Second, these methods lack the behavioral interaction of supply and demand that determines cost and price.

Grossman's work (1987) formulates a simple general equilibrium behavioral model of supply and demand for the product and for factors. Grossman makes three key assumptions. First, he uses a constant return to scale production function where the industry-specific factors of capital and labor are partially mobile out of economywide stocks. Second, the domestic-currency price of the imported good is assumed constant implying a perfectly elastic foreign supply curve and fixed exchange rate. Third, he assumes price equals the marginal cost for the domestic producer. Nevertheless, this behavioral formulation allows Grossman to examine the elasticity of employment with respect to real wages, demand growth, and foreign prices, and advances substantially the methodology used to analyze the effect of foreign competition on domestic employment. He, too, though, finds little statistical effect on employment of foreign prices. Consequently the role for tariff protection is small.

This study advances Grossman's methodology along two lines. First, it reformulates his model using industry-specific data. Second, it relaxes both the assumption of the elastic foreign supply and the assumption that price equals marginal cost for the domestic producer. Thus the model introduces both a foreign quantity variable and a foreign price variable into the determination of domestic employment. The theoretical construction is the dominant/fringe familiar from industrial organization theory.

SUMMARY OF THE MODEL

Consider the dominant/fringe model in an international framework. The dominant producer is domestic, and the fringe is the suppliers of import-competing goods.[1] The fringe firm's supply function is upward sloping with respect to the dominant firm's pricing decision. The higher the dominant's chosen price, the greater the total quantity produced by the fringe. Therefore, the dominant firm can use price to control entry by the fringe.[2]

Figure 12.1 shows the basic model. S_f is the fringe supply. (D) is the total demand. Therefore, the dominant faces the residual demand curve and marginal revenue curve D_r and MR_r. In this case using a MR_r equals MC pricing rule yields dominant output of Q_d and fringe supply of Q_f for equilibrium output of (Q).

The standard industrial organization model assumes the dominant firm knows the determinants of the fringe supply curve with certainty. What kind of uncertainty might there be about the foreign fringe supply curve that could affect the equilibrium price-output combination (and therefore labor demand) of the dominant domestic producer?

First, market share is likely to be a determinant of both the foreign and domestic supply schedules. Since it is assumed here that capital is fixed in the short run, increasing returns to scale in the short run are an important determinant of price. In addition, in monopolistically competitive industries with heterogeneous outputs, quantity is a key variable (see Chamberlin, 1957; Spence, 1976). Whereas characteristics of the foreign supply function are less detailed, foreign firms could build excess capacity with the expectation that their markets will grow into it. Export-promotion incentives would reduce the break-even price shifting down the fringe supply schedule and increasing foreign imports into the domestic market. Moreover, some industries enjoy escape-clause quota protection (leather footwear, radios and TVs, autos, some metal fabrications); we cannot assume that import price data fully reflect these quantity restraints. Therefore, quantity or market share is likely to be a determinant of the foreign supply curve as well.

Second, exchange rate changes will affect the domestic firm's optimal price-output

---

[1]This framework assumes that we can discuss firms as if they could control prices. So long as the domestic industry has a monopolistically competitive structure, price is no longer determined simply by the supply side, but also depends on other domestic firms' supply schedules.

[2]In fact, a dynamic version of the dominant/fringe model by Gaskins (1971) specifically sets out the problem as a short-run profit maximization with high price and quick entry versus long-run profit maximization with a lower price but slower entry.

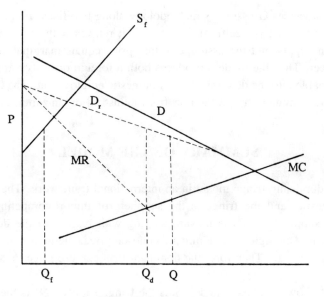

Figure 12.1. Basic model.

combination through their effect on the foreign supply curve. Given a foreign cost structure, an appreciation of the dollar allows the foreign firm to export more under the domestic firms chosen price ceiling. Thus the residual demand curve will be a function of the exchange rate.

Integrating these ideas into the formal model, we find that there are two fringe supply curves. One, the expected foreign supply, depends only on the domestic price. The other, the actual foreign supply, depends on price, market share, and the exchange rate. Figure 12.2 shows an example of what might happen if the domestic firm does not correctly estimate the foreign supply schedule. The problem may occur because the domestic firm underestimates the market share objective of the foreign supplier, or because the domestic firm has static or imperfect exchange rate expectations. S_f^P is the expected foreign supply where supply is just a function of the domestic price. Based on this perception, the domestic supply curve is MC^P defined by (w), (i), and $\bar{K}$. The domestic firm chooses (P) where perceived MR^P equals MC^P. The domestic industry expects foreign supply of Q_f^P and domestic supply of Q_d^P to fill the total demand of (Q).

However, if in fact market share is an important objective or the dollar appreciates, the foreign firm may be willing to enter the market at a price lower than that perceived by the domestic firm. One such curve would be S_f^a defined for a particular market share and exchange rate.[3]

At the decision price (P), the actual foreign supply forthcoming is Q_f^a, whereas domestic output falls back to Q_d^a. At actual marginal revenue (MR^a) equal to marginal cost, the marginal profit per unit sold is higher than before. However, the industry

---

[3]Actually, there is a family of S_a^f curves, one defined for each market share. If we assume increasing returns in foreign production, S_a^f shifts down over time as the importer grabs more and more of the domestic market.

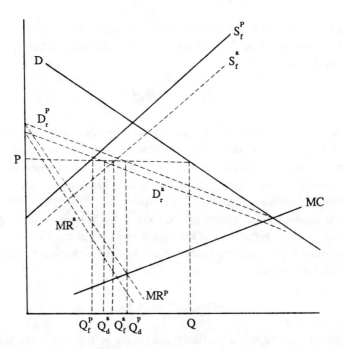

Figure 12.2. Domestic firm incorrectly estimated foreign supply schedule.

revenues and total profits must fall. Volume declines; therefore revenue falls. Profits fall because fixed capital cost must be spread over a lower output level, thus raising average costs. In addition, total profits fall since (P) is no longer the optimal price for industry profit maximization. Market penetration by imports rises. Usage of the flexible factors labor and intermediates must fall. Thus in this case where the domestic firm fails to incorporate the market share objective of the foreign supplier or the impact of an appreciating domestic currency into the pricing decision, realized market share is an important determinant of industry profits and labor demand.

This model assumes rather myopic domestic firms. In particular there is no strategic pricing behavior by the dominant producer to prevent the invasion of its market—it just makes mistakes.[4] An extension of the model should formulate more realistic exchange rate expectations so that the domestic pricing decision depends explicitly on the expected path of the exchange rate. Nevertheless, the model does advance the theory somewhat beyond the story of foreign competition under conditions of perfect competition.

A MORE FORMAL CONSIDERATION

Ultimately, the point of this exercise is to focus on the general equilibrium determinants of domestic employment when an industry is faced with foreign competition in prices and quantities.

---

[4]For a discussion of how the domestic firm might react, see Mann (1984), pp. 92–94.

The production function is three-factor Cobb-Douglas with no restriction on the returns to scale. There are two flexible inputs, labor and intermediates, and capital is fixed in the short run.

(1) $$Q_i = e^\rho L_i^{a1} I_i^{a2} \bar{K}_i^{a3}$$

Where Q_i is output of industry (i), L_i is industry-specific labor with value share in output equal to $a1$, I_i is the intermediate input for industry (i) with value share in output $a2$, and $\bar{K}_i$ is the industry-specific capital stock which is fixed at a moment of time. If it is entirely employed, it has output share of $a3$. $\bar{K}_i$ does change over time by investment and depreciation. e^ρ captures technological progress.

The firm can choose to not employ all the capital, but it must make a fixed payment based on the entire stock regardless of utilization rates. Thus the firm's objective function is to minimize short-run total costs subject to the production function constraint and conditional on demand.

(2) $$\min w_i L_i + i_i I_i + r\bar{K}_i$$

We assume factors are supplied perfectly elastically at the factor reward rate w_i for labor, i_i for intermediates, (r) for captial. Each industry is small with respect to its labor force, or alternatively, wages are set by previous contract. Therefore, labor demand and wages rates are not determined simultaneously. The intermediates market is large with respect to this industry. Finally, (r) is the cost of borrowing.

Substituting the constraint into the objective function yields the restricted short-run total cost curve.

(3) $$\min w_i[Q_i^{1/a1} I_i^{-a2/a1} \bar{K}_i^{-a3/a1}] + i_i[Q_i^{1/a2} I_i^{-a1/a2} \bar{K}_i^{-a3/a2}] + r\bar{K}_i$$

which when differentiated with respect to Q_i yields the short-run supply curve.

(4) $$MC_i = n \cdot Q_i^{1-a1-a2/a1+a2} \, \bar{K}_i^{-a3/a1+a2} w_i^{a1/a1+a2} i_i^{a2/a1+a2}$$

where (n) is an unimportant constant.

The demand function describes total demand for the domestic product and foreign substitute.

(5) $$D_i = d(P_i/P_a)^{b1}(Pm_i/P_a)^{b2Nb3}$$

Demand for the product depends on income (N) with elasticity $b3$. It depends on the relative price of the domestic item to all other goods (P_i/P_a) with elasticity $b1$ and relative price of the foreign substitution to all other goods (Pm_i/P_a) with elasticity $b2$. Thus we allow substitution between domestic and foreign products not equal to unity. Here (d) is an unimportant constant.

(6) $$Pm_i = eP_i^*(1 + v_i).$$

Pm_i is the dollar price of the tariff-ridden foreign product. (e) is the dollar to foreign currency exchange rate, v_i is the ad valorem tariff rate and P_i^* is the foreign currency price of the product.

Output supplied by the domestic firm equals demand for the domestic product, which is just total demand minus imports.

(7) $$Q_i = D_i - M_i$$

or

(8) $$Q_i = D_i(1 - m_i)$$

where m_i is the fraction of total demand supplied by the fringe given the decision price of the domestic firm.

(9) $$m_i = M_i/(Q_i + M_i)$$

Although m_i depends on the decision price, it also depends on the location of the actual foreign supply schedule, which may be either incorrectly estimated by the domestic firm or shift with a changing value of the dollar.

Suppose the domestic firm does not make any mistakes, then substituting for price in the demand function and assuming output produced, (Q_i) equals quantity demanded, (D_i) yields the expected market equilibrium output level for industry (i) (the subscript is suppressed).

(10) $$Q = h[Pa^{b1}(eP^*(1 + v))^{b2}N^{b3}]^{a1+a2/a1+a2+(1-a1-a2)(b1+b2)}$$
$$\{\bar{K}^{-a3}w^{a1}i^{a2}\}^{-(b1+b2)/a1+a2+(1-a1-a2)(b1+b2)}$$

(h) is a constant composed of (g), e^p, and factor shares.

Differentiating the short-run cost function (4) with respect to wages yields the labor demand function conditional on the output,

(11) $$L^dI_Q = j\left[\frac{a1}{a2}\frac{i}{w}\right]^{a2/a1+a2} Q^{1/a1+a2}\bar{K}^{-a3/a1+a2}$$

But the firm is likely to make mistakes in estimating the location of the foreign supply curve. Therefore, the firm's actual demand is different from (Q) by the actual import share [equation (8)]. Substituting in actual domestic output sold yields the equilibrium labor demand in terms of the exogenous variables: relative price of flexible inputs (i_i/w_i), the capital stock ($\bar{K}_i$), the relative price of the domestic product (P_i/P_a), relative price of the foreign substitute (Pm_i/P_a), income (N), and domestic market share $(1 - m_i)$. Finally, (c) is an unimportant constant.[5]

$$(12) \quad L_i^d c(i_i/w_i)^{a2/a1+a2} \bar{K}_i^{-a3/a1+a2} (P_i/P_a)^{b1/a1+a2} (Pm_i/P_a)^{b2/a1+a2} N^{b3/a1+a2} (1 - m_i)^{1/a1+a2}$$

ESTIMATION

Linearizing the model by taking logs, the estimating equation is:

$$\ln L_i^d = \beta_0 + \beta_1 \ln W_i + \beta_2 \ln i_i + \beta_3 \ln \bar{K}_i + \beta_4 \ln(P_i/P_a)$$
(13)
$$+ \beta_5 \ln(Pm_i/P_a) + \beta_6 \ln N + \beta_7 \ln(1 - m_i) + \epsilon$$

where L_i^d is employment in industry (i), W_i is the real wage, i_i is the intermediate input cost, $\bar{K}_i$ the next capital stock, (P_i/P_a) the relative price of the domestic product, (Pm_i/P_a) the relative price of the foreign substitute, (N) the level of demand and $(1 - m_i)$ the domestic market share.

The expected signs are:

$$\beta_0 ? \quad \beta_1 < 0 \quad \beta_2 < 0 \quad \beta_3 < 0 \quad \beta_4 < 0 \quad \beta_5 > 0 \quad \beta_6 > 0 \quad \beta_7 > 0$$

The sign on the relative price of the flexible inputs (β_1, β_2) depends on the relative importance of the two factors in the production process. If labor is relatively more important, then the sign should be negative. Whereas the theory constrains the coefficients on the flexible inputs to be equal, we can test the hypothesis using a Chow test on the stability of the equation across specifications.

The sign on the relative price of the product to all other goods is negative since the higher the domestic price, the greater demand substitutes away from it toward all other goods and the foreign substitute; therefore employment falls. The sign on the relative price of the foreign product to all other goods is positive reflecting substitution toward the domestic alternative, increasing demand and employment.

A negative sign on the capital stock is suggested by an excess capacity theory. If capital and labor are complementary when used efficiently, then the elasticity of employment with respect to capital should be positive. However, if capital is relatively immobile in the short run and employment is declining, then the elasticity of labor demand with respect to fixed capital is negative as employment falls, but capital does not. Moreover, Isard (1973) suggests that firms react to foreign competition by investing in labor-saving capital technology. This is further support for a negative sign on the capital stock variable.

---

[5]The assumption that supply equals demand for the domestic product requires that excess inventories $(Q_d^p - Q_d^a)$ resulting from the misperception of the foreign supply curve do not affect the next period's output choice. This might be true if the industry products have style characteristics so that last year's style cannot be sold or substituted only inelastically for this year's style.

The sign on the domestic market share and the demand variable are positive. Since this is a demand driven model, if demand for the product rises, so does employment.

Standard ordinary least squares techniques can be used since all the right-hand-side variables are exogenous to the dependent variable, at least at a moment in time. The domestic price is a choice variable, therefore exogenous. The foreign price depends on foreign cost structure, export promotion policies, tariffs, and exchange rates as before. Actual market share is determined by foreign and domestic objectives, thus is exogenous to the labor demand choice. It is assumed that factor markets are large relative to the industry, or factor rewards are determined by contracts, thus the factor returns are exogenous to employment.

Four quarterly dummies eliminate fourth-order serial correlation and seasonality. The Corchrane-Orcutt method is used to eliminate first-order serial correlation when necessary. A time trend to capture changes in capital stock productivity (either because of technological advancement or depreciation) is used.

The theoretical constraint on the coefficients of the two flexible inputs were tested using the standard F-test. However, examination of the constrained and unconstrained regression statistics show that the null hypothesis (that the coefficients are the same in absolute value) is not supported in any of the industries. Therefore, all results are shown with disaggregated flexible inputs.

The structural models do not explicitly suggest any lagged effects. However, several are created by the type of data available. First, the imports data is "general imports" not "imports for consumption."[6] Thus lagged effects of foreign prices in domestic demand might be observed as items enter as general imports, but do not reach retail until some quarters later. Likewise, the market-share variable might be lagged as imports cycle through a warehouse preparing for final sale. Since share data might signal to the dominant firm what the fringe supply curve looks like, there may be perception lags as well. Second, lack of inventory data requires real-time equating of output and demand. If the shelf-life of finished-goods inventory is long, or if inventories are large, lags on the demand side might appear. Finally, length of production process and inventory methods, both real and accounting, suggest using lagged values of input prices.

CHOICE OF INDUSTRIES AND THE DATA

Industries selected for this study come from an analysis by Schoplefle (1982). His study analyzes that industries had the greatest penetration by imports in percentage terms, and that experienced the fastest growth of import penetration between 1972 and 1976. Thus these industries are ones where the hypothesis that foreign competition reduces employment is most likely to be supported. Eighteen industries have greater than 15% import penetration into the domestic market that also have a domestic market share declining at the average rate of one percent per year or more. Of the eighteen, eleven

---

[6]"Imports for consumption" (no longer available) measures the quantity and value of imports actually entering domestic demand. It is imports arrived less imports bonded in warehouses plus formerly impounded imports newly released for sale. "General imports" refers only to imports arrived, not necessarily for sale.

do not have published employment data, and two do not have other necessary data, leaving five industries. They are: floor covering mills (SIC 227), men's and women's leather footwear except athletic (SIC 3143, 3144), semiconductors (SIC 3674), radios and TVs (SIC 3651), and plastic and rubber footwear (SIC 3021). These are industries studied in the previous literature and found to have various degrees of import sensitivity. This is an interesting group as it includes the perennially protected footwear industries, and radios and TVs. But it also includes semiconductors, which the U.S. dominated until recently and still dominates in the development of new chips.

In general, constructing consistent international data series is challenging. There are two outstanding obstacles that must be surmounted for this project. The first is the different classification schemes for imports versus for domestic products and prices. The second significant problem is that the frequency of what data are available is not the same. Finally, several of the series required for estimation had to be constructed.

Data availability bounds the estimation period from 1974 to 1981, quarterly. The proxy for the price of the domestic substitute is not available before 1974. Data for industry-specific domestic capital stock bound the analysis on the other end at 1981. Most data are available only quarterly.

Below are brief descriptions of the data used in the estimation (for more details, refer to the Data Appendix).

Price Index for the Imported Substitute (Pm_i)

The price index for the imported substitute is actually a unit-value index constructed using the Tariff Schedule of the U.S. Annotated (TSUSA) Scheme or Schedule A of customs valuation and CIF data for value and quantities. A concordance between Schedule A and TSUSA is used for appropriate tariff rates. Use of both customs value and CIF data captures, in part, the importance of transportation costs, and the overvaluation of figures by customs, and helps to minimize problems of changing composition inherent in unit-value indexes. The index is in dollar terms, thus the exchange rate is not a separate variable.

Capital Stock Data ($\bar{K}_i$)

Stock data are available only annually, and the concordance between the series available and the industries under discussion is not perfect. But only for semiconductors is the concordance problem worrisome. These data are total net stocks of structures and plant and equipment in constant (1972) dollars. Linear interpolation between end-of-year figures is used to create a quarterly series.

Domestic Market Share ($1 - m_i$)

The domestic market share variable is simply $(1 - m_i)$ where $m_i = (M_i/QSH_i + M_i)$ is the foreign market share, M_i is the quantity of imports, and QSH_i is the quantity of shipments, constructed as discussed in the Data Appendix. Due to incomplete quantity data for imports, m_i is likely to underestimate actual foreign market share. m_i will also be underestimated because shipments by domestic producers (QSH_i) are assumed to go to domestic consumers. Only for semi-conducts, however, where exports are important, is this latter bias a likely problem.

Employment (L_i^d)

The employment series is total production labor hours demanded, which is the number of production workers times the average weekly hours for the third month of each quarter, both series matched by industry.

Real Wages (W_i)

The real wages rate is the average hourly earnings for the third month of the quarter divided by the consumer price index (based to 1972). This figure underestimates real labor costs because it does not include the benefit structure.

Domestic Price (P_i); Intermediate Good Price (i_i); and All-Other-Goods Price (P_a)

These are all producer prices (based to 1972) and specific to each industry. See Data Appendix or footnotes to the Estimation Table for more details.

Demand (N)

The index of industrial production (based to 1972) is used to measure demand fluctuations.

RESULTS

The point of estimation is to determine (1) whether competition for market share, as well as in prices, is an important determinant of domestic employment, and (2) whether foreign competition in prices and quantities is *the* most important determinant of domestic employment. Table 12.1 presents the results, with details in the Regression Appendix.

First, some general comparisons with results of other authors. From the estimation, leather footwear appears to be one of the industries most affected by import competition. This agrees with Krueger (1980), Frank (1977), and Bayard and Orr (1979), but is not supported by Grossman's (1987) work. At the end, Krueger, Frank, and Grossman pinpoint radios and TVs as likely to be one of the industries more affected by import competition, whereas this estimation and those by Bayard and Orr do not reach that conclusion.

Regarding the second issue, the overwhelming impression of the results is that foreign

Table 12.1.

Regressions of Employment for Import Sensitive U.S. Industries[1]

Industry[2]	W_i	i_i	$\bar{K}_i$	P_i/P_a	Pm_i/P_a	N	$(1 - m_i)$
Radios and TVs	$-.745*_2$	$-.497_{-2}$	-1.72	$-1.135*^3_{-1}$	$.075$	$1.0*$	$.071_{-1}$
Floor coverings	$-.268_{-1}$	$-1.404*$	-1.527	$-.384$	$-.019$	$1.663*$	1.425
Rubber footwear	$-.461_{-1}$	$-.217$	-1.224	$-1.039*$	$.320*$	$.733*_1$	$.016$
Leather footwear	$-.576_{-2}$	$-.108$	1.494	$-.079$	$.244*^4_{T,-2}$	$1.385*$	$.372*$
Semiconductors	$-.593_{-1}$	—	$-.319$	$-1.665*_1$	$.0303_T$	$1.003*$	$.204$

[1]For more detail, see Regression Appendix.
[2]*Variable definitions for industry (i):*
  W_i—real wage.
  i_i—intermediate input price.
  $\bar{K}_i$—capital stock.
  P_i/P_a—relative price of domestic good.
  P_{Mi}/P_a—relative price of foreign good.
  N—demand.
  $(i - m_i)$—domestic market share.
[3]$()_{-L}$—variable logged L times.
  $()_T$—variable divided by time (to capture changes in quality).
[4]*—significant at the 10% level.

competition, whether it be in prices or quantities, is less important as a determinant of employment than are domestic variables, particularly domestic economic activity and the relative price of the domestically produced good to all other goods. There is some evidence that excess capacity, because it increases the cost of production, reduces employment through feedback effects. On the other hand, there is mixed evidence as to whether high real wages or high intermediate input costs are the more important cause of high marginal costs, lower equilibrium output, and lower employment. Real wages do appear to be a relatively more important determinant of domestic cost for radios and TVs, and both types of footwear.

Although the foreign variables are only marginally significant, it is useful to examine how much these elasticities imply for employment losses given foreign competition either in prices or quantities. Table 12.2 shows the calculations for annual job losses due to competition in prices and quantities using the elasticity estimates from Table 12.1. Employment in the floor coverings industry is hardest hit, as was suggested by the Bayard and Orr (1979) study. A 1% per quarter decline in the relative price of the imported substitutes and the actual annual decrease in import penetration as measured by Schoepfle (1982) yields a decline of 2,100 jobs, fully 4.1% of industry employment. For semiconductors, similar calculations yield 1,000 jobs lost, 0.5% of industry employment. The bulk of the loss to employment in these two industries comes from increases in import penetration. Both of these industries may be more captial-intensive suggesting that foreign competition for market share leads to an inefficient scale of production at home, higher costs, and employment losses.

On the other hand, calculations for both types of footwear and radios and TVs suggest that competition in both price and quantities is important for determining employment levels; price competition appears relatively more important. These industries may be more labor-intensive such that foreign producers with cheaper labor can consistently

Table 12.2

Annual Job Losses

SIC	Name	(1)	(2)	(3)	(4)
227	Floor coverings	32	2,064	2,095	4.1
314 3/4	Leather footwear	996	558	1,554	1.5
3021	Rubber footwear	281	18	299	1.4
3674	Semiconductor	270	766	1,036	0.5
3651	Radios and TVs	239	56	295	0.4

[1]Annual job loss associated with 1% per quarter decline in relative price of imported substitute.
[2]Annual job loss associated with annual average market share penetration as reported by Schoepfle (at between 1 and 2%).
[3]Total annual job loss from price and market share competition.
[4]Total annual job loss as a percent of 1981 industry employment.
Source: Regression Appendix and Schoepfle (1982).

set their prices below domestic production costs leading to employment losses at home. The two footwear industries lose about 3% of industry employment, whereas radios and TVs lose only 0.4% of industry employment. Radios and TVs have received substantial protection in the last several years, so the small impact of foreign competition may be the evidence of successful protection. Similar successful protection of leather footwear (also protected with quotas) was not possible perhaps because footwear is a labor-intensive industry whose long-run comparative advantage is the developing countries with large unskilled labor forces.

CONCLUSION

The response of domestic industry to foreign competition occurs both through foreign price and through market share competition. Therefore, previous research that did not analyze market share competition ignored an important determinant of employment and underestimated the impact of foreign competition.

However, the role of domestic economic conditions, flexible input prices, and capital stocks overwhelm the effects of foreign competition in determining employment. Real wages are not the most significant determinant of employment for some of these industries, even the most labor-intensive ones, whereas the cost of intermediate inputs is. Therefore, the argument that high labor costs led to import pressure does not receive unqualified support. The costs of fixed capital and excess capacity are high and have important effects on employment opportunities especially in the more capital-intensive industries. Therefore, it is quite possible that the uncompetitiveness of several of these domestic industries comes from capital stocks that are too large and too expensive to maintain.

Overall, these results suggest that protection will be an inefficient mechanism for aiding domestic employment because foreign factors affecting employment are dwarfed by domestic factors. Whereas wages and employment are perhaps the only factors that the firm can control in the short run, the importance of capital suggests that an appropriate policy is selective disinvestment and abandonment. The focus on import protection as a way to solve the employment problem may be an indication of a failure to recognize that the source of the problem is internal, not external.

DATA APPENDIX

More fundamental than acquiring or constructing data of similar frequency is the problem that domestic input, output, and cost data are classified according to the SIC code system, whereas import data are classified according to the Tariff Schedule of the U.S. Annotated (TSUSA) scheme or the Schedule A commodity classification.

The SIC code classification is an industry classification as opposed to a product classification scheme. Thus goods are aggregated according to the production method of the industry, not necessarily according to any notion of demand substitutability. Most of the data are available at the four-digit level. Within a four-digit grouping we are likely to find a rather homogeneous set of products based on production methods. However, these products may or may not be good demand substitutes. For example, there are five different categories of women's shoes in SIC 3144. We would expect these to be quite similar in production technology and relatively highly substitutable in demand. However, in SIC 3674 (semiconductors), whereas the basic production process for semiconductor manufacture is virtually identical across chips, there may be no demand substitutability across different kinds of chips.

The import data are classified by commodity. Schedule A seven-digit classifications are available for quantities, custom valuation, and CIF valuation for each imported commodity. Tariff rates are classified by TSUSA seven-digit number. The concordance of the seven-digit TSUSA to the seven-digit Schedule A is not one to one. In fact, there are often a number of different TSUSA categories, sometimes each with its own tariff rate, assigned to a particular seven-digit Schedule A number. In these cases, it is impossible to correctly assign tariff rates to the Schedule A number. An arithmetic average of pertinent tariff rates is used when necessary.

The first stage of data preparation involved forming a concordance between the TSUSA and Schedule A, and then matching Schedule A and SIC categories. The task was made more difficult by a change in 1977 of both Schedule A and SIC classification and coverage. However, these concordances provide a set of domestic wage, employment, price, and capital stock data matched with a foreign quantity and value data set.

The next step creates the price indexes for imported substitutes. Clearly it is quite important to get this price as close as possible to the correct price. However, we are limited by published data. The price index, which is actually a unit-value index is constructed using Schedule A data values and appropriate tariff rates. It is weighted by contemporaneous-year CIF-valuation weights and summed over the weights to get a single unit-value index to match with the single SIC industry code.

$$(A.1) \qquad Pm_i = \frac{\Sigma_j\{(CV_t^j/QU_t^j * TR_t^j + CIF_t^j/QU_t^j) * CV_t^j/\Sigma CV_t^j\}}{\Sigma_j(CV_{72}^j/QU_{72}^j * CV_{72}^j/\Sigma_j CV_{72}^j)}$$

where CV^j is the custom-valuation of the product, which is that value to which the appropriate tariff rate (TR^j) is applied, and CIF^j is the certified-insured-freight valuation of the product and QU^j is the quantity. (j) indexes the seven-digit Schedule A categories that are included in each SIC classification for good (i), and (t) is the end of quarter month, and 1972 is the base year.

This index is designed to capture the importance of transportation costs (CV-CIF) in foreign price, or, in the case when $CIF < CV$, the gross over-valuation of the item using the CV number. The weighting by $CV^j/\Sigma CV^j$ is to allow as much as possible for the changing composition of the Schedule A items in the SIC code so as to minimize the lack of substitution opportunities often assumed by unit-value indices. Since volume data are not available for every Schedule A item, only itmes where both values and volume are available could be used in creating the index. We must assume that the ignored items have the same average unit-value as the included items. Table 12.A.1 shows the coverage by CIF-value by industry.

It is a question as to how well customs-value data measures the U.S. importer's actual purchase price or CIF measures the true cost of transporting the good into the United States. Customs valuation is based on a myriad of prices supposed to reflect the "arms-length" price, a particularly pertinent concept in subsidiary-parent sales. The CIF value should include transportation and insurance. But when the CIF value is less than the customs value, which is true for some years for semiconductors, clearly one valuation is incorrect. Nevertheless, the index is constructed to come as close as possible with existing data to a true tariff-ridden price index for the imported substitute.

For several of the industries, there has been a significant improvement in the quality of the foreign substitute. We cannot be sure that quality changes will be reflected in the unit-value index. Therefore, for these products (leather footwear and semiconductors), the unit-value is deflated by a time trend to capture the quality adjusted price changes.

Capital stock data creates another hitch. Stock data are available only annually, and only at the three-digit SIC level. For some industries, the analysis covers the entire three-digit SIC category (floor coverings and rubber footwear) so the match between capital stock and other SIC data is one to one. Four-digit data are available for radios and TVs. For the remaining two industries, the concordance between the capital stock data and the rest of the data is not perfect and it is out of line by varying degrees.

In industry 314, leather footwear, where the analysis covers only women's and men's

Table 12.A.1

CIF Value by Industry

SIC	Name	Percent[1]
227	Floor coverings	4.4
314 3/4	Leather footwear	0.0
3674	Semiconductors	4.8
3651	Radio and TV	0.0

[1]Percent of SIC excluded due to incomplete volume data. By CIF valuation, December 1981 benchmark.
Source: U.S. General Imports Schedule A.

footwear, the concordance between the employment and wage data and the capital stock data is acceptable. Whereas the ignored classifications account for 23% of the three-digit classification by value in 1981, we would expect the capital/labor ratio and output/capital ratio to be similar in the excluded categories (house slippers and footwear).

For semiconductors (SIC 3674), capital stock data are available for only SIC 367, electronic components and accessories. The excluded categories account for fully 63% of output by value. The measure of the elasticity of employment with respect to the capital stock is likely to be biased upward as the labor force appears to be working on a very large capital stock. It is also possible that within the electronic SIC, capital technology is most important for the semiconductor industry.

The capital stock data used are total net stocks of structures and plant and equipment in constant 1972 dollars. Using net stocks accounts in some limited way for technological progress and also allows capital to decline via normal depreciation and abandonment. To make a quarterly series, linear interpolation between end-of-year figures is employed.

Industry output data also creates problems. Value of shipments by four-digit SIC is available annually, except for category 314, which has four-digit quantity of production data available monthly and radios and TVs for which value shipments are available monthly. Value of shipments by broader industrial category (textile mill products, rubber and plastic products, electronic components) is available monthly. The average share of the four-digit SIC in the broad industrial group is shown in Table 12.A.2.

For semiconductors and radios and TVs the shares are large. For rubber footwear and floor coverings, the percentages are low, suggesting the constructed quarterly data series might be very noisy. In order to get an industry-level quarterly data series, the annual share of the four-digit industry in the broad industrial group is assumed to be representative of the quarterly share. Thus

(A.2) $VSH_i = (VSH_i/VSH_{big})_{annual} * VSH_{big\ monthly}$

Table 12.A.2
SIC (Broad Industrial Group)[1]

Year	227 (textile mill product)	3021 (rubber/plastic product)	3674 (electrical components)	3651 (radio/TV)
1974	.105	.0211	.316	1.076
1975	.104	.0208	.301	.870
1976	.104	.0170	.345	.868
1977	.109	.0140	.317	.757
1978	.118	.0100	.313	.691
1979	.127	.0102	.324	.678
1980	.119	.0106	.342	.659
1981	.115	.0105	.341	.642

Share of SIC in broad industrial group by value of shipments.
Source: Annual Survey of Manufactures.

where VSH_i is the four-digit SIC value of shipments and VSH_{big} is the value of shipments for the broad industrial group.

Finally, in order to derive output data, the value shipments data must be divided by price data to get quantity shipments.

$$(A.3) \qquad\qquad QSH_i = VSH_i/P_i$$

where QSH_i is the quantity shipments of the SIC, and P_i is an estimate of the actual price. P_i is the wholesale price index for the four-digit SIC code based to 1972 times the 1972 actual unit-value of imports for the appropriate SIC industry. (Price levels, not indexes, are not available by SIC code.)

In addition, it is assumed that exports of products by the U.S. industries are negligible such that quantity shipments are entirely for domestic demand. Table 12.A.3 suggests that the assumption is to varying degrees acceptable. The electronics group is the largest exporter—12% of output is exported. The data are simply not available to even contemplate constructing an estimate of export shipment by SIC. Therefore, we must assume exports are not significant.

Construction of the variable measuring import penetration uses this quantity shipments data and quantity of imports data.

$$(A.4) \qquad\qquad m_i + M_i/(QSH_i = M_i)$$

where M_i is quantity of imports. Due to incomplete import quantity data, m_i likely underestimates actual foreign market share. m_i will also be underestimated because all quantity shipped by the domestic firm, QSH_i, is assumed to be available for domestic demand and not get exported.

The employment series is total production labor hours demanded per week. Thus

$$(A.5) \qquad\qquad L_i^d = PR_i * H_i$$

where PR_i is the number of production workers and H_i is the average weekly hours for the third month of each quarter.

The wage rate is average hourly earnings for the third month of the quarter, which underestimates labor costs by the benefit structure. This could be significant in some of the more unionized industries and industries with older workers: the coefficient on

Table 12.A.3
Exports' Share of Production

SIC Name	Percent
22 textile mill production	3.4
31 leather/leather production	3.9
36 electronic/electronic equipment	12.4
30 rubber/misc. manufacture	4.0

Source: Annual Survey of Manufactures. "Origin of Exports of Manufacturing Establishments."

the real wage would be biased toward zero. Nominal wages NW_i are deflated by the consumer price index to derive real wages.

(A.6) $W_i = NW_i/CPI$

Intermediate input prices and all other goods prices are producer price indices, based to 1972. For certain of the SIC industries, there is a likely third input—textiles for floor coverings (TEX = producer price index for industrial commodities, SIC 103), for leather footwear (LEATH = producer price index for industrial commodities, SIC 042), and for rubber and plastic footwear (RP = producer price index for industrial commodities, SIC 07). For radios and TVs, the producer price index for intermediate inputs to the manufcturing process (PIMFG) is used. An input-output tale supports these choices for third input.

Semiconductor industry is the only departure from the three-input model. The third major input to the semiconductor industry is research and development. There is no price index for R&D so a simple two factor capital and labor production function is used.

Substitute final goods prices, also based to 1972, are tailored to the type of good—whether producer or consumer, final or intermediate. Thus the consumer price index (CPI) is used as the all-other-goods price for both footwear industries, and radios and TVs. Consumer finished-goods index (CFG) is used for floor coverings. PIMFG is used for semiconductors.

For the general demand variable, the index of industrial production based to 1972 is used.

REGRESSION APPENDIX

$$\ln L_i^d = \beta_0 + \beta_1 \ln W_i + \beta_2 \ln i + \beta_3 \ln \bar{K}_i + \beta_4 \ln(P_i/Pa) + \beta_5 \ln(Pm_i/Pa)$$
$$+ \beta_6 \ln N + \beta_7 \ln(1 - m_i) + T + q1 + q2 + q3 + \epsilon$$

Table 12.A.4.
Statistical Variable by Product (4-digit SIC)

SIC 3651—radios and TVs

Right-hand Variable	Estimated Coefficient	Standard Error	t-Statistic
constant	15.4316	15.5667	.991323
$\ln W$ (−2)	−.744897	.230097	−3.23732
$\ln K$	−1.72039	2.50258	−6.87449
$\ln PIMFG$ (−2)	−.496577	.431650	−1.15042
$\ln N$	.999803	.206370	4.84470
$\ln P/Pa$ (−1)	−1.13517	.441289	−2.57240
$\ln Pm/Pa$	.75443e-1	.587006e-1	1.28522
$\ln(1 - m)$ (−1)	.709914e-1	.6960743e-1	1.01988
T	−.195870e-1	.202332e-1	−.968064
$q1$	−.993034e-1	.142799e-1	−6.95406
$q2$	−.695229e-1	.183702e-1	−3.78455
$q3$	−.303737e-1	.205425e-1	−1.47858

Table 12.A.4. Continued
Statistical Variable by Product (4-digit SIC)

SIC 3651—radios and TVs

Right-hand Variable	Estimated Coefficient	Standard Error	t-Statistic

1974q3-1981q4

R-bar squared (adj for DF) = .938173	Cochrane-Orcutt
sum of squared residuals = .986300e-2	final value for rho = .7507138
std error of regression = .240686e-1	std error of rho = .1226755
F-statistic (11, 17) = 39.6251	t-statistic for rho = 6.1195105

SIC 3674—semiconductors

Right-hand Variable	Estimated Coefficient	Standard Error	t-Statistic
constant	.699653e-1	6.57579	.106398e-1
ln$W$ (-1)	$-.592751$	.495837	-1.19546
ln$K$	$-.319329$	.625709	$-.510347$
ln$N$	1.00262	.395426	2.53555
lnP/Pa (-1)	-1.66485	.542025	-3.07153
ln$Pm/Pa/T$	.302980e-1	.834647e-1	.363003
ln$(1 - m)$	.204345	.122086	1.67378
T	$-.202908e-1$	.235152e-1	$-.862879$
q1	$-.112891$	.299320e-1	-3.77157
q2	$-.976710e-1$	.346132e-1	-2.82178
q3	$-.106114$	.358467e-1	-2.96021

1974q2–1981q4

R-bar squared (adj for DF) = .951684	Cochrane-Orcutt
sum of squared residuals = .450130e-1	final value for rho = .4743287
std error of regression = .486734e-1	std error of rho = .1607288
F-statistic (11, 17) = .58.1213	t-statistic for rho = 2.951112

SIC 3143/4—leather footwear

Right-hand Variable	Estimated Coefficient	Standard Error	t-Statistic
constant	-7.14638	7.97130	$-.896514$
ln$W$ (-2)	$-.576201$	.391800	-1.47065
ln$K$	1.49486	1.27960	1.16823
ln$LEATH$	$-.108357$	.931641e-1	-1.16304
ln$N$	1.38590	.221580	6.25460
lnP/Pa	$-.786149e-1$	.460462	$-.170731$
ln$Pm/Pa/T$ (-2)	.244323	.633711e-1	3.83124
ln$(1 - m)(-2)$	.371911	.139197	2.67183
T	$-.169251e-2$	.698174e-2	$-.242419$
q1	$-.113745$	.164354e-1	-6.92069
q2	$-.294064e-1$	.187143e-1	-1.57133
q3	$-.534505e-1$	.215651e-1	-2.47856

1974q3–1981q4

R-bar sqaured (adj for DF) = .923421	Cochrane-Orcutt
sum of squared residuals = .128924e-1	final value for rho = .5719034
std error of regression = .275386e-1	std error of rho = .1523298
F-statistic (11, 17) = 31.6942	t-statistic for rho = 3.7543765

Table 12.A.4. Continued

Statistical Variable by Product (4-digit SIC)

SIC 227—Floor Coverings

Right-hand Variable	Estimated Coefficient	Standard Error	t-Statistic
constant	16.1377	8.98869	1.79533
$\ln W\,(-1)$	−.268414	.439819	−.610978
$\ln K$	−1.52752	1.29608	−1.17857
$\ln TEX$	−1.40405	.199177	−7.04923
$\ln N$	1.66314	.194777	8.53866
$\ln P/Pa\,(-1)$	−.384189	.293285	−1.30995
$\ln Pm/Pa/T$	−.192746e-1	.521758e-1	−.369417
$\ln(1-m)(-1)$	1.42491	1.94554	.732399
$q1$	−.951388e-1	.220437e-1	−4.31593
$q2$	−.109773	.285918e-1	−3.83931
$q3$	−.100784	.305610e-1	−3.29781

$1974q2–1981q4$
R-bar squared (adj for DF) = .923862
sum of squared residuals = .138182e-1
std error of regression = .269680e-1
F-statistic (11, 17) = 36.1889

Cochrane-Orcutt
final value for rho = .1897142
std error of rho = .1792585
t-statistic for rho = 1.0583276

SIC 3021—Rubber and Plastic Footwear

Right-hand Variable	Estimated Coefficient	Standard Error	t-Statistic
constant	14.0928	8.94540	1.57542
$\ln W\,(-1)$	.461300	.527116	.875139
$\ln K$	−1.22375	1.14699	−1.06693
$\ln RP\,(-1)$	−.216934	.447129	−.485171
$\ln N\,(-1)$	.733511	.188812	3.88487
$\ln P/Pa$	−1.03929	.418293	−2.48459
$\ln Pm/Pa$	.319985	.866008e-1	3.69494
$\ln(1-m)$	.158095e-1	.115645	.136707
T	−.271123e-1	.818590e-2	−3.31207
$q1$	−.531614e-2	.383752e-1	−.318530
$q2$	−.357814e-1	.244391e-1	−1.46410
$q3$	−.193341e-1	.383371e-1	−.504317

$1974q2–1981q4$
R-bar squared (adj for DF) = .724060
sum of squared residuals = .370934e-1
std error of regression = .453954e-1
F-statistic (11, 17) = 7.91775

Cochrane-Orcutt
final value for rho = −.4889532
std error of rho = .1592613
t-statistic for rho = −3.0701324

References

Bayard, Thomas O., and James A. Orr. 1979. Trade and Employment Effects of Tariff Reductions Agreed to in the MTN. U.S. Department of Labor, Economic Discussion Paper No. 1, Office of Foreign Economic Research, Bureau of International Labor Affairs, June.

Chamberlin, E. H. 1957. Monopolistic Competition Revisited, in *Towards a More General Theory of Value*. New York: Oxford University Press.

Frank, Charles R. 1977. *Foreign Trade and Domestic Aid*. Washington, D.C.: Brookings Institution, 23–39.

Gaskins, Darius W., Jr. 1971. Dynamic Limit Pricing: Optimal Pricing Under the Threat of Entry. *Journal of Economic Theory* 3(4).

Grossman, Gene M. 1987. The Employment and Wage Effects of Import Competition in the United States. *Journal of International Economic Integration,* vol. 2.

Isard, Peter. 1973. Employment Impacts of Textile Imports and Investment: A Vintage Capital Model. *American Economic Review* 63(3).

Krueger, Anne O. 1980a. Protectionist Pressures, Imports and Employment in the U.S. *Scandinavian Journal of Economics* 82(2).

Krueger, Anne O. 1980b. LDC Manufacturing Production and Implications for OECD Comparative Advantage, in I. Levison and J. Wheeler (eds): *Western Economics in Transition: Structural Change in Adjustment Policies in Industrial Countries*. Boulder, CO: Westview Press.

Krueger, Anne O. 1980c. Impact of Foreign Trade on Employment in U.S. Industry, in J. Bleck and B. Hindley (eds.): *Current Issues in Commercial Policy and Diplomacy*. New York: St. Martin's Press.

Mann, Catherine L. 1984. Employment and Capacity Utilization in Import Sensitive U.S. Industries, in *Trade and Finance Relations Between the Industrial and Newly Industrialized Countries,* doctoral dissertation, MIT.

Martin, John P., and John M. Evans. 1981. Notes on Measuring the Employment Displacement Effects of Trade by the Accounting Procedure. *Oxford Economic Papers* 33(1).

Schoepfle, Gregory K. 1982. Imports and Domestic Employment: Identifying Affected Industries. *Monthly Labor Review,* August.

Spence, Michael. 1976. Production Selection, Fixed Costs, and Monopolistic Competition. *Review of Economic Studies,* vol. 43.

U.S. Department of Commerce. 1977. *Census of Manufactures,* Vol. II. *Industry Statistics.*

U.S. Department of Commerce. *Current Industrial Reports: Manufacturers' Shipments, Inventories, and Order,* 1977–1982 and 1958–1977.

U.S. Department of Commerce. 1980. Foreign Trade Division, *U.S. Foreign Trade Statistics Classification and Cross-Classifications.*

U.S. Department of Commerce. 1982. *History of the Tariff Schedules of the U.S. Annotated* and *Supplements.*

U.S. Department of Commerce. U.S. International Trade Commission, *Tariff Schedule of the U.S. Annotated and Supplements,* various years.

About the Contributors

Khosrow Fatemi is professor of business administration at Laredo State University, Laredo, Texas, where he teaches graduate courses in international trade and international business. He has previously taught in Europe, the Middle East, and the Far East. Dr. Fatemi is the founding editor of *The International Trade Journal*. He has published more than twenty books and articles and has presented a large number of papers at different professional meetings around the world. His writings have appeared *inter alia*, in *The Wall Street Journal, The Middle East Journal*, and *Issues in International Business*. His most recent books include *International Trade: A North American Perspective*, and *U.S.-Mexican Economic Relations: Problems and Prospects*. He is the editor-in-chief of the International Business and Trade Series for Taylor and Francis International Publishers and a founding member of the International Trade and Finance Association, presently serving as executive vice president.

Contributors

Jack N. Behrman is the Luther Hodges Distinguished Professor of international business at the Graduate School of Business Administration, University of North Carolina, where he has taught international business, ethics, and comparative management, and is associate dean of the faculty. Previously, he held faculty appointments at Davidson College (North Carolina), Washington and Lee University (Virginia), and the University of Delaware, as well as visiting professorships at George Washington University (Washington, DC) and the Harvard Business School. During 1961–1964, Dr. Behrman was assistant secretary of commerce for domestic and international business—responsible for the international trade and investment programs of the department, trade with Soviet bloc countries, and domestic industrial promotion and mobilization. He has published more than 100 articles and some forty books and monographs on international economics and business issues. His most recent books include *Industrial Policies, International Restructuring and Transnationals, The Rise of the Phoenix: The U.S. Role in a Restructured World Economy*, and *Essays on Ethics in Business and the Professions*.

Robert Carbaugh is professor of economics at Central Washington University, Ellensburg, Washington. He is the author of *International Economics* (3rd ed.) and the co-author of *The International Monetary System*. His publications in journals and other books are primarily in the areas of international economics and industrial organization. In 1984 Professor Carbaugh was selected as the University Teacher of the Year at the University of Wisconsin-Eau Claire.

John H. Dunning holds a joint appointment as ICI Research Professor in international business at the University of Reading, England, and State of New Jersey professor of international business at Rutgers University. Since the mid-1950s, Professor Dunning has written or edited thirty-four books and published reports, mostly in the area of international direct investment and the multinational enterprise. He is chairman of two London-based economic consultancies, Economists Advisory Group (EAG) and EAG-Access. He is also the senior economic advisor to the executive director of the United Nations Center on Transnational Corporations. He is currently working on a four-year research project on multinationals, governments, and competitiveness. Professor Dunning is serving on the editorial boards of several professional journals, including *The International Trade Journal*. He is also the immediate past president of the Academy of International Business.

H. Peter Gray is professor of economics and management and chairman of the department of management policy and organization at Rensselaer Polytechnic Institute, New York. He is also professor emeritus of economics and finance at Rutgers University. He has previously held faculty positions at Rutgers, Jilian University (China), Wayne State University (Detroit), and Thammasat University (Thailand). He has also conducted seminars in Europe and in the Far East. Dr. Gray has published sixteen books and about 100 articles. His most recent publications include *International Economic Problems and Policies* and *Free Trade or Protectionism? A Pragmatic Analysis*. His articles have appeared in, among others, *The International Trade Journal, Weltwirtschaftliches Archiv,* and *The European Journal of Political Economy*. Dr. Gray is the current president of the Eastern Economic Association and the president-elect of the International Trade and Finance Association. He serves on the board of several journals including *The International Trade Journal*, and has served as referee for many others.

Ad Koekkoek is a senior lecturer in international economics at Erasmus University (Holland) and also a senior policy adviser on trade policy at the directorate general for development co-operation in the Ministry of Foreign Affairs of the Netherlands. During 1973–1975 he was a visiting lecturer at the University of Lagos, in Nigeria. He has published several articles on different aspects of trade structure and trade policy to various academic journals. His current research primarily consists of studies on comparative advantage for the Netherlands and the European Community, the international division of labor in selected industries, and the concerns of the developing countries in the Uruguay Round of GATT negotiations.

James M. Lutz received his Ph.D. from the University of Texas at Austin in 1975. He is presently associate professor of political science at Indiana University-Purdue University at Fort Wayne. His research has involved work in comparative politics, the international political economy, and the adoption of public policies. His recent publications include *The United States and World Trade: Changing Patterns and Dimensions* (co-authored with Robert T. Green), and *Protectionism: An Annotated Bibliography*. Professor Lutz' current research includes continuing work on the product life cycle, protectionist practices and their effects, and the political uses of trade.

Craig R. MacPhee is professor of economics at the University of Nebraska-Lincoln, where he has taught courses in theory and international trade and finance since 1969. He received his Ph.D. in economics from Michigan State University in 1970. Professor MacPhee has authored several books and numerous articles in academic publications, as well as a series of monographs published by the United Nations. He has served as a consultant to several private and governmental organizations and has represented the United Nations in consultations with the Commission of the European Communities in Brussels and in the Tokyo Round of multilateral trade negotiations in Geneva. He has lectured at Oxford University, the Australian National University, Zhongshan University in China, and Academy Sinica in Taiwan.

Catherine L. Mann is an economist in the division of international finance at the Federal Reserve Board of Governors in Washington, DC. She has most recently been on the staff of the chief economist of the World Bank. She has previously taught international economic classes at Boston College, Georgetown University (Washington, DC), and the University of Maryland. She received the Special Achievement Award from the Federal Reserve in 1986, and a Ford Foundation Fellowship for research at the National Bureau of Economic Research in 1987. Her recent publications examine the effect of politics on protection, micro and macroeconomic explanations for the emergence and persistence of the U.S. current account deficit, and the effect of exchange rates on the prices and profit margins of internationally traded goods.

Franklin R. Root is professor of international business and management at the Wharton School in Philadelphia. A graduate of Trinity College, he has an M.B.A. from the Wharton School and a Ph.D. from the University of Pennsylvania. Professor Root has lectured in several countries in the fields of international business and economics. He has also served on the faculties of the University of Maryland, the Copenhagen School of Economics and Business Administration, and the Naval War College. Professor Root is engaged in extensive consulting with business and government agencies. He has led several workshops sponsored by the American Association of Collegiate Schools of Business (AACSB), to "internationalize" business schools in the United States. He is a past president of the Academy of International Business, and is the current dean of the Fellows of the Academy. Professor Root's recent publications include *International Trade and Finance* (5th ed.) and *Entry Strategies for International Markets*.

Bernard Sarachek is professor of international business at the Henry W. Bloch School of Business Administration at the University of Missouri-Kansas City. Previously he taught at Clark University (Massachusetts), Detroit University, and Rutgers University (Queens Campus). He has held Fulbright-Hays teaching appointments at the University of Karachi, in Pakistan (1977–1978), and the Universiti Kebangsaan in Malaysia (1981–1982). He has published numerous articles in a variety of academic journals.

Darwin Wassink is professor of economics at the University of Wisconsin-Eau Claire. He has previously taught at Sophia University in Tokyo, Japan, and at the University of Iowa. He has served as an economist for the United States Agency for International Development in Pakistan and for the Ministry of Finance and National Economy of Saudi Arabia. His publications have been in the fields of international economics and economic development.